A LIGHT IN THE DARK

A LIGHT IN THE DARK

A HISTORY OF MOVIE DIRECTORS

———

David Thomson

ALFRED A. KNOPF

NEW YORK

2021

THIS IS A BORZOI BOOK PUBLISHED BY ALFRED A. KNOPF

Copyright © 2020 by David Thomson

All rights reserved. Published in the United States by Alfred A. Knopf,
a division of Penguin Random House LLC, New York, and distributed
in Canada by Penguin Random House Canada Limited, Toronto.
Originally published in hardcover in Great Britain by
Weidenfeld & Nicolson, an imprint of
The Orion Publishing Group Ltd, London, in 2020.

www.aaknopf.com

Knopf, Borzoi Books, and the colophon are registered trademarks
of Penguin Random House LLC.

LIBRARY OF CONGRESS CATALOGING-IN-PUBLICATION DATA
Names: Thomson, David, [date] author.
Title: A light in the dark : a history of movie directors /
David Thomson.
Description: New York : Alfred A. Knopf, 2021. | Includes index. |
Identifiers: LCCN 2020017733 (print) | LCCN 2020017734 (ebook) |
ISBN 9780593318157 (hardcover) | ISBN 9780593318164 (ebook)
Subjects: LCSH: Motion pictures—Production and direction—History. |
Motion picture producers and directors—History and criticism.
Classification: LCC PN1995.9.P7 T485 2021 (print) |
LCC PN1995.9.P7 (ebook) | DDC 791.430232—dc23
LC record available at https://lccn.loc.gov/2020017733
LC ebook record available at https://lccn.loc.gov/2020017734

Jacket image by Shutterstock
Jacket design by Orionbooks

Manufactured in Canada
First American Edition

For Jon Segal

. . . the actors hated doing it. They felt terribly uncomfortable at the way in which they had to cling to each other. I said, "I don't care how you feel; the only thing that matters is the way it's going to look on the screen."

—ALFRED HITCHCOCK, TALKING ABOUT *NOTORIOUS*

. . . the funny thing is that Bogey fell in love with the character she played, so she had to keep playing it the rest of her life.

—HOWARD HAWKS, TALKING ABOUT LAUREN BACALL

I must have complete total final annihilating artistic control over the picture.

—STANLEY KUBRICK, NOTES FOR A CONTRACT NEGOTIATION, 1964

CONTENTS

A LIGHT IN THE DARK

DARKNESS VISIBLE

A light in the dark! It sounds such fun and so encouraging. Isn't that the promise of enlightenment rescuing us from obscurity and the condition we learned to call noir? The plan lets us feel directors are visionaries and pathfinders. Won't there be treasure in the light?

Consider the title carefully. Is it entirely cheerful or positive? Or does it feel the enclosing pressure of darkness—the state of mind Milton called "darkness visible" in *Paradise Lost*? Isn't that a message in noir? Is the light enlightening or a way of holding off our fear of the dark?

One thing seems clear: these people who lit up the dark might be storytellers, prophets, supreme entertainers, or heroes—yet they were also calculating magicians, manipulators, fakes, and dictators in the making. Such heroes might need very careful watching. They could turn out as Fritz Lang's character Dr. Mabuse, as Hitler's dream for Herr Lang . . . or Charles Foster Kane, a lord of misrule.

So suppose you want to take a photograph. It may involve your dog or some human beloved; it could be the light on the water or the mountains a few miles away. In all cases, this enterprise requires a subject, you, and a camera. You may have read instructions for the camera; your beloved has perhaps been shy, or the opposite of shy. So you have decisions to make about the picturing, so small or delicate you hardly notice them. The apparent naturalness of life is invaded by the grid of choices and decisions.

But getting on for two hundred years into the history of photography, you don't expect some cocksure Other to intervene and tell you, *No, not like that. Do this instead.* It's your show, so you do not want to be directed.

This book is a critical history of how the big enterprise of movie yielded to those intruders, the directors. They were unknown once; then they became heroes and masters. And now it is possible to see that they might even fade away, because the process and the cameras have minds (or a mindlessness) of their own that cannot be denied.

In the first part of this book I have chosen exemplary figures because, one way or the other, they pulled off the intrusive trick by charm, dominance, vision, luck—and other people's money. These are big figures by most standards, auteurs. But that means I have omitted others who would have seemed essential once—Cecil B. DeMille, Sergei Eisenstein, even Charlie Chaplin. They are referred to, but not in the depth I have allowed Fritz Lang, Luis Buñuel, Jean Renoir, and so on. My personal judgments could be left looking silly in history. Opinion can't be afraid of that.

I have chosen classic directors as understood from an era

when I was in film school (1960, more or less, when that kind of education began). That status has lasted, even if "classic" now needs a pinch of salt or a Turner brand image. Even in 1960, some reckoned Hitchcock was just an "entertainer," instead of an insanely calm obsessive. The directors in this book represent their decades, and the attempt to work wherever fate blew them—or directed them.

Still, I have had to omit valuable others—Boris Barnet, F. W. Murnau, Jean Cocteau, Mitchell Leisen. Film Studies can tell you it has such figures taken care of. But if you've ever encountered a 2015 film student who didn't know who Gary Cooper was then it's easy to wonder if those "in the know" have lived properly with Jean Vigo, Josef von Sternberg, King Vidor, or Dziga Vertov. You can look those guys up, we say; or make a note to do so some other day.

Once upon a time, we did not know the names of directors. Then they became essential. And now? Try this: Who directed *Ozark*?

I

———

WAITING FOR THE MONOLITH

We sat in the dark for nearly a century; we were traveling together. We hoped we were going to have fun, a good scare, or just be occupied. We were strangers there, but fellow pilgrims, and the cinema was a palace for our wondering.

But it was like a prison, too. Wasn't there a sinister air, a feeling that someone must be in charge—working the machinery, dimming the lights, taking our money? Yet there was no one in sight except for people selling tickets and wistful usherettes. Instead, there was this feeling of being alone in the dark place, exposed to the searchlight of the projector, and the suddenness (quicker than saying "cut") with which a nice family picnic might be invaded by a tiger, a tidal wave . . . or even a black monolith.

Do you remember that moment in Stanley Kubrick's *2001*? There we are in a semi-desert (in Utah perhaps, or Namibia), at "the dawn of man," where ragged apes battle for futile power. Then all of a sudden a monolith appears, before our eyes (made by Brancusi or HomePlastics, Inc.), dominating the scene and proving that something is in charge. That's ominous (the apes chatter in fear), but it's a relief, too (they gather beneath the black intrusion, waiting for the feature), because the world is more frightening for apes if no one is running the show. That could mean there's no show. And as educated apes gave up on God, so we were left open to uncertainty.

The suddenness of the monolith is a sublime intervention, as if fate or advertising had told those apes that Las Vegas was just over the magic-hour horizon, with Dean Martin and Jerry Lewis opening at the Sands tonight. Or as if that fluttering kite of shadow in the western sky might be an asteroid approaching, like the one we believe hit the Yucatán 66 million years ago.

The monolith was a religious experience and such awe does call a god into being. But who could be that god? It might be the light, the money, or the haunting apprehension in being part of a movie crowd. But then directors said, *It's me. I'll be God!* The arrival of that thin black screen (really, that's what it is), was Kubrick's way of saying, *C'est moi, Stanley. Just see what comes next!* And we were left having to decide whether this was arrogance, pretension, or the wonderful wizard of cinema.

Directors shouted "Action!" and "Cut!" Those bold words were meant to signal they were in control, and that shaky confidence has worked from D. W. Griffith and Alfred Hitchcock to Ingmar Bergman and Martin Scorsese. This is a book about that assumption of authority and our hope that it promotes cinema into a great entertainment for the world, or even an art. It's the history of a job and the arc of magic. Without those optimistic explanations, "cinema" might be just a machine that teaches people they are deluded, alone and insignificant. So direction was what the word suggests, a determination about not being lost, a filling of the void.

At first, there was no such thing as a theory. There wasn't even directing. There was a camera and the light. Just photography, a sensationalism: having lovely faces to look at when there was no one actually there.

Imagine you are nineteen in 1890. You have a camera and you are so intent on taking pictures that other people believe you are obsessed. (Film directors are expected to be obsessed—it goes with their not heeding so much of real life.) At the end of the day in your room, in London or Chicago or Calcutta, you are studying the picture of your girlfriend, present and absent at the same time.

Cut there, because my 1890 assumption is tricky now. I'm making the male gaze our origin legend. My editor suggests adding "or boyfriend" to be "more inclusive." I'm happy to do that, but it leads back to historical matters. In the early days of the picture business, it was invariably a man wanting to photograph a woman, and the sad record of our fine art has to face how often that was a path to seduction, exploitation, and the control lurking in the phrase "directed by." By now, women are a little more likely to hold the camera and direct a film, but seldom do they gaze at men the way my 1890 guy was fixed on his girlfriend. Doesn't "gaze" have a note of rapture? Our photographer felt that she was there for him, and in 1890 that was still an orthodoxy. It follows that the romantic pressure in movies—their thrust, their hope for meaning—was different for men and women. We are determined to repair that imbalance, but watch carefully: it is possible that "cinema" might vanish in the reformation. Suppose the cult of directors could be ending, swept aside by CGI, streaming, and correctness in a medium that often edged into the illicit.

You're going to have to follow that line. We're going to have to live by it.

The young man has a snapshot; he took time and trouble over it; and now he has the image even if the romance has ended. He made the picture the year before, on an excursion to the countryside. He asked the girl to stand just so, under that sycamore, but in a soft light—and would she take her hat off and let her hair be free? Then he saw the sun had clouded over just a touch; it put her face in a more pensive light. So then, as she was thinking, or so it seemed, he *took* the picture (that word is important, for theft can be authority). The snap was a record of the light, of her, and of our new power over the momentary. But looking at the picture put us on the edge of once upon a time. Perhaps the young man would tell a story about this woman and where she went, an odyssey, and how he followed her for years and thousands of miles, and rescued her from being lost. (At 16 snaps a second, you might have a ninety-minute story . . . with 86,400 snaps. This was the industrialization of the split second, fifty years or so before man, or Man, split the atom.)

He began to be moved by the way this slip of photographic paper could overcome time and mortality and might grip strangers. "Action!" he ordered; it sounded so positive. Perhaps he was directing this girl and real life, just because he had chosen them. Didn't he want her? But perhaps the medium— its isolation and its worship of something seen—was directing both of them. He had never had so intense a relationship with a stranger. He realized that properly once she left him. But don't rule out the possibility that she thinks he dropped her once he had the photograph to be in love with. There is an intimacy in photographs that may challenge human closeness.

"Action!" was like an open sesame. It started with this young man or a few other geniuses, but in ten years the world was hooked on the word, its energy, and that black monolith of desire.

How quickly this new medium began to fuel our longing for stories, dreams, and self-deception. I am talking about a total culture, and this quaint imagined anecdote from 1890 fits just as well with how we are using selfies and smartphone images in 2020. Who is directing your smartphone? Is it you, or your friends, or is it the corporations that preside over such media and call them social, as opposed to merely revenue-generating? Or is it the transaction of seeing and being seen that is in charge?

Come to that, is anything "in charge"? And is it frightening when that question has no sure answer? Is that what alarmed the girlfriend, so she left him? Did she get the idea that he was more moved by the photo than by her?

If you were a kid in 1890, that was not so far from David Wark Griffith (born in 1875) or Erich von Stroheim (born in 1885). They are examples of the early movie director, though that was not either one's first ambition. They were pioneer failures with egos that rebelled at being put down. Griffith was born in rural Kentucky ten years after the end of the Civil War. His father had been a colonel in the Confederacy, and then a state legislator. But he had died when D.W. was ten and the mother moved them to Lexington, where she opened a boardinghouse. This was on the edge of survival, when some of her boarders were traveling actors or people in theatre. Griffith the boy listened to them and thought he might be an actor—so many film directors have come to the set as would-be actors, afraid of being nobodies.

Directing defines the practice of film, but it also embodies the desire to be "someone." So many directors are tempted to be actors: Jean Renoir, Charlie Chaplin, Orson Welles, Erich von Stroheim, Vittorio De Sica, Laurence Olivier, François Truffaut, John Cassavetes, Woody Allen, Roman Polanski, Clint Eastwood, Marlon Brando, Barbra Streisand. Don't forget Jerry Lewis, or his longing to become (and to deride) Dean Martin in *The Nutty Professor.*

Don't write off the famous Hitchcock cameos as gimmicks: the fat man dreamed of being with slim actresses. When Martin Scorsese took on the one-scene role of the bloodthirsty passenger in *Taxi Driver,* he was laying claim to the dread and violence of his film. Deeper still, some directors envisage themselves as *all* their characters. In his great film *Persona* (1966), Ingmar Bergman was invested in the women played by Liv Ullmann and Bibi Andersson. After all, both would be his lovers in actuality, in his head, and on his screens.

D. W. Griffith wasn't good enough as an actor, so he took up writing—scripts and plays—to survive. That's how he got a few small parts at the Biograph studio, and that's where the bosses concluded that he was wooden as an actor and uninspired as a writer. But if he still wanted a job he could "direct."

What does a director do? Griffith wondered. We are talking

about a time, the 1900s, when the distinctive creative force in filmmaking, the power, was split between the cameramen and the actors. This was a reenactment of what our young man went through in 1890 with the young woman. The cameraman and the camera were joined at the hip. And by 1890, it was common knowledge that some photographers were so remarkable they might be artists.

But few people knew how a movie camera worked—how to load the film without its being spoiled; how to be sure that the film ran through the camera at a steady speed, with the sprocket holes fitting the claws exactly; and then how to unload the film and get it processed—making the negative positive. Some cameramen processed their own negative because they were unwilling to let the film out of their hands. But sooner or later labs sprang up, and in those labs there might be a genius who sidled up to a cameraman and said, "Look, if you underexposed the film by a stop, say, and then I pushed it twenty seconds longer in the developing—no need to explain this, but trust me— then I think the film could pick up an extra intensity, a feeling beyond mere reality. You'll see it. Interested?"

So Kodak and their rivals were like directors, and if one day Gregg Toland would teach Orson Welles all he needed to know about the camera, I doubt he explained the full wonder of extra-wide-angle lenses, with depth of focus so that the middle ground felt irrationally stretched out and expanded, with astounding emotional impact: it's part of why *Citizen Kane* feels so grand and so lonesome, so megalomaniacal. Welles saw or felt that but he couldn't talk turkey to the lab.

You can guess the other key role: someone to stand under the tree to be photographed, and to look pretty, noble or funny or villainous—someone the public could "get" in an instant, someone who fit in with the emerging scheme of being good-looking or bad-looking in melodrama. Prolonged dramatic acting, such as people revered in the theatre, was not easily managed in movies because it needed context and preparation. But a girl could be enchanting on the spot, and there were comics who made you laugh out loud in three seconds. Quickness became a decisive directorial touch, like a glance or a knockout punch.

It was said that the camera loved some people (though not others, and that was the source of a discrimination—it might become a fascism—that has always challenged democracy). In practice it also meant that people doing the filming loved or desired some people being photographed. That was not indecent; it was the prelude to having strangers in the dark love the filmed faces. Something else followed from that: if there were a dozen pretty girls waiting for a chance at Paramount or Universal, why not "entertain" half of them? The direction of the process permitted a certain promiscuity and it was taken for granted. In your imagination, you can do anything. That's another fascism, or the risk of control getting out of control.

D. W. Griffith had always been a historical convenience—until he was suddenly reassessed as inconvenient. More or less, historians have said that in the beginning there was frontier disorder in the enterprise of movie and in its narrative potential, but then David Wark Griffith, tall, courtly in an old Southern way, and wearing a broad-brimmed hat to indicate where he was, intervened and said, begone chaos—we will have shots that fit together in a tidy story; we will make a movie a series of compelling instants or moments; we can school the pictured faces to find a level of sentimental delivery that is coherent and appealing; we will convert motion into emotion, just like the way electricity is provided. We'll make a couple of these one-reel tales a week. I'll be in charge. And then the business can go out in the world and sell the pictures and we'll take a portion of the revenue to make more pictures.

Very well: we'll get just a fraction back and the business will keep the portion, the meal, the diet, and all the corn the country grows. We'll call that a compromise.

It is a pretty story, and not inaccurate. But all over the movie world there were hundreds of people—not always men—who were engaged in the same unmapped treasure hunt. Griffith had the acuity (it is vital in movie directors still): he could organize the untidy set and the larking around of the players; he could tell his cameraman, Billy Bitzer, there was a plan and a story, even if he was making it up as he went along. *I am in charge!* Someone had to be, otherwise the hundred questions every hour would go unanswered and the project could dwindle into inertia. Directors did not really have time to rehearse or revise an intimate scene; those niceties got lost in all those infernal questions that have to be answered: Will Lillian Gish be back from the doctor's in time to do the ice-floe shot? How do we get the cat to drink the milk? Is the actor Bobby Harron drunk or just happy? Should Mae Marsh wear the floral dress or the cloak? We need $11,300 in cash by six o'clock.

Griffith played or occupied the role of the director, a He Who Must Be Obeyed (and whose answers should be acted on), because he was a genius, or a mastermind, or perhaps just there, wearing the hat. The "genius" lived somewhere between moral authority and public relations. But Griffith was very good in his time, and he had a fine gentlemanly way with his actresses that placed them in a Victorian scheme of romance, guilt, and suspense. Just as Griffith organized the set and its jobs, so in history the pandemonium of movies before 1915 was reconstructed around his lofty figure and ill-defined example. No one answers a hundred questions an hour correctly, but he has to have the nerve to provide answers and make the questioners gamble on believing them.

None of this trick would have worked but for *The Birth of a Nation* and its wild guess that crowds raised on ten-minute movies might sit still for three and a half hours for what was an "event" picture. D.W. had a part in the raising of the money to do the film ($100,000), and he had a smaller share in the colossal revenue it brought in. But he would be set aside in ten years or so by the industry his picture had created and funded. (We say it maybe grossed $100 million, but we don't really know, because the accounts were not kept properly.) He could run a set, but cash flow was out of his control. Never mind: Lillian Gish would strive to get him on a U.S. postage stamp (in 1975) and the history books emerging in the 1960s would identify him as a pioneering father. Film studies in universities depended on geniuses: therein lay departments and majors, tenure and respect. The torrent of raw cash could be overlooked and it has seldom been taught.

The respect was encompassing. In the 1960s and 1970s, as America battled over what were called civil rights and the race issue, it was as if no one really saw *The Birth of a Nation* as an imprint of reality instead of for its creative consequences. This could not last. Gradually truths took apart the legend. It was easier to appreciate that Griffith the narrative innovator had a trite mind; his sense of human story had little interest in the complex underliers of how we lived. He did raw melodrama in 1915, but he would have been lost with an intricate narrative like Ford Madox Ford's *The Good Soldier*, published in the same year.

Griffith was a crowd pleaser with ticket sales high enough to make someone like Ford bitter. Griffith was a racist, too. Suddenly and belatedly, it seemed, we caught up with the understanding that *The Birth of a Nation* was intolerable, ugly, and all too American. The church of cinema shrank from it and when the centenary of the film arose—2015—it was hard to see the film itself. You can say it had dated badly, but in fact we had dawdled in our education. Movie is such a sensation and so inherently melodramatic in its juxtaposition of darkness and a bright light that we have to get used to our own slowness. Griffith's stress on his managerial personality had helped obscure what his film was about.

If we crave geniuses (because they help us believe in ourselves), then we should recognize that 1910–15 was also the age of Picasso, Joyce, and Mahler. Those fellows are still being attended to, whereas D. W. Griffith is now an outlaw or a genius we cannot own up to.

Stroheim was different. He was Jewish, from Vienna and the lower class. His father made hats. He only picked up the "von" as he came to America, but he had learned how an upstart needed to act grand and forbidding. Stroheim was a hustler, an intimidator, a self-advertised "brute," and an opportunist who would make his own bad luck. He had understood the need to direct how people thought of him.

So he was an actor before taking up directing. Now, since his death (in 1957), it is clearer that he will be remembered more as an actor—a ham, yet endearing and expert, above all as the prison commandant in Jean Renoir's *La Grande Illusion* and as Max von Mayerling, the ex-director, former husband turned butler, and minder to Norma Desmond in Billy Wilder's *Sunset Blvd.*

He had not set out to be a director. In America by 1909, he wandered until he came to Los Angeles in 1914, and on the rising tide of hostility toward Germany he had the wit to see that he might get small parts as a classic or cliché Prussian officer. Once war films began to be made, he announced that he was an expert on military uniforms—to be on the Von's side is to trust that he made up this fussy etiquette, as if designing costumes for a picture. But this work brought him to Griffith and he was an assistant of all trades to the great man on *Intolerance*. Assistant of all trades is not to be taken lightly as training for a director.

So Stroheim did anything asked of him, and had the ingenuity to convert impossible orders into something he could do, while congratulating his bosses on their acumen. He might agonize over costumes, and get the right pair of French sofas for a scene; he could ensure that Griffith had a flattering speech for his dinner with theatre owners; and then urge a nervewracked actress to get some sleep, or the drugs that put rest in her eyes. He might write a new scene five times overnight. He would be expected to handle the extras in a crowd scene and be sure they all looked sixteenth-century. He would get actress Miriam Cooper's Afghan hound to the vet. I am making this up, but this wilderness of tasks is what assistant directors are raised to do. And he might plot the future when he would be the great man, a sardonic, cynical master, and a director who could out-stare the infant studios and a boss as young as Irving Thalberg (just twenty-three when he first encountered Stroheim).

Like Griffith and so many men born on the far side of electricity, automobiles, and telephones, the Von loved the past. He was unrelievedly sexist, and he encouraged his own reputation for perversity. He shaved his head and affected a suntan, and he had a way of staring at and hesitating over beautiful women that made for conquest—or a polite version of it. He said he was in charge but he had a sardonic, ironic air that said honestly there was nothing there to run. It was all fate. His ambitions were pretenses (another key in directing—be ruthless and obsessive but know it doesn't matter). He made a couple of extravagant, old-fashioned movies that did well—*Blind Husbands* and *Foolish Wives,* not least for the supercilious dandy he played on screen.

Foolish Wives is the more arresting of the two. It has Stroheim as a bogus count, a con artist; he is a sardonic, heartless womanizer for our amusement, yet graced by Stroheim's suave self-love. So we respond to his leering wickedness—just as the publicity encouraged, the Von was "the man we love to hate." But suddenly this misanthropy feels out of control: this director-actor is set on self-destruction (as much as Orson Welles would be on *Citizen Kane*—or Picasso in his late, rueful sexual drawings). Stroheim was a master of his art; he relished the power he had discovered. But he had glimpsed the dead end in directing and the way its heroes might be dangerous to know or trust. In the end, *Foolish Wives* is too slick to be tragic, too smug to deliver inescapable ruin. But it is still unnerving in its astute self-loathing.

Yet his work as a director might have faded away by now—he

is not as interesting as Mauritz Stiller and Victor Sjöström in Sweden, or Abel Gance and Louis Feuillade in France, or Fritz Lang and F. W. Murnau in Germany—but he established his legend by the decision to film Frank Norris's novel *McTeague*, published in 1899. It is a dogged realist saga about commonplace Americans at the start of the twentieth century being destroyed by their lust for gold. So it is one of the few great American movies about money, the secret passion of the nation that prefers to hide behind violence, sex, and doing the right thing.

Greed (the blunt title Stroheim adopted) is a two-hour drama, with good location scenes, emphatic acting, and a tidy moral warning to us all. That was not his plan, and he was curiously shy about his intent. He understood how Griffith had transformed fifteen- or twenty-minute entertainments into three hours. He saw how that had brought a business of film distribution to life that had required the building of theatres. So he imagined a picture that might be six or ten hours—like Wagner's *Ring* cycle, if you like—that could be seen over several nights. Or did he foresee that at this scale he was setting out on a personal disaster?

Greed is as if made by another man in its remorseless concentration on the real: in the dentist's office on Polk Street you can still see the real life of San Francisco passing by. The film cannot escape all the clichés of silent melodrama, or not until it needs to, as when it delves into the madness of Treena (ZaSu Pitts), whose fixation on money has taken on a sexual glamour. She has nightmares that are closer to Luis Buñuel's psychic dreamscape than to the comforting naturalism of most American movies. But it is when *Greed* gets to Death Valley (they shot in temperatures over 100 degrees), when the desert becomes a metaphor for the monolith of gold, that the melodrama rises to a new pitch that still terrifies American moviemaking.

What followed is a story of genius or wildness being tamed, of a director being redirected. The project went from the Goldwyn Company to being a pickup for Metro-Goldwyn-Mayer, led by Irving Thalberg, who had already crossed swords with Stroheim at Universal. So *Greed*'s initial length was seen as excessive and resisting control. From ten hours, bit by bit, the picture shrank to the two-hour version we have today. As such, it is still one of the most important American movies, a triumph of its time and a blatant offense in the eyes of its business. The industry was teaching America to assess imagination as a commodity just as every news report on your smartphone is preceded and humiliated by some advertisement. It is orthodoxy now to see *Greed* as directorial aspiration being overridden by Hollywood as a mere function. But don't let that obscure the hammy indignation with which Stroheim was calling for a curse on the house where he worked and on that stealthy compromise in pictures, of doing his story and being his genius, on Other People's Money. *Greed* could have been made yesterday. Which makes it harder to imagine it being attempted tomorrow.

The Von was a warning and an inspiration to other directors and a guide to how the job of directing needed to be acted out. It was a show that endorsed Command, Vision, or simply Me! What follows in the body of this book begins as a line of notable directors, statues in the history, if you like. From Fritz Lang and Jean Renoir to Howard Hawks and Alfred Hitchcock, these men helped define the medium in their being directors. Some said they were just professionals; some preferred to be seen as artists. But companions on the edges of their striving thought they had to be crazy to be doing what they did.

Directing a movie is so ruinously stressful, it's a marvel that some seem so calm about it while living past forty. But plenty have behaved badly, recklessly, or so close to obsession as to seem disturbed. Of all the reasons that prompted people to become film directors—especially the shy guys hiding in the dark—don't forget its opportunity to be out of control and then be rewarded for it. Directors cannot get over the urge to be an outlaw. That sometimes accounts for their everyday behavior, but it's why they created Cagney in *Public Enemy* and *White Heat,* Charles Foster Kane and Clyde Barrow, Brando and his boys in *The Godfather,* and even the sad veterans in Martin Scorsese's *The Irishman.* For good and ill, these respectable gangster-types did it their way.

"Made it, Ma! Top of the world. It's me!"

2

TO BE A MASTER: FRITZ LANG

Herr Lang was only five years younger than Stroheim, but he was as artful a careerist as the Von was self-destructive. Lang stared down mere people—actors and crew—and used his monocle to pick up the light and dazzle them. He knew what had happened to Stroheim, of course, but he was not daunted. So he made the biggest film ever attempted in Germany: his *Metropolis* (1927) cost over 5 million reichsmarks. It is prodigious, prophetic, crazed, and foolish. But beautiful. And it earned only 75,000 reichsmarks. Somehow Fritz was not exiled to Death Valley. The disaster made him all the more glorious and imperious. He did something film directors need to learn—he got away with it.

No one liked him, but he didn't give a damn. Perhaps he didn't notice. He gave orders and expected to be obeyed. That habit would spread in Germany. In going from Berlin to Hollywood he moved from a culture devoted to unlikeable but unassailable authority to one that wanted to persuade itself that everything was a team effort to make stories in which audiences could rely on knowing who were the good guys and the bad. This was going from the UFA studio in Berlin in the era before sound, to talking pictures in Hollywood where the moral fables sent audiences home humming and contented. Lang was the maestro who could see how the anxious Weimar Germany and an America free from fear were two sides to the same coin of power and control in the world. His journey spelled out the vagaries, the thrills, and the humiliations in being a movie director.

But he never had control of his American pictures, and control was what moved him the most. The thing that sustains *Metropolis* is its suspense over who can direct this future world. When you look at his pictures now, their bleak passion is in the ominous interior shapes: the design of a room; the sardonic balance in a storyline; and the meanings that the system is too fearful or too cheerful to draw out. The most interesting question about Lang as an artist is how fully he understood that trap he was in, and what it did to his longing. Longing seems a strange word to use about him, because he was the kind of person who never told you what he wanted or how naked desire can make you. But we cannot contemplate his German films without feeling the pulse of a vision so full of danger and pessimism that . . . well, perhaps that was what appealed to Goebbels and Hitler and made them want to hire Lang for their movies.

We'll come to that. But first consider his best-known Hollywood picture, and in many ways the most effective. *The Big Heat* (1953) was a tidy, routine Columbia production; ninety minutes long, it made a decent profit. It was as well-behaved a piece of studio product as *Metropolis* was outrageous. Lang would say he had struck out for freedom in coming to America, but on screen the opposite was the case.

In an unnamed American city, a high-power policeman kills himself. We never know why but an atmosphere of corruption hangs over the suicide. His widow takes the letter he had left on the desk where he shot himself, and she is cold-bloodedly prepared to deal with the city—both its crime boss and its chief of police: she will keep the letter in her bank in return for a suitably amplified pension. That is the way this city works. The mobster and the chief of police are so alike.

But another cop, Dave Bannion (Glenn Ford), is as sentimental as he tries to seem tough. He suspects what the widow is doing and so he investigates the case. His superiors warn him off that mission, but he is dogged—the way we would like our cops to be. He pushes so hard that the dark forces in the city put dynamite in his car. You know that ignition trick—movies have always loved it and the bright bang it brings. But instead of taking out Bannion, the bomb kills his wife (played briefly with warmth and enthusiasm by Jocelyn Brando, Marlon's sister).

The wife's death frees a vengeful energy in Bannion, the fiercer because he realizes he will get no support from the police system. His moral determination seems justified; it's something audiences could admire and identify with. But Ford, normally a rather placid actor, turns up his intensity until we feel his anger, a withering disdain for law and order. His feeling is frightening, a little dangerous, and I suspect Lang wanted to explore it. But the safe film from 1953 cheats that resolve.

Bannion becomes involved with Debby (Gloria Grahame), a blithe whore, the mistress of a cruel gangster, Vince (Lee

Marvin), who works for the crime boss. On an impulse, to rebuke her flippant independence, Vince throws scalding coffee in Debby's face. She feels ruined, an outcast—she had nothing else but her youthful sexuality. So Debby and Bannion become weird allies and we all want Vince punished. Doesn't he deserve at least some coffee in *his* face? The film nags at our violent impulse.

There's a scene in a bare hotel room where, without saying so, Debby offers herself to Bannion, but he is too pristine or Hays Code–controlled to take up her invitation. At that point, the nasty vitality of the film halts. Those two ought to have an embrace; it could involve him looking at her scarred face, taking off her bandages like clothes; it could be a hell of a scene, for two people who recognize their kinship as wounded outcasts. That could make for a climax where together they dispose of Vince, even at the cost of their own lives. The logic of the "heat" needs those three corpses left in the penthouse suite, with some certainty that the city's corruption will continue, like the weather, the stock market, the rhetoric of freedom, and the film's brilliant observation that Debby and that widow at the start are sisters under the mink coats they wear. Something in the film knows that corruption is the human way, while reform is a white lie.

But the city's dilemma is said to be settled; that's part of Columbia's tidiness. The boss and the police chief have been indicted. Bannion goes back to his job and his young daughter, an honest man in a rehabilitated police force. But there is still as little daylight and vitality in this city as Lang had allowed from the start. The big heat clashes with the coldness of the setting. This is not the film to ask: does Bannion really have the temperament we want in a cop? According to the Hollywood code, it tells itself that everything is going to be all right. His city, and yours, is safe.

That was 1953, and you know how all right and safe turned out. I suspect Fritz Lang had few doubts about the way the new world was going. But he was not allowed by the American system to spell out that despair, in the way that in *M* (1931) he had constructed a piercingly lucid equation between the forces of law and the underworld, with a pathetic but hideous murderer (Peter Lorre) caught between them. Lang's vision and the beauty of his films disdained reassurance and trusted that the human beast would endure.

The German Lang is like Hyde compared with the cramped Jekyll he became in Hollywood. Born in Vienna in 1890, the son of an architect-contractor, he could afford to travel the world in the years before the Great War. He drew in the bold, sensual style of Egon Schiele, and he had thoughts of architecture for himself, but he came home at the outbreak of war and joined the Austrian army. He fought in Romania and in northern Italy (he seemingly faced the young Ernest Hemingway during the Piave campaign) and he was wounded several times. It was in hospital when he was on the mend (there was an eye injury) that he began playing with the idea of writing film scenarios. After all, he was a child of the new movie age and always fascinated by the fast-moving action adventures of early serials. He is one of a generation of educated people transfixed by the surface speed, romance, and violence of sensational cinema. All his life, he preferred that ferment to depth of character or theme. The ideas in Lang are in the action and the rigor of architecture-school compositions. His philosophy was very simple: people are trapped in compositions. But the richness in that principle never failed him, and it was often the life force in narrative shapes that resembled corpses, or stiffs. Lang's characters are uninteresting, until they feel walls, doorways, and constructed geometry closing in on them.

Was Lang such a person himself? The question needs to be asked as a general matter: movie directors often create a world in which they might like to live, or escape into. That comes out of their fusion of fantasy and reality. Lang seldom disclosed much inner warmth or personality beyond that of an opportunist or survivor. He lived in tortured and challenging times. His characters have little reason to trust their fellows. But as he began to make movies, he married a young woman, apparently named Lisa Rosenthal. She may have been his nurse in the hospital (Hemingway had such a liaison). She may have been Russian and Jewish. We know too little because Lang never advertised the union.

No sooner were they married than Fritz moved out on her because he had begun an affair with Thea von Harbou, a successful novelist and screenwriter from an upper-class family. He was sleeping up. Lisa discovered them in bed together. She was distraught. At which point there are two scripts to choose from: she killed herself in misery, or something else occurred, prompted by the report that Fritz and Thea were slow in calling for help. There is even research that claims Lang may have shot Lisa himself and tipped her body into the bath. Some people at the time never got over that suspicion, and after he married von Harbou, Lang dropped Lisa Rosenthal from memory, talk, or existence itself. Not everyone believed the dark story, but few who knew Fritz ruled it out. He was a locked-up person who went his own way, and his work is preoccupied with vengefulness and guilt.

The Lang–von Harbou partnership prevailed from 1921 for eleven years. She was Lang's screenwriter on everything he made. That means she was part of the narrative inspiration for *Der Müde Tod* (1921), a solemn meditation on death; *Dr. Mabuse the Gambler* (1922), the crucial introduction of the arch-criminal figure (played by Rudolf Klein-Rogge, who had been von Harbou's previous husband); *Die Nibelungen* (1924), the two-part film adaptation from Wagner, the first about Siegfried, a golden Nordic hero, the second, *Kriemhild's Revenge,* still one of the most unrelenting and delirious combat films ever made; *Metropolis,* derived from a novel Thea had written; *Spies* (1928); *Woman in the Moon* (1929), a significant adventure in science fiction; *M* (1931); and *The Testament of Dr. Mabuse* (1933).

This is an astonishing body of work, the core of Lang's greatness, and a monumental assertion of will and creative personality in a German film business that was regularly shaken by economic distress. We speak of the vision of *Metropolis* in its creation of a world where a numb superclass presides over the slavery of the underground worker community. We marvel at that juxtaposition being delivered through art direction and futuristic construction. We are still thrilled by Brigitte Helm playing both the saintly Maria who seeks to organize the workers and the diabolical robot doll ready to seduce anyone and everyone. We are impressed by the length and scale of *Metropolis,* and the way it had been inspired by Lang's visiting Manhattan and imagining future cities. But don't forget its huge losses and how they confirmed Lang's instincts about doom.

The film was a disaster by the blunt test of measurement that hangs over every director. Yet Lang made it seem like a colossal cultural event, not just in Germany but all over the world. It was a venture that indicated the screen excitement and philosophical madness that might be possible in epic cinema. There was a prospect of realism being tossed aside by frenzied poetry. The story's resolution, that the good heart could reconcile the warring head and the hand, was trite fortune-cookie nonsense. H. G. Wells, an approved futurist, was one of many who called it fatuous. But *Metropolis* was felt in 1927, and ever since, as a portentous, scary vision of where modern urban society might be going. Its mixture of trash and prophecy, impact and nonsense, is most prescient—and most indicative of Lang's artistic temperament. The film has survived because of its headstrong mixture of social violence and philosophical pretension.

But it had needed Thea von Harbou, just as she had created Dr. Mabuse as both a monster and a beguiling authoritarian. And it was she who had had the idea—not just innovative but potentially perilous—of making a serial murderer, and a killer of children, the protagonist of *M*. Directors have often disdained their screenwriters; they want to believe the whole work is theirs. But that is a sign of how some of them feel crippled in their dependency on writers—some directors cannot write themselves. It is not just a matter of fluent, credible dialogue. It also means the creation of story arcs that can be the arches to support enterprises as immense as *Metropolis*. In America in the years ahead—the years of freedom, as Lang sometimes said—he never found a writer like von Harbou who had sustained him through ten pictures.

In addition, Lang came to America with very poor English at

the moment when actors had to talk for themselves and seem natural as the medium gave up the declaratory captioning of inter-titles. The naturalism of talk would expose the shrillness in *Metropolis*—it needs forbidding or operatic titles.

When Lang quit Germany, von Harbou stayed behind (she was having an affair with another man). Lang had had many affairs himself during their marriage; the working bond meant more than any romantic feelings. On the few occasions Lang had to film a love story he proved not just helpless but immune. But von Harbou then became a Nazi—that was where her heart lay, as one might judge from her dread and rapture for Mabuse and his warped omniscience. She did no more good work in Germany: she needed Fritz the picture-maker and the dramatist of her ideas. But one can argue that he always missed her naive literary drive. A von Harbou might have been the screenwriter who saw how in *The Big Heat* detective Bannion could become an ugly force of vengeance, locked in an obsessive relationship with Debby the whore—even while his sweet wife was still alive (it's akin to having the two Marias in the same space). Suppose it became a film in which the honest cop became caught up in an illicit affair?

Von Harbou is now a discarded figure in film history, but after Lang's departure she directed a couple of films and wrote at least twenty more. They are no longer seen or remembered. She was imprisoned after the war as a Nazi supporter, and she directed a production of *Faust* in the prison. She died in 1954, one year after *The Big Heat*.

There is another point to make. As was inescapable in the 1920s, Lang's films had to have valiant, handsome, and would-be entertaining heroes who oppose the figures of evil. There is Paul Richter's Siegfried, Gustav Fröhlich as the rich man's son in *Metropolis,* and Gustav Diessl in *The Testament of Dr. Mabuse.* But these men only surpass their enemies in synopsis. On screen, in performance, they cannot compete with the wicked forces whose abiding ambition is universal destruction. There was a taste for Götterdämmerung in Lang—it is there in Mabuse, the temptress robot, and even in Peter Lorre's terrible killer in *M*—and surely that was something the Nazis felt in their souls when they offered Lang the chance to be the director of movies for the Third Reich. They understood his dark energy and fatalism, and they wanted that glamour.

At the time, in 1933, and immediately thereafter, Lang told a story about how he had been invited to lead Nazi cinema and had immediately known that he had to get out of his death-driven country overnight. It wasn't that tidy. The research by Patrick McGilligan for his book on Lang makes it clear that the Austrian needed several months to make up his mind, that he took care to secure as much of his money as possible, that he took a few trips outside Germany before making his grand departure. I don't doubt his self-protective instinct, or his sense of where Germany was headed, but Lang was a professional and a careerist who had always had his eye on Hollywood. There could be a great play about his 1933 hesitation—or a film worthy of Renoir.

America had already been the destination of his two obvious rivals in German cinema: Ernst Lubitsch and F. W. Murnau. Lubitsch had gone west in 1922, and in time his unique satirical touch had won him a production chief role at Paramount and then delivered superb American comedies in pastiche European settings—*The Shop Around the Corner* and *To Be or Not to Be,* pictures of such warmth and emotional intelligence as to leave Lang looking like a chilled kid. Murnau had died in California in 1931 but only after he had made *Sunrise* (1927), a rare amalgam of expressionist European cinema and American romantic idealism. Lang was never the man to make films in that Hollywood mood. He had so little feeling for love, and no respect for America's faith in it. He was—if I can say this—too close to being a fascist.

America did its best to welcome and absorb Fritz Lang. There was talk about how important he could be, and MGM wanted to cash in on the story that this brave man had given up Nazi success to make wholesome American films. That never quite worked out, though his Hollywood debut, *Fury,* is a truly frightening picture, in which an ordinary Joe (Spencer Tracy) gets caught up by a stupid legal system and is then apparently burned to death by a lynch mob in an ugly middle-American town. This portrait of America and its citizenry is alarming. Tracy is very good as the burned man who seeks vengeance. But the film is so diagrammatic and so disconcerting that audiences didn't like it. And something in Lang did not seem able to catch an American idiom or the way Hollywood pictures had to serve the box office. *Fury* did well enough for MGM (with Joseph L. Mankiewicz as its unlikely producer), but the hope for a prestige production fell flat. It seemed unbelievable when Tracy's somber figure went back to being a nice guy, and it was nowhere near enough in correcting the baleful portrait of an odious Middle America. Fritz didn't always get where he was, or what Americans might sound like. He was in a world that needed everyday screen heroes, but he couldn't muster that belief or find a necessary rapport with his actors.

Norman Krasna had done the screenplay for *Fury,* spurred by a real lynching in San Jose, California, in 1935—and his story got the only Oscar nomination that *Fury* received. Lang had wanted the victim to be black (as in the San Jose case) and he was too innocent to realize that Hollywood was not that liberal. The supposedly prestige production subsided in compromise. Lang had thought to end the story bleakly, but he was compelled to stage a reunion and a final kiss between Tracy and his girlfriend (Sylvia Sidney). You could tell his heart wasn't in it. If Ford and Gloria Grahame had ever got it on in *The Big Heat* it could have been heated and a touch perverse. But Hollywood didn't do perverse—at least not in its pictures.

Lang had arrived with the reputation of a freedom fighter, and of a very effective director of action. He tried to be businesslike and obedient. And this was the era of the factory system when many directors lodged themselves with long-term contracts at a studio and began to gather a friendly crew of craftspeople and actors: John Ford at Fox, Frank Capra at Columbia, George Cukor and Vincente Minnelli at MGM, Preston Sturges at Paramount. But MGM did not want Lang for more pictures: they said he was "difficult"; he claimed he was a perfectionist. Later he said he was banned from the studio.

He never found a home or a base. In the next two decades, after *Fury,* he worked for Walter Wanger and United Artists, Paramount, Fox (three films), United Artists, Paramount again, then to International, to Universal, to Warners, to Walter Wanger again, to Republic, back to Fox, two at RKO, two at Columbia (*The Big Heat* was one of them), to MGM, to RKO again, and then finally a return to Universal for *Beyond a*

Reasonable Doubt, a striking work in which the hero is finally revealed as a killer.

So he didn't work enough with the same writers, cameramen, or art directors, let alone actors. Except for his partnership with producer Wanger and Wanger's wife, the actress Joan Bennett, there was no creative thread. And threads worked in Hollywood: the Wanger films are very interesting (*You Only Live Once, Scarlet Street, Secret Beyond the Door*), while Lang's most valuable player in Hollywood was Joan Bennett (*Man Hunt, The Woman in the Window, Scarlet Street, Secret Beyond the Door*). He had an affair with her and used her on screen as a femme fatale, a brave hooker, or a slut. They had a bitter chemistry together, but no warmth.

Lang never earned more than $50,000 for a directorial assignment; some other directors made four times that sum. He never had residuals on his pictures, but he never had what anyone could agree on as a hit. Only vivid supporting players suited to be American villains liked him, people like Dan Duryea, Lee Marvin, and Dan Seymour. Stars like Henry Fonda and Gary Cooper despised him. Fonda said he was just a puppet master; Cooper pretended to be deaf if Lang tried to talk to him. They found him meticulous on props, demanding physical imitation, blank on character or talk. They also noted a degree of sadism in his treatment of vulnerable actors: this had begun with Peter Lorre on *M,* where Lang had seemed to believe in humiliating and hurting the actor to make the killer he played more abject or unbalanced.

That had worked, but for the most part Lang's American heroes are uninhabited costumes, mouthing the lines and not much more. Ford is better than that in *The Big Heat.* But when

Columbia was excited by Ford and Grahame in that film and immediately paired them again in *Human Desire,* the result was a travesty of its blunt title. The actor worth treasuring in Lang's America is Edward G. Robinson as the bourgeois figure lured away from his safe life and into the arms of a risky temptress in *The Woman in the Window* and *Scarlet Street.* Those are not great films; Lang himself admitted that *Scarlet Street* was a lot less than its original, Jean Renoir's *La Chienne.* But they have a feeling for the dull guy aroused by movie sensationalism, and that theme is important in so much cinematic experience. I can never quite shake the feeling that they are set in some European city. That could be because Robinson (born in Bucharest) is fussy, tender, middle-aged, and anxious in un-American ways.

Those two films thrive on Lang's eager eye for enclosing spaces—the obsessive trap that he believed in, as if it was a Ouija board. The high mark of that vision is *The Ministry of Fear* (1944), a symphony of enigmatic doorways and treacherous rooms (it does include a séance). It is also a silly, complicated thriller, where Ray Milland is like a sleepwalker in what Graham Greene would declare was one of the worst movies ever made from his novels. *The Ministry of Fear* did nothing at the box office, but it is a masterpiece if you care to think of motion pictures as if made by Mondrian.

There are some flat-out bad pictures in Lang's America: *You and Me* (an awkward attempt at comedy—he rarely did jokes); *Western Union* (a hollow Western); *House by the River; American Guerrilla in the Philippines* (a listless war movie on location—Lang preferred the studio); *Rancho Notorious* (an inflated Western made on sets with Marlene Dietrich as a vain prop); *The Blue Gardenia* (an inert thriller); *Clash by Night* (a triangle romance from Clifford Odets done without feeling); and even *Moonfleet*. I say "even" because this adaptation of John Meade Falkner's boyish adventure, set in the eighteenth century, in color and CinemaScope, was revered by Lang's French admirers. And it was in that odd alliance that Lang would be rescued in film history.

In the 1950s, in *Cahiers du Cinéma* and *Positif*, Lang was acclaimed as the master he wanted to be. There was a fringe element of French enthusiasm, the MacMahonists (named for a cinema on the avenue MacMahon), who could see the iced grace of Lang's compositions and may not have heard the lameness in his dialogue. They ignored the narrative shortcomings and responded to the pure, cinematic vision. They wrote articles and books about Lang, and used him as a model in condemnation of the alienating Hollywood system. There was truth in that theory—and Lang lasted longer in Hollywood than most of the European refugees: Lubitsch, Renoir, Max Ophüls, Robert Siodmak. When Jacques Rivette made his first feature film, *Paris Nous Appartient* (1961), he used a scene from *Metropolis* to identify the mounting paranoia in a society on the edge of nuclear catastrophe and conspiracy theory. That reference added to the sinister atmosphere of that remarkable New Wave film, which managed to balance cinema verité with the surveillance threat of a Mabusian society. Rivette also wrote a fine essay on Lang's use of hands, a great insight of a sort that could not register in Hollywood. Then there was *Le Mépris*.

More commonly known as *Contempt* (1963), and adapted from Alberto Moravia's novel *Il Disprezzo,* this is Jean-Luc Godard's wintry yet summery-looking dismay over the picture business. Michel Piccoli plays a depressed screenwriter who feels he is selling out to the system, and is subtly offering his wife (Brigitte Bardot) to the rapacious producer (Jack Palance, as a tyrant worthy of Lang). Piccoli is writing a script for a version of *The Odyssey*, and the director of that epic, "Fritz Lang," is played by Lang himself. He was in his early seventies at the time, but he seems older or runic, a man who might have had coffee (or a whore) with Homer.

Contempt is the tragedy of the screenwriter and his wife. As such it has some bearing on the marriage of Godard and his wife, the actress Anna Karina. The director is not presented as a power on this film, or as its creative energy. Indeed, for a man who had once filmed Wagner, this "Lang" was an admission of how far epic cinema had become a colossus of commercial greed and vulgarity exceeding any artistic intention. Godard uses Lang as a forlorn seer, a man who has seen his own ambition overtaken by futility. It seems admiring of Lang to a point of worship, and it added to the cult of a veteran director who would make no more films. But it is like an obituary for Lang and his age of cinema.

Lang did not die until 1976, at the age of eighty-five, in his house on Summit Ridge Drive in Beverly Hills. It was deco, all in white, sparsely furnished, austere, and neurotically tidy. There were just four people at his funeral. He had had no known children. But he had a toy monkey, Peter, that he talked to and put to bed at night. There was a living companion of several decades, Lily Latte, and one of her tasks had been to order in the prostitutes Lang required. He was professional—if that's how you want to put it. He died a year before *Star Wars*, and truly George Lucas was one of his children, if not in artistry or intelligence then in seeing how the cinema of special effects could give us future worlds. *Metropolis* and *M* live on. Both films have their flaws, but they subscribe to Lang's instinct, filled equally with dread and admiration: that authority would shape the world through technology and design; and that murderers might yet become our heroes.

He was the first searing pessimist in a medium given over to crowd-pleasing and sentimentality. In Germany, at least, he had held to desperate visual poetry as a director's duty. I suspect the American Lang regarded himself as a failure, and he made a lot of films that uphold that view. He never had a commercial success. He did not share in the optimism of American cinema. He could not regain his Germany from the 1920s. But he is crucial to an understanding of how Weimar collapsed into fascism. If you want to appreciate Fritz Lang the prophet, you should study the German television series *Babylon Berlin* (on Netflix). It has the energy and fevered precision of his great work, and it leaves us apprehensive about who may be running our show.

3

EVERYONE'S FRIEND: JEAN RENOIR

By contrast to Lang, Jean Renoir was regarded as a good man who understood how real people often lied to themselves in seeing life from their point of view. He was as lovable as his movies seemed tolerant. If you want a quick sense of this man, watch his Octave in *La Règle du Jeu,* an untidy connection in a muddled world, trying to make everyone's life easier—and having little left for himself. It's as if a director could not resist stepping forward and joining in his own picture. For decades he was hailed as a humanist and a model that other directors aspired to.

"When I first came out of the theater, I remember, I just had to sit on the edge of the pavement; I sat there for a good five minutes, and then I walked the streets of Paris for a couple of hours. For me, everything had been turned upside down. All my ideas about the cinema had been changed."

That's the future director Alain Resnais, describing an experience from 1944 (he says, though he may have got the year wrong). Somehow, he had just seen a version of Jean Renoir's

La Règle du Jeu. It cannot have been the full picture the director intended. That had opened in July 1939, an edgy movie in a summer of unease. So the picture had been badly received. In a week it was cut and interfered with. Then it vanished.

It's more likely that Resnais had seen the picture in 1946, when the original version was revived. He does mention a theatre and a curb where a young man could sit and marvel without being arrested. Resnais was twenty-four in 1946. Who can be sure? Memories are our code of faith with history—and memory would be a lasting subject for Resnais, as the thread of both hope and insecurity. Recollection is so emotional; it slips and slides. Everyone has their reasons or their versions of what happened—so they must be brave enough to believe they are remembering truly.

At nineteen, in 1960, I believe the only Renoir film I'd seen was *La Grande Illusion,* at a repertory theatre in south London, when that film about Great War prisoners, French and German, was regarded as a humanist classic, a monument. But I wonder if I had seen *The River* at ten or eleven; I have no way of being sure of this, and it's easy to imagine that film, set in India, seeping back into my childhood, like water finding cracks. As the female narrator says at the end of the film, contemplating the Ganges:

> "*The river runs, the round world spins*
> *Dawn and lamplight, midnight, noon.*
> *Sun follows day, night stars and moon,*
> *The day ends, the end begins.*"

Did I have those lines in my head in 1960? Renoir was not established then. In the book I clung to as an account of film history, Roger Manvell's *The Film and the Public,* published in 1955, there was just one mention of *La Règle du Jeu* and its "tragic burlesque." Manvell was more impressed with another French film from 1939, Marcel Carné's *Le Jour Se Lève,* starring Jean Gabin and Arletty—his book was dedicated to her. But in my deficient French, trying to read *Cahiers du Cinéma,* I was realizing that a generation of young French critics were giving up on Carné and honoring Renoir as their godfather.

Accordingly, in 1958, two enthusiastic French archivists set about recovering and restoring *La Règle,* and thus the film reopened in its best possible form at the Venice Film Festival in September 1959. By 1960, it was in release in London; it was in New York by 1961. That year, at the National Film Theatre in London, Richard Roud (soon to be co-creator of the New York Film Festival) curated a large season on French cinema where Renoir emerged as a central figure. At the same venue in 1962 Roud put on a Renoir season, more or less complete. In the 1962 *Sight & Sound* critics' poll on the best films ever made, *La Règle* was second to *Citizen Kane.* Those two films seemed to be the new portals for a great history. The cinema was properly defined at last. Or so we told ourselves.

For about three decades, Renoir reigned. His films were available and admired. People wrote books about them. One of the happiest classes I taught at Dartmouth was a seminar on Renoir, where I talked about Jean being the son of the painter Pierre-Auguste, growing up in a creative household, and being a subject of some of his father's portraits. That was not just an insight into impressionism, but a threshold to understanding how in being seen—even by family—there was a kind of theatre.

So Renoir the moviemaker was joining hands with French painting of the late nineteenth century. If you wanted to believe in art as a way of getting through life, then this link was so encouraging. It was enhanced by two books Jean wrote: *Renoir, My Father* (published in 1958 in French and 1962 in English), and later a novel, *The Notebooks of Captain Georges.* In setting and attitudes, this was a nineteenth-century work in which a cavalry officer falls in love with a whore. The easygoing sensuality in the sentimental education was more erotically candid than Renoir's films. It felt as natural to love Jean as it was to admire Renoir.

He died at his home in Los Angeles, a naturalized American, in 1979. Orson Welles wrote a fond and discerning obituary for the *Los Angeles Times* that called him "the greatest of all directors." In truth, Renoir seemed a more balanced or warmer person than Welles, and a more mature or less vain storyteller. As I said, we reckoned that his bumbling, emotional confidant to all, Octave, in *La Règle du Jeu,* was the man himself as well as an example of how some people go through life as directors of the action. I saw Renoir once in person at the National Film Theatre and he was the definition of gregarious, attentive and encouraging, yet shy, watchful, and oddly insecure. He was so like Octave there was no need to think of him acting.

There's a key in that hesitation that takes us into Renoir's style as a director—and the persuasive thought for several decades that he had created a way of seeing stories, people, space and relationships that had (and has) never been surpassed.

Renoir was born in 1894, effectively the dawn of the movie process. There is a generation that seemed inevitably suited to the medium and it includes Fritz Lang, Luis Buñuel, Alfred

Hitchcock, and Howard Hawks. They were infant cameras, if you like; they grew up looking to see. But Jean was not immediately set on pictures. He wanted to be a ceramicist first, a secondary art in the life of his father, that unrestrained painter of hedonism, light, society, and female nakedness. That last motif makes people uncomfortable now, and there is a nervous regret that Renoir the painter hired servant girls to take off their clothes and be his models and his dreams.

Who knows? Who can feel what that meant to Jean or to the women? The old man was infirm; he had bad arthritis that crippled and restricted him. The photographs of Pierre-Auguste show a man wizened by pain, even anger, because of it. Jean stands beside him like a loving sentry. But the painter was not helpless. He painted and he had three sons: Pierre (who became an actor—he played Simenon's Maigret in Jean's *La Nuit de Carrefour* and Louis XVI in *La Marseillaise*), Jean (born when his father was fifty-three), and Claude (born when he was sixty). For decades, connoisseurs and the public alike were in awe of his peaceful, statuesque nudes, as steady as trees and patient while time passes. Nowadays we are not as relaxed. In presenting a Renoir show at the Clark Art Institute, curator Martha Lucy said Renoir had come to stand for "sexist male artist." "Who doesn't have a problem with Pierre-Auguste Renoir?" Peter Schjeldahl asked in *The New Yorker* in the summer of 2019.

We don't know what happened in his studio beyond the fact that at eighteen Andrée Heuschling was one of Pierre-Auguste's last models, in a household where Jean was recovering from war wounds. Jean and Andrée fell in love; he may have seen her naked first in his father's brushstrokes. They mar-

ried a month after the father's death, in 1919, and she became
Catherine Hessling, the lead actress in several of Jean's earliest
films, including *Nana,* from the Zola novel.

Hessling is a conventional silent screen actress; she's pretty,
or photogenic, but she has limited herself to being an intense
projection of appearance. So intent on being a burning light,
she seldom grasps the inwardness in which the light of self may
flicker out, like a flame—in which the intensity could be more
vulnerable or liquid. This is a way of saying that Renoir only
discovered cinema with sound, and the way its enriched naturalism allowed actors *to be,* instead of projecting. The famous
Renoir motto, that everyone has their reasons, is prelude to
a way of photographing people in groups in which they have
their reasons, or their space, when company can slip into chaos.

To be precise: in a film, actors do what they can to look like
a character: take this given pose and gaze at the distance; now
turn to the right, and in doing so you cannot stop revealing
something else, an edge of doubt or anxiety going from one
pose to another. Now walk across the room—live in space—
and we can begin to see how complicated you are, how ordinary as well as good-looking. You have your reasons, but you
have so much more: your clothes, your expressions—the way
you react to being looked at—your room, the view through the
window, the breeze that stirs the curtains and your hair: the
open-ended entirety of your possibility.

I want to keep this analysis vague, or gentle, because Renoir
was never dogmatic about it and may never have had it as a
textbook approach in his head. Nevertheless, in the 1930s, in
black-and-white, he fashioned and improvised a way of looking at life (call it mise en scène) that amounts to a credo: look,

this is what cinema can be—the same as life. Without any of the melodramatic stress Welles felt for deep focus in *Kane*, Renoir had been pushing focus and its tenderness with real space for years. For Welles, deep focus resonated with vibrato, just like his voice. For Renoir, seeing more, and placing figures in their context, was matter-of-fact; it was lifelike as well as cinematic, and it was an unconscious harking back to paintings by his father that reveled in group situations in the open air—I'm thinking of pictures like *Bal du Moulin de la Galette* (1876) and *Luncheon of the Boating Party* (1882), where fifteen or so people are caught in a casual situation, without seeming crowded or composed, but in a latent theatricality that is a perfect comparison to the frantic group scenes, the tragic burlesque of the farce at the close of *La Règle du Jeu*.

Even if you feel you know the 1939 film quite well, if I asked you to name the cast I suspect you'd have some difficulty. Yes, you'd know it was Renoir himself as Octave, and Marcel Dalio as the marquis, Robert de La Chesnaye. But who plays Christine, Geneviève, Lisette, Schumacher, Marceau the poacher, or André Jurieu?

There's no reason to feel guilty, or to doubt Renoir's affection for his players. But he did not care to make movies about movie stars. His characters are attractive sometimes, but they are not picked out in close-ups with sculpted romantic lighting; they are faces in a gallery of faces. If everyone has their reasons— even the small-part players—then no one rises above the others or has a charisma that can subdue the needs of society or the group. *La Règle du Jeu* applies to an untidy gathering of people, a party, in which servants and masters can easily change places, in which we are not trapped in a fantasy identification with a

Cary Grant or a Garbo. Not that that impulse is unpleasant or unrewarding. But movie star films do assert a hierarchy of beauty or greatness or blessed aloneness. And Renoir says no to that. We are not alone; we are all alike, and in deep focus and group shots you can't help seeing that bystanders or onlookers believe they are as much a center of attention as the apparent leads, like the marquis, Christine, and all the rest. His deep focus knows that life is about all the rest.

Not that there isn't an extraordinary level of performance in Renoir films. As the marquis in *La Règle,* Dalio gives one of the most beguiling performances in all of film, an uneasy aristocrat, a dapper Jew, a dandy but a mess, a womanizer longing to be in love, a master who likes servants, a character actor who has backed into a lead role. It's worth recalling that within a few years of *La Règle,* and his enforced departure from France as a Jewish actor, Dalio was re-established at Warner Brothers—as the croupier at Rick's place in *Casablanca,* as Frenchie in *To Have and Have Not.* He had shifted from lead roles to cameos and supporting parts. He may have sighed over this, but perhaps he understood Renoir's attitude, that everyone is a supporting player. And that the thing being supported—call it existence and misunderstanding, as much as rapture or happiness—is what films should be about.

Equally, Renoir could find a player who was so compelling that he might build entire films around him. Michel Simon was a year younger than Jean, and he seemed ugly or unsuited to movies. This was not just a matter of his looks; it had to do with his liberated ungainliness, his sense of other, odder rhythms and darker thoughts than those shown by most actors; his eccentricity. Simon had the reputation of being a rascal, a libertine, and perverse, all things he encouraged the way a tramp might let the rain and the light fall on him. Renoir used Simon in *Tire au Flanc* (1928) and *On Purge Bébé* (1931), modest comedies. But then he put him in *La Chienne,* Renoir's first inadvertent masterpiece. I say that because it has all the air of a regular film.

La Chienne is about a lowly bank cashier caught in a bad marriage who meets a prostitute. He falls for her and a melodrama follows, though Renoir keeps it at the level of a small newspaper story, not a grand passion. But he opens up space and depth before our eyes and the actuality of this anecdote becomes so compelling that . . . well, Simon fell in love with Janie Marèse, the actress playing the whore. It is an example of how the magic of film can turn its players into ghosts of their screened selves.

But in this process, Renoir was captivated by Simon and his unexpected being. That led to casting him as the tramp in *Boudu Saved from Drowning,* in which a would-be suicide, thinking to drown himself in the Seine, is rescued by an alert bookseller and proceeds to disrupt that good man's life. *La Chienne* and *Boudu* preceded Simon's famous role in Jean Vigo's *L'Atalante,* and I think they nourished it, for we are talking about a film climate in which filmmakers learned from the pictures they were seeing.

Simon's infatuation wasn't tidy. Janie Marèse had fallen in love with Georges Flamant, the actor who played her pimp. They went off together and she was killed in a car crash with him driving. At the funeral, Simon threatened Renoir for having caused this tragedy—but then they reconciled and made *Boudu* together. It's hard to believe decades later that no one has ever tried a movie about what happened on *La Chienne.*

La Chienne and *Boudu* are landmarks, too offhand to live comfortably as masterpieces but ravishing displays of how cinema—with sound and a natural, unstressed way of seeing things—had become the essential modern way of telling short stories. Few remarked on this at the time (but few in America noticed how a Howard Hawks was altering the possibility of Hollywood movies without grabbing attention or many Oscars). Renoir's line of work carried on with *Madame Bovary, Toni, Le Crime de Monsieur Lange, La Grande Illusion, La Marseillaise, La Bête Humaine,* all the way to *La Règle du Jeu,* at which point hostilities intervened. *La Règle* rattled French fears when audiences craved comfort—so few had the calm to recognize its glory.

There's another work to include in this line, a broken or unfinished film, *Partie de Campagne.* It's from a Guy de Maupassant story—Maupassant was an influential source for the movies—in which a Parisian family goes to the country on a summer's day. The daughter has an impulsive romantic adventure that amounts to one of the director's most resonant glimpses of passion on screen. It's a film about windows opening and things being seen, about a river and a nearly crushed treatment of eroticism (Sylvia Bataille is one of the most pained, lyrical faces in film). It suggests that wistful irony is the only possible defense in life, and it regards a river as a bloodstream. Renoir was developing a theory that we are all like corks bobbing along on a river, self-important of course, but no more significant than the passing scoops of light on the surface of the flowing water, always different, always alike.

Intruded on by bad weather and other assignments, *Partie de Campagne* never made it to full length. Let's say it could be the greatest forty-minute picture ever attempted. Though filmed in 1936, it was left unfinished until the producer Pierre Braunberger released it in 1946, as if a true film is ever quite finished, as if the river stops when someone calls "Cut!" Renoir was close to a feeling that passing time meant a movie should never stop. We think of this condition as surveillance now, though that is seldom as warm as Renoir wanted. There is a chill in all cameras (as Christopher Isherwood foresaw), and it can affect the tone of their stories.

So Renoir and his companion, Dido Freire (his continuity assistant), left for America. So many talented people were getting out of Europe in a muddle of terror and fatalism. Renoir would say later how *La Grande Illusion* had been called the greatest antiwar film ever made. It was actually nominated for the Best Picture Oscar—the first time for a foreign-language film (it lost to Frank Capra's *You Can't Take It With You*)—and then two years later war broke out. Corks or common lives have so little agency, without engine, rudder, or sails.

If Renoir is your hero, then you want to be confident about the bold line of his life and you can foresee that he would become American, living in Beverly Hills instead of in the Renoir country house in the Sologne. In truth, I think his life was always so untidy he only acted bold. That is the survivor's way, and in 1939 survival could mean everything. He might have stayed in France. He might have been killed because of that. He could have faced the tough test of collaboration or resistance. He might have rubbed shoulders with Jean-Pierre Melville and Chris Marker and even the youthful Alain Resnais, filmmakers who had some attachment to the Resistance. Let's just say that in his own artistic conscience there were seldom unequivocal heroes.

His American pictures are not to be forgotten, or overrated, just because they are Renoir. There's *Swamp Water, This Land Is Mine, The Southerner, Diary of a Chambermaid, The Woman on the Beach.* You can say that they all resist Hollywood even as Renoir strove to be American—*Swamp Water* and *The Southerner* are rural pictures, under the sway of Robert Flaherty and even William Faulkner. They are deserving curiosities, but I feel they are lost and unsatisfactory. I think *Diary of a Chambermaid* is the best, and the most French, for all the flair of Paulette Goddard and Burgess Meredith. Charles Laughton is cripplingly humble and ingratiating in *This Land Is Mine,* a huge star the more disconcerting for his attempt to be commonplace. The film has no naturalism, and that's a signal omission in these American years. It's as if Renoir never quite found or trusted the real in America. In a way, Fritz Lang (the two were not friends) adjusted to Hollywood's requirements better than Renoir and in that time he remade *La Chienne* as *Scarlet Street,* with Edward G. Robinson, Joan Bennett, and Dan Duryea. *Scarlet Street* is very watchable but about twenty-five percent of *La Chienne.*

Lang stayed in Hollywood another ten years after the end of the war, never quite sure if he was as much a prisoner as he might have been in Nazi Germany. During that time, he made *Human Desire,* a failed remake of *La Bête Humaine,* as if to demonstrate crucial cultural differences. Even with Glenn Ford and Gloria Grahame, the title was a travesty next to the heat Renoir had found between Jean Gabin and Simone Simon.

Renoir was in prison, too, in Hollywood. *The Woman on*

the Beach seemed the most promising of his American films—
it's a triangle melodrama, with Robert Ryan falling for Joan
Bennett, who is wife to a blinded painter played by Charles
Bickford. It shrank to seventy-one minutes, a complete failure.
The studio head Darryl Zanuck was heard to say that Renoir,
though talented, "was not one of us."

Still living in Beverly Hills, Renoir read Rumer Godden's
novel *The River*, and his urge to make another film returned
after depression. But a producer said why make a film in India
without a jungle and tigers? For a moment, Renoir toyed with
the thought of Marlon Brando as the wounded American soldier trying to rehabilitate in India. But that fell through the
cracks and eventually Renoir went off to Bengal itself and settled for a cobra instead of tigers.

It is a film about watching three young women in a wild
garden, and it was Renoir's first film in color, photographed
by his nephew Claude Renoir. The girls are Patricia Walters,
Adrienne Corri, and the Indian actress Radha, and they play
young women contemplating being in love with their wounded
American, played by Thomas E. Breen. Then one hot afternoon as they are taking a nap—the camera sinks in and out
like breathing—the little boy of the household, Bogey, is bitten
by the cobra he wanted to make friends with.

The film was paid for by a Los Angeles florist. In the making, Renoir met and encouraged a young Bengali, Satyajit
Ray. Radha became president of the Theosophical Society of
India. Patricia Walters made a few more films. Adrienne Corri
went on as a flamboyant actress—all of which is promised in
her headstrong presence in *The River*. I could say it is a great
film about adolescence and romantic yearning; don't forget

how glorious it is in color, music, and dance. Still, I don't quite know why I'm weeping about it as I write.

Surely I saw it as a child, or have I not grown up yet?

The three young players were more or less nonprofessional actors. Corri had made one film and she would have a career (she was sensational as Nastasia in a TV adaptation of *The Idiot* in 1966). You feel she was determined about that at twenty. But Renoir loved them all as amateurs and he said you could do wonders with such unshaped talent so long as you never gave them their set story. Rehearse them in other parts or possibilities. Let them become acquainted with the scheme of pretending. Only then give them their character and their lines, and set them free—perhaps in just one take. I think Renoir regarded India itself as another nonprofessional player, and that's testament to the way he had appreciated life as a series of *contes,* or scoops of light on the surface of the river. There is a short film, twenty-two minutes, hard to find, made in 1968, in which Renoir rehearses an actress (Giselle, the wife to Pierre Braunberger). I don't know why it is hard to find when people are so interested in acting. But being inaccessible or lost in cinema is not to be overlooked or wasted. In a medium obsessed with all we can see, the invisible or the out of frame may hold great secrets.

Acting had become Renoir's subject and his pilgrimage in the three films of his late glory: *The Golden Coach* (1952), *French Cancan* (1954), and *Elena and Her Men* (1956). They are all period films in color, exotic exercises, unlikely but made with absolute assurance.

The Golden Coach concerns traveling players in a South American country (it is said to be Peru). The viceroy has a golden coach which he thinks to give to his mistress until he meets Camilla, the lead actress in the commedia dell'arte troupe. She is embodied by Anna Magnani in a diagram of desire and deception. The lifelike fluency of the 1930s is now fixed in color and procedural camera movements that lift the action into a kind of ritual—a play. Unless that sounds like the curse of theatre, let me add that in the 1950s, in France, Renoir had become absorbed in stage work. To that end he directed productions of *Julius Caesar* and Clifford Odets's *The Big Knife* (with Daniel Gélin in the lead), and he also mounted a play of his own, *Orvet,* with Leslie Caron in the lead (he had thought of casting her in *The River*). As for *The Golden Coach* (adapted from Prosper Mérimée, but Mozartian in its way; Mozart is a deep dramatic influence on *La Règle du Jeu*), it should be seen as a screwball comic romance, and one of the airiest syllabubs Magnani ever allowed herself.

Still, I think it is preparation for the magnificent *French Cancan,* which may be based in fact or legend, but let it soar unencumbered. It claims to be the situation that introduced the cancan to Parisian society in which Danglard (Jean Gabin) is an impresario always looking for a new attraction and a fresh female he can present. Thus, he abandons one mistress (María Félix) to "discover" a young laundress (Françoise Arnoul) who can cancan. But then, as the dance triumphs in Paris, Danglard is a river that moves on and finds another woman. The laundress is hurt and angry at this—for a moment she won't dance—and it may be today that a concerned public would be indignant to see a late-middle-aged lecher grooming and having young talent just to keep his show alive.

So maybe the film has dated or moved into a gloomy, disapproving light. Maybe its mood and dynamic are simply show business, and maybe that is a bad place now for virtuous people to go. You must make up your mind over such questions. But what you are seeing (try the film day after day for a week) is a unique movie musical (there is a cameo with Edith Piaf), an amused pastiche of the Paris celebrated in impressionist paintings, and something like exhilaration. If it's a scandal to be so excited, so be it.

There were more films: *Elena and Her Men* (a showcase return for Ingrid Bergman after she had left Roberto Rossellini); *Le Déjeuner sur l'Herbe,* a flagrant paean to sexuality and female nudity, a film for Pierre-Auguste, some of it shot in his garden at Cagnes-sur-Mer; *Le Testament du Docteur Cordelier,* where Jean-Louis Barrault is uncanny as the Jekyll-and-Hyde figure; *The Elusive Corporal,* a rather leisurely return to the comradeship of prisoners of war; and *Le Petit Théâtre de Jean Renoir,* a film of episodes that finds room for Françoise Arnoul and Jeanne Moreau, an actress who might have been imagined by Renoir long before he worked with her. By which I mean to say that she was a player born for the avid, nervy way of looking that Renoir had identified, and which he had shared with Truffaut, Godard, Rohmer, and Rivette.

In that spirit, he was not just the director of the allegedly second-greatest film ever made, but also the father to a tide of new waves. But the theory of waves and rivers says that only in paintings and photographs can they be stilled. Renoir is unique and most influential in teaching us how movies have told only part of the story.

Reputation is made to be undermined. There are small signs: in the *Sight & Sound* poll of 2012, *La Règle du Jeu* dropped to fourth. That's hardly bad, and if Ozu's *Tokyo Story* was now ahead of it one could fairly say that that story of parents being passed by was a film Renoir would have cherished. But is *Vertigo* better than *La Règle*? That seems to be opting for neurosis over reason—and that is a useful way of assessing recent cinema history. More to the point is my feeling that people today, cinephiles, whatever we want to call ourselves, are not seeing Renoir as much, or not thinking about him.

We have to recognize that stylistic history has moved on. The cinema of mise en scène, honoring time and space in the unfolding of a plausible story, has yielded to the engine of editing, to special effects, and to a reverence for things on screen such as no one has seen in life. To be solemn about that, you can say that fantasy is suppressing visibility. Even a Renoir believer, like Godard, played a leading part in that deconstruction. *Pierrot le Fou* is a Renoirish story reassessed in a chilly mood of film analysis. I think it's a great film, but it points toward an emotional nihilism that Renoir would have rejected—in his amiable way.

My unease over this unannounced tendency in film appreciation was added to by the publication in English, in 2016, of Pascal Mérigeau's book *Jean Renoir: A Biography*. It had appeared in France in 2012 and won prizes there for its meticulous research into a life that had not been that fully attended to before. Had it been trusted too much? When a translation appeared in English it came with a one-page foreword from Martin Scorsese, that began, "There are very few artists in the history of movies who are undeniable. Jean Renoir is one of those few. If you're dealing with cinema, you're dealing with Renoir."

Mérigeau's book proves much better than that, and far more questioning. At 942 pages, published by Brett Ratner's Ratpac Press, it is a big book. But it was barely reviewed: once upon a time it would have been recognized as an event. I found it poorly written and translated, and that adds to its nagging, remorseless quality. For the book has set out to strip Renoir of the sentimental veneration that treats him as a great man and a good guy. I felt this because I realize that I had myself huddled in that uncritical fondness. I admire Mérigeau's stringency and his mounting lack of affection for Renoir the man. Jean could be mean, sneaky, conniving.

He had his reasons. I'm grateful for the book. Not all film directors are good people. Mérigeau helps us see that Danglard was selfish, obsessed, too distant, while pretending to be everyone's friend. I can live with that; it applies to me too. But I am glad to think that I won't live to see Renoir slipping to the neglect that Marcel Carné now inhabits—and which he does not deserve. So we cling to the moments when an Alain Resnais staggered out of the dark in turmoil and a feeling of being changed.

Once upon a time, Renoir was the model of humanist cinema, an informal genre that included Frank Capra, Vittorio De Sica, Satyajit Ray, and even Chaplin. But today, it's harder to find humanist contenders. Many of our most renowned directors have been wary of human society—think of Kubrick, Polanski, Ingmar Bergman, Michael Haneke, Scorsese, Jane Campion, Bong Joon-ho. Even a masterpiece of compassion, Pedro Almodóvar's *Pain and Glory,* was sometimes shrugged off as too soft-hearted. So it says a lot about the trial of being a director that we are less trusting in the community of the medium now. In the age of Covid, we had to see how steadily for years the crowd was less drawn to going to the movies.

There was an era when we wanted to admire movie directors, and so we overlooked their desperation and the way they assumed power. We are less forgiving now about that authority. Anyone in the film business knows how much it is a power game. But humanists in the dark are inclined to idealize creative figures. So Ingmar Bergman may have been a great artist, *and* a sacred monster.

Can we handle that double act?

4

IN DREAMS: LUIS BUÑUEL

Renoir was in love with the facts in photography and its stunning appearance. He was his father's son, and in the 1930s, as he did his great work, he had the young Henri Cartier-Bresson as an assistant. Jean reveled in Pierre-Auguste's light, but there was a deeper spirit awake in cinema, one that felt the psychic currents beneath appearance. So it's not enough or useful to insist on seeing Luis Buñuel in the clear and reliable light of fact. One needs to slip into his kind of dream.

I am trying to describe the start of a Buñuel film. An open landau with two horses is coming down a long road in a rural estate. This carriage feels older than the young couple it holds, a man and a woman, modern and chatting amiably. Séverine and Pierre. The two coachmen wear black, buttoned uniforms, with top hats, riding boots, and dress coats. They seem like policemen or custodians from an earlier age (before 1914?) and a different code of obedience. They are controlling the carriage, making a pleasant ride for the couple. She is blonde in a red dress, so lovely her very point seems being an adorable emblem. Isn't she set to be our "belle"? He is youthful, dressed in safe gray, a suitable husband. This is all very nice, and we can hear faint bells as if from the harness of the horses. Wedding bells? What else would you expect on a honeymoon?

Then the carriage halts—we are in remoter country now, near florid trees and undergrowth. Attitudes have shifted; secrecy is set free. Some darker plan is ready. We feel the suspense in watching. We don't want to miss anything. This is getting close to the nature of cinema.

The husband and the coachmen now drag the woman from the carriage. This is outrageous, but we do nothing about it. Are we accomplices? She protests—she thought she was the wife—but her treatment is remorseless. No rescue is at hand—only us, and we know we are not responsible; that is not our thing. We see her stockings collapsed around her ankles. She is gagged. The husband says he will kill her if she screams. What can we do but watch?

Is this a masterpiece or something that should not be allowed?

Ropes bind her wrists, and when the rope is pulled she is nearly hanging from a tree. The husband tears down the top of her red dress and then rips away her white bra. We see her naked back and her blonde hair. This is all done "tastefully"—please don't be afraid. The husband gives a signal and the coachmen move in to whip her. This is not exactly pleasant, but somehow it seems allowed or available for us. We feel we should not be watching, but there we are. Perhaps you should not be reading? Our best protection is that this could be a dream.

We hear the lashes. She reels in anguish. But her skin stays flawless. "Enough!" decides the husband. Is he going to forgive her? (Forgive her for what?) Instead, he tells the younger, tougher coachman to take her. This man removes his top hat and unbuttons his tunic. We might as well understand the imminence of his blunt service. He goes up to the tethered woman, dips his rough head into her bare back, and kisses her. Her pained face, that wild hair, are thrown back in some fusion of submission and desire.

It is a piercing scene fifty years after it was made, but I doubt *Belle de Jour* could be delivered now as a fresh festival offering. Presented at Cannes, even with the mature Catherine Deneuve in the audience (she is past seventy-five, a monarch in France), it might prompt howls of outrage as if the MeToo audience felt it was being challenged. The film won the Golden Lion at Venice in 1967, but now . . . ?

Then the husband's voice asks, "What are you thinking, Séverine?" and there they are, at home, the two of them, ready for bed. She is already lying there in a pretty nightdress, her long, brushed hair spread out on the pillow. She smiles, she was thinking of him, of them, she says, and she does look prepared for love, or whatever these two call it.

But they have separate single beds—are they from Hollywood's Code or some antique European upper class? The hubby—he is so boyish in white pajamas—does think of getting in bed with her. Then alarm invades her lovely face, and she tells him no, not now.

As she was about to be humiliated by her postilion, she had asked her Pierre, the husband, "Don't let the cats loose." As if worrying over what small sharp teeth could do in a dream.

We hadn't seen or thought about cats until that line, but now we can't forget a hint of danger attached to them. They are like the smothered impulse to ravish this carnal statue in her Yves Saint Laurent clothes and that Catherine Deneuve face.

The story of Séverine and Pierre may start like this, as a rule, but that is not a normal way of beginning a celebration of a film director. In due course I will get to a synopsis of Buñuel's career, but that outline wouldn't impress him. Being useful goes only so far if you are willing your own postilions to ravish your wife. I could tell you how Luis Buñuel came to be in Paris to make this film in 1966–67; I could fit it in place in a sensible way. But I wouldn't put much trust in being so workmanlike.

Instead, I feel drawn to a lingering close-up of Jean Sorel (Pierre) as he looks away, beyond the frame, at the idea of an outrage visited on his wife. There's such innocent longing in his face, such aspiration: he could be Columbus seeing Las Vegas (instead of Hispaniola). I have a similar wish to dwell on the smoothness of Deneuve's skin (not so much young as eternal or impossible), that sound of small bells in the distance, and what those cats may mean.

Not that there's going to be a tidy equation: the cats = Zoroastrianism, the Cuban Missile Crisis of 1962, or Luis's admitted addiction to secret passageways. Rather, the cats mean anything and everything. At any point, in any film, you could cut to a shot of cats getting loose and it would work. Suppose *Citizen Kane* murmurs "Rosebud," the glass ball shatters, and cats are seen escaping. It's less a matter of what that means, than meaning hanging in the theatre air like perfume or longing. You could take that close-up of Pierre, add a view of Séverine bound and whipped, and then the cats, slinky, low-slung, tentative but lethal, getting away from confinement. Put those three shots together *in any order*—and you'll have a movie, with audiences in a frenzy if you don't continue it.

That suggestion of violence may seem fanciful, but you never know: the whips do come out. Make human beings desire something and there's no way of being sure you can control them. In *That Obscure Object of Desire*—Buñuel's last film (1977)—Mathieu is quite desperate to get his hands and other moving parts on Conchita. His desire is so profound and humiliating he cannot see that she is two actresses! When Maria Schneider was deemed "unfit" for that project, Buñuel had replaced her with two actresses, Ángela Molina and Carole Bouquet. This seems absurd, yet magical, and suddenly we see how casting has always been a trick of desire in which any man or woman serves a fantasy.

Nearly forty years before *Belle de Jour,* in Paris still, Buñuel and Salvador Dalí presented *Un Chien Andalou,* just seventeen minutes long. It is a jazzy fable about the desperate gestures of desire and all its variations. Male hands touch a woman's clothed breasts. She resists. He tries again. The dress dissolves to bare breasts. And close-ups of faces behold the idea of such actions, not just as real events, but as daydreams, like cats, curled up on the sofas of polite society. You could cut these shots into *Belle de Jour* and they would make a marriage— except that Buñuel knows official marriage is just the pretty vehicle in which desire rides. He was fixed on the simplest, witty threats, like the outrage implicit in seeing and being seen. He understood this as the forbidden transaction in cinema. *We really shouldn't be watching,* because that could make us recognize our deluding myths. So cinema is always hovering over the illicit—the male gaze. The doubling of Conchita is a provocative joke, but it does insinuate that for this kind of man all women are alike, and in a kind of servitude.

The mention of Salvador Dalí may have alerted you to saying: of course! Dalí and Buñuel were surrealists—there's your answer, or your way of evading unsettling implications. Those surrealists were deliberately crazy, downright naughty. They did whatever they thought of, and left decent, hardworking police to tidy up the mess. So you can speculate to your heart's content over what means what, because these fellows had *no thought of anything meaning anything.* They were so silly!

But you have felt some efficacy in fleeing cats at the start of *Citizen Kane.* No, Orson Welles didn't intend that, but think how he does poeticize that moment of the ball slipping from Kane's hand and becoming shards of glass through which we see a nurse in white coming into the room after the "Rosebud," the word everyone will claim they heard. Don't rule out the chance of Kane dreaming. With a cat on his lap?

You are already too vulnerable to the associations in any film to be fobbed off with excuses about the surrealists being frivolous. Perhaps they understood movie better than anyone and the chance of any cut being poetic. Weren't they in the habit of walking in on a movie in progress, waiting in the dark while they worked out what it was "about," and then leaving to seek another film and submit to its intense but clouded visions— until some drab plot resolution shut down interest? It's reasonable or optimistic to speak of film being a narrative medium, but the more neurotic the plot impulse the quicker our interest drains away. If films last in our minds it is because of their mysteries.

By the way, if it occurred to you that that surrealist habit of entering a film after it had begun was a proof of silliness, be cautious. Try it yourself, and notice the exciting creative vulnerability you feel with a film that is already running. Just because a movie starts on time is no reason why you have to be obediently "on time" or forget "once upon a time." How else are you meant to understand the affinities between *Un Chien Andalou* and *Belle de Jour,* and to recognize their fascination with fascination? You see, they are both one film, just as Luis Buñuel really had no other subject or process than filming ardent faces beholding objects of desire and attempting to balance propriety and abandon.

Buñuel used different stories, but he never departed from the irony in frustrated desire. In *Un Chien Andalou,* the male and female want to be independent, to be themselves, but they cannot resist the biological allure of coming together. *They cannot help looking at one another.* In *L'Age d'Or* a man and a woman are lifetime aspirants to—but confirmed failures in—the perfect fuck club. They are so in love. Yet they perceive that the surest stimulus to desire is in being thwarted. In just the same way, in *Belle de Jour* Séverine experiments with sexual satisfaction (she goes professional) and sees how hard it is to reconcile that obsession with bourgeois contentment. She is so austerely pure—that is the air of Deneuve's blancmange skin—that she needs to be a depraved whore trading on her virginal propriety. She has her perfect young husband, but she cannot resist a swaggering young gangster, an inscrutable Japanese man with a magic box full of . . . is it a mechanical cat?, the gloomy attention of a perverse friend, or the lesbian caress of the brothel keeper. Sex is not particular or sentimental. It is the wind or the air. Thus it is necessary to abandon the formality of having it with just an "ideal" partner.

That last is no small liberty and it may lead us to the damning problem, the ultimate detachment, in Buñuel, the thing that takes his slippery genius too far for our culture.

He may be the most provincial of the great film directors, having been born in Calanda, in Teruel province, Aragón, in 1900. His father was rich from trade in the U.S. and Cuba but in his forties he came back to Calanda and married a beautiful, seventeen-year-old aristocratic girl in the flawless spirit of bourgeois accomplishment. So the boy emerged from Calanda, a town he would later describe as existing in the stupor of the Middle Ages until 1914. He grew up in Zaragoza, attended the University of Madrid, and after that he was in Paris as a hanger-on in avant-garde circles. But he never lost his reliance on well-to-do male characters, childlike in their privilege, and their lofty view of life, women, and their daft sexual eminence. *Él* and *The Criminal Life of Archibaldo de la Cruz* feature such handsome puppets who know very little of the world they control.

Then, in his last years, Buñuel found that the impeccable but thoroughly guilty Fernando Rey was made for such a corrupt paragon, libidinous but curiously innocent in *Tristana, The Discreet Charm of the Bourgeoisie,* and, above all, in *That Obscure Object of Desire,* where his Mathieu is a complacent Don Juan, a gentleman who has never thought to work a day in his life, cultivated but not educated. These are men used to riding in carriages in the fragrant avenues of a lost world. Buñuel was often known as a radical and a leftist, even an insurrectionary, but time and again he exults in conservative attitudes and would no more give them up than he might abandon caviar, solitude, or collecting firearms.

As he worked his way in Paris from the Middle Ages to modernism, he served as an assistant to Jean Epstein on *The Fall of the House of Usher* in 1928. In the same spirit, but with money from his mother (that favored bourgeois scheme for getting ahead) he and Salvador Dalí made *Un Chien Andalou*—it was brief, pungent, and erotic, with that opening scene of a razor slicing a young woman's eye and thus providing jacket illustration for so many thrilled celebrations of the new medium. Note, it *was* a female eye; it was a rape, no matter that the eye seemed unfazed until the razor bit.

The cheeky pals said the whole venture was meant to be senseless and automatic or improvised, but they relied on the surrealist awareness that you can't put random things together without some rabid spectator detecting a link. So breasts become buttocks and desire rhymes with despair, a watching face is a horizon, and so on. Ninety years ago, *Un Chien Andalou* insulted the bourgeois idea of a motion picture business—the orgy is here, desire anything you see—and the hell with polite seeing. It was the first dangerous film, and arguably still vital enough today to be the last, rolling along on the tango records Buñuel played at the Paris screening.

A year and a bit later, on his own, but with money from the Vicomte Charles de Noailles, Buñuel enlarged *Un Chien Andalou* to sixty-three minutes and called it *L'Age d'Or*. It is different, with two thwarted lovers (Gaston Modot and Lya Lys), but it is a strained operatic version of the shorter film, and its bigger bang, with references to the Marquis de Sade and a debauched Jesus Christ, was calculated to provoke the modest riots that ensued. Orderly idiots yelled and threw ink at the screen.

This is Buñuel, sui generis, of course, but it's also almost decadent and humorless. And not nearly as sexy—even if it had an extensive influence, not least on Jean Renoir's celebrated *La Règle du Jeu,* which adopted several of its themes and images (a gamekeeper, a gun, and an orchestral conductor, as well as Monsieur Modot).

Then Buñuel stopped, as if bored. So much for the principle of the obsessive artist compelled to make pictures and feed his appetite. Perhaps his private funding dried up. Perhaps the debut outburst had sated him: some directors give up their all on a first picture. Or was he out of ideas and impulses? He did make a short documentary, *Las Hurdes,* about peasant hardship in an "unbelievably backward" area in Salamanca. It's a grim, depressing, and obligatory piece of protest certain it can do nothing to mend the unforgivable world.

From 1932 to 1947, Buñuel roamed or dithered. They were years of instability: the civil war in Spain, and then the larger conflict. His name was attached to a few projects: he worked on dubbing American films for Spain; he was at the Museum of Modern Art in New York for a spell, doing very little; he does seem to have devised a scene—of a severed but live hand—for Robert Florey's *The Beast with Five Fingers.* But then he came to ground in Mexico for *Gran Casino,* and suddenly he took root on low-budget pictures of increasing interest. It was as if, nearing fifty, he had decided to have a career, and chose to site it in one of the least promising film industries where he could be understood, and freer from censorship than in his own Spain.

Some of the Mexican pictures are as light as the setting made likely. But some are departures, as Buñuel had his first chance to learn the craft. In 1950, *Los Olvidados* was an apparent piece of neorealism, in which the exposed dreams of young beasts in Mexico City slums went way beyond conventional socialist hopes on their behalf. Buñuel never believed people could be saved, or really wanted it. He did not foresee a healed Séverine or a rational Mexico. But the film was noticed: attacked in Mexico, it won the prize for best direction at Cannes, got international release, and was startling enough in its raw fantasies to remind cinephiles of *Un Chien Andalou*. Film buffs took heart at realizing their man was working steadily again.

Buñuel found a friendly producer in Mexico, Óscar Dancigers. They did *Gran Casino, Los Olvidados, Susana, El Bruto, Robinson Crusoe, Abismos de Pasión* (from Emily Brontë's *Wuthering Heights,* a favorite fatal romance for the surrealists), and *Él,* and there's reason to think the director was nourished by this support and funding, and being free from those chores. *Robinson Crusoe,* shot on a wild coast, gained special attention, because of its literary subject, because of his debut with color, and because Dan O'Herlihy got an Oscar nomination for his work as Crusoe. It is an adventurous film but aware of the existential loneliness of the castaway. There is a Man Friday (played by Jaime Fernández), but no Girl Friday. It's hard to see a Buñuel desert island without that phantom, and Friday does dress up as a girl in one scene.

One gem of the Mexican films is *The Criminal Life of*

Archibaldo de la Cruz, or *Ensayo de un Crimen,* a title that does not patronize the hero's obsession over trying to murder someone, anyone. Archibaldo is a child-man (played by Ernesto Alonso) neurotically drawn into tasks of murder but always frustrated. This block is akin to what other Buñuel heroes feel with impeded sexual release. Play this 1955 feature with *Un Chien Andalou* and one can admire Buñuel's sentimental respect for idiot maleness unable to inhabit its own garden of delights.

He seemed comfortable in Mexico, but he did admit longing for better budgets, more expansive art direction, and star actors. They were a way to study ordinary human fraudulence. Most directors seek sincerity or commitment in star players, but Buñuel liked them for their helpless furtiveness, as they tried to breathe within their smothering image and reputation. No one else had really used the idea of marbled corruption waiting in Deneuve. Polanski had noticed it in *Repulsion,* but he disapproved of it. Buñuel was protective of her serene glaze. So in the 1950s, even in Mexico, he sometimes had proper French stars like Simone Signoret, Charles Vanel, or Gérard Philipe. You can feel him gently probing for cavities in their glamour.

Then in 1959, he released *Nazarín,* with Francisco Rabal as a priest of compassionate intention who determines to live among the poor seeking to redeem them and his own calling. But this priest is seen as a helpless bungler—this is in contrast with the saintly model from Bresson's *Diary of a Country Priest,* made a few years earlier. Buñuel's priest has to go undercover and at last he becomes unsure of his own sanity. It is not that *Nazarín* is anticlerical or atheist. But Buñuel recognizes how schemes of sin and forgiveness, guilt and redemption, are simply narrative constructs—fantasies—that we impose upon reality in an attempt to control it. "Thank God I'm an atheist!" he used to tell interviewers.

There was a new focus in *Nazarín,* and it grew out of Rabal's traditional angst as a performer. The film won the International Award at Cannes, and that led to an invitation to return to Spain (Franco was still in power), as if its Church had seen no more than a film about a valiant priest instead of an autopsy on self-deception. The Spanish invitation was to make *Viridiana,* about a novice (Silvia Pinal) taken in by her landowner uncle (Fernando Rey for the first time) who means to marry her or rape her. She will make an alliance with the uncle's bastard son (Rabal) as she tries to help the local beggars, only to discover that they have rapist ambitions too. It had a famously sacrilegious scene where the beggars fall into the pose of the Last Supper. So the official Spanish view was outrage and disgust, but then the film shared the Palme d'Or at Cannes (with Henri Colpi's *Une Aussi Longue Absence*). At last, Buñuel was reunited with scandal—and with Europe. He reveled in both, and liked to say he was just a simple man who filmed what he saw.

There was one more film in Mexico, and it was meant to be a movie about a rich house with costumed diners—though Buñuel was irked that it ended up looking rather tawdry. He was especially irritated that the production made do with common table napkins. He was emerging as a fetishist of the "nice" relics of bourgeois life. Séverine's pristine bra in *Belle de Jour* was made of the same stock. The Mexican finale was called *The Exterminating Angel,* and its hysterical predicament meant something all across the world in 1962 as claustrophobia turned to conspiracy and impatient cats clamored for release.

In the film, socialites gather for a splendid dinner. They realize the servants are quitting. In that ominous mood, will they have to look after themselves? They stay, and then find they cannot leave. This is a neurotic impediment. In black-and-white the mansion becomes a purgatory, then a slum, and the people turn into refugees from a commercial reduced to decay and degradation. One day, this may seem Buñuel's great film—but first we have to appreciate our difficulty in getting back into that other old mansion, the one we called Cinema.

The early 1960s were the moment of new waves, and the Spaniard slipped into that bracing water. He was at a point where his absurdist parables might reactivate screwball comedy in a modernist mode of abandon. To that end, he found a new pal, Jean-Claude Carrière, in a collaboration that began on a dull remake of *The Diary of a Chambermaid,* with Jeanne Moreau as the sour-insolent Célestine. (Renoir had done the story better in Hollywood in the 1940s.) Carrière was born in 1931, and he was already a novelist and a screenwriter, smart enough to understand how he might help Buñuel. He was the "doctor" the great man needed. As such they were co-scenarists on *Belle de Jour, The Milky Way, The Discreet Charm of the Bourgeoisie, The Phantom of Liberty,* and *That Obscure Object of Desire.*

Buñuel admitted his gratitude to Carrière, but no one else knows exactly how they worked. Carrière had other good credits, but he gave his great master significance or focus on exceptional films, and he made Buñuel's more abrupt (or harsh) inventions a touch more commercial. He opened up the Don's indiscreet charm. After Buñuel's death (in 1983), the prolific Carrière did many more screenplays, including Jonathan Glazer's *Birth* (2004), one of the most natural surreal explorations of Manhattan's emotional tensions. He also earlier did the script for Nagisa Oshima's *Max, Mon Amour* (1986), in which Charlotte Rampling takes a chimpanzee as a lover. *Max* was produced by Serge Silberman, who was Buñuel's fond producer on the last films.

That trio—Buñuel, Carrière, and Silberman—had their triumph with the foreign film Oscar for *The Discreet Charm of the Bourgeoisie* (the surreal picture with the best box office). But Buñuel delivered one more personal masterpiece with *My Last Sigh,* his memoir, published in 1983 with this note: "I'm not a writer, but my friend and colleague Jean-Claude Carrière is. An attentive listener and scrupulous recorder during our many long conversations, he helped me write this book."

My Last Sigh is unexpected yet predictable. It is lofty in its lack of ego and self-explanation. The work of movie seems necessary but incidental, next to the digressions and reveries. There is a chapter, "Pros and Cons," in which we learn that Buñuel hated statistics, the proliferation of information (he was taken just before that onslaught broke), politics, newspaper reporters. He edges away from any pretension to making sense. On the other hand, he adores small tools, obsessions, snakes and rats, and sword-canes. He doesn't mention cats; some things can go unsaid.

Does it diminish "Buñuel" (or any director) that he had pals? Or does he spell out a way of organizing friendship, and providing a helpful window on the nature of film directing—as if it was busy traffic being directed? Don Luis has been treated as a splendid lone figure in the cinematic landscape; that's appealing but erroneous. It leaves subtle lessons: if Fernando Rey hadn't had Buñuel he might be no more than the suave master criminal, Alain Charnier, in *The French Connection* (1971). But if you feel the affinities in filmmaking, and the way any whoring screen must carry so many pictures without awkwardness or crowding, then you can see how the Friedkin film is attentive to Buñuel. Out of the Middle Ages and the desolate prairies of Aragón came one of the most ambiguous masters we will ever have, more a tease than a teacher. (He should have directed *Lolita*.)

Yet Buñuel's rating on the movie stock exchange is slipping. No matter that so many of us seem always hurrying after a meal that does not materialize. Despite the settled marriages in which the partners are somehow looking off-screen. Still, his seasons or fêtes are less often now. Perhaps his insights are too unsettling for a community content with dreams and white lies. I fear his status is passing out of reach—and there are other directors for whom that shade has arrived: Josef von Sternberg, King Vidor, Mizoguchi, and even Jean Renoir. If those masters fade away now will they come back? Even as dedicated cinephiles come and go, talking of Tarantino? Or is film culture possessed by the spirit of amnesia? How about a movie—like *Citizen Kane*—on a great man, with this small extra: no one alive can quite remember why he is supposed to be great.

There is the other issue, the one I mentioned earlier: whether we are prepared to look at sweet wives being abused any longer.

More or less, *L'Age d'Or* is the epitome of a late 1950s feeling that one day soon for all of us there had to be a Great Love Fulfilled, the crowning of desire with completion and orgasm, with pleasure superseding pregnancy . . . and a nice cigarette afterwards. This was part of the gradual way in which common people were claiming sex as a right along with the terminal days of movie censorship, the liberation of Lady Chatterley and "Love Me Do."

But Buñuel intuited a perverse cracked foundation in that longing—true for scorpions, ants, and cats, as well as us— whereby desire was an energy that depended on never being satisfied. So sex reigned in the head, never mind our moving parts.

That is harder to take nowadays, because it leaves us wondering if our partner in life, our beloved, is just a carnal input-output system or a fleeting phantom of cherished liberty. The act, our *it,* can be so easily renewed or replaced (the way one image or picture follows another on movie screens). Does that make the act trivial or disappointing compared with the imagining? We understood how the sadomasochism of Séverine being stripped and abused *was* the cats being let loose. And we felt a thrill, as if they were tigers.

But now our carriage ride can be uneasy—truly it has become shaming to be at some movies. It does not help the new wave of feminism to be told how fickle we are, how unprincipled. Really, should we be witnessing such dreams?

In the imminent orgy of 1966, Deneuve's pale bride on the brink of outrage was houseproud enough to warn her hubby about the cats. Once that was funny, but today it hovers over another kind of disgrace. I doubt that *Belle de Jour* would be shown now—or made—if it wanted to be new. It is retrogressive and predatory because a project is on now for men and women to exist in benign reciprocity. Can that brave new world throw out our shameful fantasies, or are we always at a dinner party we can't escape, or endlessly on a country road expecting a Michelin meal to turn up? We may be our own cannibals, but eating people is wrong now, or for the moment. Séverine is a warning name.

5

A NATURAL LIAR: HOWARD HAWKS

Does a natural liar lose sight of his lies? Do some dreamers believe their dreamscape is commonplace and real? Do we know what is happening, or do we just tell stories?

Howard Hawks would never have done surrealism, or created Séverine; that would have been un-American or unacceptably uncommercial. But he might have given Stephen Sondheim a cue for his song "Pretty Women" and the thought that "Something in them cheers the air!" He did get a nineteen-year-old to ask eternal questions about just putting your lips together and . . . how to have and have not.

Hawks liked to be thought of as a tough realist; he preferred men testing their mettle under real circumstances. Wasn't that how Hollywood functioned, the factory that made Busby Berkeley musicals, horror fantasies, noir romances, and Westerns? Those cowboy pictures looked as real as Arizona scenery, but the fables were raptures as much as Frederick Austerlitz ghosting across polished floors in the guise of Fred Astaire. Just say that stage name and you feel the dream, like satin or wealth.

Where does one begin? Let's acknowledge that Howard Hawks never won the Oscar for best director. Only once was he even nominated for that award, for *Sergeant York,* which is one of his least watchable and most uncharacteristic pictures. That means—I break this to you gently—that he was not nominated for *Scarface, Twentieth Century, Bringing Up Baby, His Girl Friday, To Have and Have Not, The Big Sleep, Red River,* or *Rio Bravo.* So, at the outset, you have to understand the foolishness of the world in which he carried himself with a fixed yet relaxed coolness or indifference. As if he was dreaming, or as if it didn't matter. He wasn't *so* far from surrealist irony.

My introduction to Hawks came long before I understood what a director was. It was sufficient that up there on a big screen in *Red River* I had the "West," an expanse of territory in which it seemed nearly impossible to drive a large herd of Texas longhorn cattle to a railhead, somewhere in Kansas or thereabouts, so the cows could be put on trains and delivered across America. This task seemed such a compelling thing, and as its harsh problems gripped the enterprise, so Tom Dunson, the head of the ranch, grew increasingly severe and tyrannical to a point where his adopted son, Matthew Garth, had to take the herd from him and move on in an enlightened democracy, leaving a wounded, chagrined Dunson as the spirit of revenge that would come pursuing Garth. That crisis duly occurred in Abilene, which was not the first destination, but how it worked out.

There would be a fight to the death on the streets of Abilene, with the weary cattle as onlookers. So it came to be, until the girl Matthew had acquired on the way, Tess Millay—by removing an Indian arrow from her upper breast and sucking out the poison so that Tess felt the need to slap him in the face—observed the two men fighting and told them to stop and grow up because anyone could see they loved each other. Then the two battered chumps gazed at the peremptory woman—she was so much more confounding than the cattle, the river, the Indian attacks along the way—and accepted that more or less she was going to dispute and educate their stupid, stoic supremacy all the way.

Age eight, I was not deceived: I understood the difficulties—the stampede, the Indians, the weakness of some men, getting a cloud to pass over the sun at a burial, the quest for Groot's false teeth. I was quite prepared to feel the immense job that had been done, the cattle drive, one of those things that made America—but also made it into a fantasy camp. Still, it seemed fatuous to emphasize the difficulty. The cattle drive was a paradise, a rapture, in which black-and-white prevailed, and a searching eye could ascertain that the entire journey had been done in the same pleasant valley. I wanted the drive to start off on a second lap, where Matthew would have his Tess to cuddle up to at night, and where his adopted father would give him grudging grace and respect, as well as sour words and implicit challenges. The drive, the dream (both words reconciled one day by David Lynch in *Mulholland Dr*) was a grand place to be. It was the screen, and I had never seen a movie that understood its romance as much as *Red River*.

The screenwriter of the movie, Borden Chase, was indignant afterwards, and several historians have joined this cause: they have said that the dramatic logic of the story was such that either Garth or Dunson—or both of them?—should have been killed in that confrontation. I think that misses the point, that after all the fuss of their conflict has been resolved, this is a movie screen and not the real Wild West and its heat and dust. The theatre seemed perfumed. The function of the exercise was not to put beef on the table for dinner in Newark and Los Angeles, it was to provide a dream of male prowess, courage, and that deft, offhand knack of knowing that, after all, the drive didn't matter any more than it was vital to get an Oscar for such bliss. I sat in the theatre in south London and saw the film a second time. In the seventy years since, I keep seeing it, as if it is a delightful carousel to ride on.

Red River, in some sweet map of the mind, flows into Renoir's rivers and all the fluent passages of cinema. Getting from the Rio Grande to Abilene, Kansas, was about eight hundred miles—if you cared to measure it—or it was somewhere between two hours and the rest of your life.

There was a real or provable Howard Winchester Hawks. He was born in Goshen, Indiana, in 1896, and he died in Palm Springs, California, the day after Christmas in 1977. His family was rich in the paper manufacturing business and the father moved them to snooty Pasadena when the boy was ten. They were rich enough to own orange groves, and Howard went to Phillips Exeter Academy in the East, and finally to Cornell where he got a degree in engineering. He was a tennis player, elegant, a dandy. He said he raced cars and had enough flying hours to be an instructor when America got into the Great War. I say "said" because he was also a line shooter, a fantasist, and a calm liar. For all the aura of a man doing a job, and what men must do, it is the awkward truth about Howard that his forte was in making stuff up, and telling dry, laconic stories about it, especially to pretty women. His engineering training did not lead him into making automobiles; it was directed at manipulating our feelings through the agency of imagined travel, the best frictionless kind—going by screen.

Some of this may seem disparaging, and it does describe an unreliable man. But I find it hard to be disapproving, not just because Hawks gave, and still gives, me such pleasure, but because he exemplifies an attitude to life that was prevalent in film directing in his time, when making a story work on screen surpassed so many shortcomings in life. For example, *Red River* was a hit, and it had been a bold venture into independence for Hawks (and his wife; they were partners in his production company for a film made outside the studio system). But the immaculate job on screen, and the orderly way in which herds of cattle trudge from one end of that valley to another (near Tucson, Arizona) belie the actuality in which Howard's cattle were regularly rustled and depleted by his own wranglers and stunt riders, leading him into prolonged legal actions that ended up eroding his profit on the picture.

So there could be another *Red River,* a screwball version, where the dream of prowess is undercut every day by his attempts to look after the damn cows and battle with a local lawyer (played by Ann Sheridan or Lauren Bacall?). It's not that Hawks would have been averse to that wry comedy (though he might have thought of a young, spiky Grace Kelly as the lawyer and Cary Grant as the harried director trying to salvage dignity in the dung).

You see, he never really made a single-minded or unequivocal drama, because he could not help feeling the ridiculous side to solemn matters. On *Red River,* in its confrontation of Garth and Dunson, there was always the knowledge that the gay Montgomery Clift and the resolutely straight John Wayne were not suited to being father and son. Sometimes Clift could hardly stand up with the weight of loaded six-guns on his slender hips. Hawks relished such ironies; he never had a hero who didn't deserve to have his leg pulled or to be out-talked by an insolent woman half his age.

Forget the engines dismantled and reassembled in engineering classes at Cornell—the abiding impulse in Hawks's films is men and women needling each other as the only way of decently delaying or averting plain sex.

Howard was a society guy, a snob, ready for polo, croquet, and any game on which fellows could gamble. In Hollywood, marriage was often one of those games. So, in 1928, Hawks married Athole Shearer, the older sister of actress Norma Shearer, who had become the first lady of the picture business in 1927 when she married Irving Thalberg, the forbiddingly brilliant but fragile production head at Metro-Goldwyn-Mayer.

Athole had been married before; she had had a child by that marriage. Howard took on that boy and then had two more kids with Athole as his eye began to wander. It was said that Athole was not entirely well (in the mental or emotional sense), yet she would live till 1985, so that there were some suggestions that her anxiety had been aggravated by Howard's infidelity. After all, he was in the picture business, where power, money, good clothes, a great house, a Duesenberg, and "attractiveness" were so close to turning people into international icons. Athole had wanted to act, but she lacked the extra edge or need on screen that Norma possessed. Howard was making silent pictures at the time, one of them *A Girl in Every Port* (1928), which did a lot to promote Louise Brooks as the wanton figure G. W. Pabst invited to Germany to play Lulu in his *Pandora's Box*. Did Howard get involved with Louise? Did he have a thing for intelligent, provocative dark-haired women with knowing eyes? Athole would have had to wonder. (Not that he was ever against blondes.)

Howard Hawks directed seven other silent films, and they are patient, waiting. When asked how he had felt about doing sound films, or talking pictures, Hawks declared, "I thought it was so easy." He had found himself. That does not just mean the naturalism of talk, and realizing that some dialogue was better than others. It is not simply the teasing between men and women, with caustic instruction on whistling. Rather, it is a matter of flirt, of calculated, stylized seductiveness between mouths that are ready to kiss and be kissed. Not that this was merely heterosexual. So often, when men talk to men in Hawks, the exchange has that at-the-net air of smart, sexy tennis and droll one-upmanship: think of Philip Marlowe and General Sternwood at the start of *The Big Sleep;* listen to Dude, Stumpy, and John T. Chance bickering in the jailhouse in *Rio Bravo;* hear the guys cooped up together in *Air Force*—and we haven't even got to the clear-cut romantic pictures yet.

Then think of how Hawks guessed that the rattling exchanges between the editor and the reporter in the play *The Front Page* (both male) might be reassessed as banter between a man and a woman for *His Girl Friday*. For Hawks, flirt was the natural competitive way in which characters fenced together. It was a profound, cherished notion that we had tongues to be witty, personal, and surprising.

In the early 1930s the would-be master was learning. His *Scarface* is a famous film, and worth seeing, but its problem is that Tony Camonte, its gangster lead, is a bore, unsmart, and driven by psychological urges that encourage the worst in actor Paul Muni. There are adventure films, with cocksure toughies like *Ceiling Zero* (flying) and *The Crowd Roars* (motor racing), both with Cagney as the guy. But neither of those movies counts next to the lyric effrontery and sexual cannibalism of *Twentieth Century,* in which the central couple are actors through-and-through, never mind professionalism. John Barrymore was the kind of brilliant fraud Hawks admired, and Carole Lombard was apparently his second cousin—once removed and then reunited? He started *Come and Get It* for Goldwyn. But when the producer went into the hospital, Hawks changed the girl's part for Frances Farmer ("the best actress I ever knew"—brilliant but "difficult"—who went from stardom to breakdown, institutions, and a lobotomy). Goldwyn was miffed and Hawks had to quit the picture, but there's enough left of Farmer to grasp his point.

Then one day, he bumped into Nancy Gross at the Clover Club, a high-class gambling establishment off Sunset. He was twice her age. She was tall, blonde, ravishing, smart, and a cool dresser. He could have invented her or been waiting to, with his fingers and his lips crossed. They fell in love, or whatever it was called. He would be divorced from Athole and marry "Slim." That was Nancy's nickname, which was carried over for Bacall's pioneering role in *To Have and Have Not,* where Bacall also had clothes modeled on those worn by Slim, just what every impoverished nineteen-year-old in Martinique was wearing in 1944.

Not that Howard was single-minded, even if he had *the* knock-out girl in a town that picked knock-outs like peaches.

By the time of *To Have and Have Not,* no matter that Slim had recommended Betty Perske after seeing a photograph of her in *Harper's Bazaar,* Howard thought to conquer Bacall (she was under a personal service contract to him), and that was maybe happening when she fell for Humphrey Bogart, her illustrious but miserable costar on that film.

Never mind, Slim and Howard were not made to retire to Palm Springs in harmony, playing bridge and reading thrillers together. They both had roving eyes. But Slim was a purring motor for Howard's best years: he had just made *Bringing Up Baby,* still a pioneering, dark screwball comedy about an educated nerd and a quite mad girl. All he did in the next few years—the Slim years—were *Only Angels Have Wings, His Girl Friday, Sergeant York, Ball of Fire, Air Force, To Have and Have Not, The Big Sleep,* and *Red River.* You can talk about the seven films von Sternberg made with Marlene Dietrich; there are the things Ingmar Bergman did in the mid 1950s to mid 1960s; there are the giddy years of Scorsese and Godard. Still, the Slim films are a body of work that could have turned Hollywood into a forest of Arden for irony and ambiguity. Of course, the system was too solemn for that, and too fearful of being thought un-American. But the films remain. *Sergeant York* is the deadbeat at the party, but don't erase it, because it was the biggest hit Howard would ever have ($8.25 million box office on about a $1.7 million budget). At least three films in that run are masterpieces—and you are old enough to pick which ones yourselves. Meanwhile, don't lose sight of how these rhapsodies of flirt and lethal match play were made in the proximity of world war, over which we were supposed to be gloomy and anxious.

So while *Air Force* was made at the height of hostilities, it soars on the certainty that these guys will come through. The real war was nastier than that. For Hawks, *Air Force* is like a musical on comradeship, skill, and technology. Its B-17 bomber is an enclosed sanctuary, like the jailhouse in *Rio Bravo* or the Barranca airport in *Only Angels Have Wings*. It is threatened but secure in its romance.

Hawks was as far from the theatres of Auschwitz, Stalingrad, Bataan, and Hiroshima as a Bonnard breakfast table. These films are serenely frivolous. *To Have and Have Not* makes polite gestures towards Vichy-ite skullduggery and the war effort, but it is not interested in any effort that requires strain. It is a reverie on how Bacall stands in a doorway, the zigzag pattern in Hoagy Carmichael's shirts, and the chance of cross-talk innuendo between Harry and herself. Truly, "innuendo" is a sexual word. It's only later in life that you realize how Bacall was not even a good actress and then you see the miracle of a mocking, sultry presence, the allure and Wildean intelligence that she rose to with Hawks, Bogart, and his screenwriters, Jules Furthman and William Faulkner.

Hawks preferred to work from a script which was then sharpened and pushed further in improv rehearsal. The small group of actors talked it out; the methodology was trying to conjure up a spur-of-the-moment wit that felt fresh yet natural or conversational. It was essential to Hawks that his players be comfortable with this scheme. Still, in a career survey it is dumbfounding that Bacall could sound so arrestingly smart at nineteen when she often labored in later years. It's as if in his best films Hawks had created a small circle of wordsmiths trying to get a line in edgeways. One cannot grasp *His Girl Fri-*

day for its speed without realizing that the talk is what Hildy and Walter have instead of making love. There have never been more adroit or agile minds in contest in an American film. And that was nearly eighty years ago.

Hawks favored certain writers. I think Faulkner was there as a drinking buddy and for the snob appeal of his literary career. Not that it's easy to imagine Hawks struggling with *The Sound and the Fury* or *Light in August,* much less attempting to re-create those dense atmospheres on screen. We know that Faulkner worked on scenes; we believe in their mutual respect. But Jules Furthman is the more interesting and useful collaborator.

Hawks had heard the sharp edge of Furthman in some von Sternberg films—he had worked on *The Docks of New York, The Case of Lena Smith, Thunderbolt, Morocco, Shanghai Express,* and *Blonde Venus.* His spirit hovers over *Underworld,* which was credited to Ben Hecht. It was Furthman's trick to put a man and a woman in attraction, and then have them resist that situation, by cross talk, argumentativeness, and the play of hostility. What Hawks took from that—and it is gold—is that a couple telling themselves they are in love, and so happy about it, is often doldrums on screen. They need to fight about something. So Furthman was there, with credit, on *Come and Get It, Only Angels Have Wings, To Have and Have Not, The Big Sleep,* and *Rio Bravo.* By reputation, Furthman was contrary and even unpleasant. But he was the most influential of Hawks's writers, and one longs to have been an eavesdropper on story conferences that involved not just Hawks, Faulkner, and Furthman, but also Hecht, Charles MacArthur, Charles Lederer, and Leigh Brackett (who was female and a sci-fi short-story writer who got tempted by the movies and knew how to do them).

What emerged from this process included the scene at the Acme Book Store in *The Big Sleep,* the one where Marlowe (Humphrey Bogart), pursuing a bibliographical inquiry, realizes that the woman in the store, with spectacles and her hair tied back, probably with several degrees, is also Dorothy Malone, ready to slide the blinds down on the shop door, find a friendly bottle, and be closed for the afternoon. Yet open too, so that these days there could be complaints at the sexism of the scene and the way this unnamed clerk has made herself available for the male gaze and its fantasies. We shouldn't be having so much fun with the scene, and I fear it reflects on Howard's characteristic way with women. The film of *The Big Sleep* is full of cabbies, hat-check girls, and librarians ready to give Marlowe a swift eye. This is in a film where the central dream is that Bogart and Bacall were made in heaven—or was it just Burbank?

That Acme scene as filmed is not actually in Raymond Chandler's novel. In Chapter 5, Marlowe asks the clerk a scholarly question and she fills him in. Cigarette smoke and wry charm are in the air, but "I thanked her and left." Howard could not be that brusque, not with Ms. Malone, twenty-one, standing there. He dismisses Chandler's very wary, if not neurotic, suspicions about available women. Hawks, in part at least, was in pictures because of their access to women, and he made movies in which the promiscuity inherent in the glamour of the film world depends on the camera's susceptibility to whichever pretty woman comes along. Cameras are not loyal. We are training ourselves now to disown that facility, and it is possible one day that Hawks will be blackballed. But along that tricky way, we have to recognize that the conversations between John Wayne and Angie Dickinson in *Rio Bravo* may be the most beguiling examples of romantic cross-purposes in American film.

One has to reconcile the charged mood of such scenes, in which Malone and Dickinson never had better opportunities, with the alleged "realism" of Howard Hawks. More than ten years after Howard's death, and a year before her own demise, the real Slim—Slim Keith by then—told me that Howard had been a gambler, a liar, and a fantasist, but was rather limited in bed. This was not said with malice or lack of fondness. Slim believed Howard had been a great filmmaker; she was happy about her association with him in his best years, and there were stories that Jules Furthman liked to hang around waiting to hear and use some of Slim's own funny lines from life. But Howard was a chronic womanizer, always "discovering" new actresses, and invariably on the mark with his choices. You have to be locked into hero-worship not to see how far his movies are extensions of the womanizer's romance with himself. *His Girl Friday* is a masterpiece, but it also indulges a restless male adventurism that takes it for granted that the favored female (the best in sight) will always come back, no matter how badly a man behaves. The secret to *His Girl Friday* is that this couple are bound to a destiny of always breaking up so that they can regain the thrill of wooing and being wooed—so long as no one ever owns up to being in love, that embarrassing movieland swamp where intelligence and aloneness may drown. This mannered attitude is like "the right stuff," that code in Phil Kaufman's 1983 film, in which the ineffable condition will be killed if anyone mentions it. So an austere male shyness is protected, but sometimes that leaves it seeming stupid and selfish.

It's like never admitting that movie's lifelike glamour has little in common with the perplexity of life, except for being some fleeting consolation.

Perhaps it was his training as an engineer, but Hawks liked a film style that was functional, unobtrusive, and matter-of-fact. He had begun his filmmaking at Fox in the late 1920s, when that studio was under the sway of German expressionism, thanks to F. W. Murnau and *Sunrise* (1927). Hawks never heeded that influence, and in his entire work there are few shots or moments that draw attention to themselves. Just occasionally a piece of action stands out, like behind the frosted-glass window when Harry Jones takes poison in *The Big Sleep*, or the difficult plateau landing of a plane in *Only Angels Have Wings*. In that case Hawks insisted on the whole circling in one shot, taken from another plane, but that was a tribute to Elmer Dyer, the aerial photographer, and even to his brother Kenneth who had been killed in an accident on a flying picture in 1930. Whatever, it was a repressed concession to the right stuff.

Hawks was generally content to film conversations in the regular way, or in what the French called *"le plan Américain,"* full or three-quarter figures. That neutral point of view was a studio convention, of course, but Hawks was happy to adopt it as a basic structure in life or understanding. If A was talking to B, they needed to be in AB adjacency—you can try it yourself in life. But if this seems simpleminded, pay attention to how our phone systems have undermined the AB bond. More and more, people do not quite meet in life, in shared space. For Hawks that was not just heresy, it was against nature.

He preferred group shots to close-ups. He did not believe people went through life in close-up soliloquy. They were talking to each other, noticing body language, and as interested in listening faces as in those that were speaking. It's possible that Hawks told himself and his collaborators that all of this was done to keep things "real." It's just as likely that he had concluded early on that film itself—the whole thing—was such a charade that you didn't need such extras as soft focus, angled shots, slow motion, thrilled string music, or that "right stuff." Sitting in the dark with the straight fantasy was the real nature of the dream. I don't recall a flashback in all of Hawks or what I'd call a neurotic close-up—and that shot is the backbone of Hitchcock films. Hawks liked to think he was straightforward—the same tight-lipped pipe dream that keeps Hemingway's taut prose trembling.

Not that that writer warmed to the director. We may regard *To Have and Have Not* as a transcendent movie romance, apparently hard-boiled yet tender at its center. Nevertheless, it butchers the most socially realistic of Hemingway's novels (published in 1937) and the least glamorous. But here's a key point about Hawks, the consequence of his fantasizing: he was resolved to leave the audience feeling happy and settled. Hemingway's *To Have and Have Not* is a critique of wealth and mindless privilege, but Hawks was too rich and conservative to get into such matters. He served Hollywood and the philosophy that films were meant to make us feel good. So, even as I note his lack of Academy recognition, it needs to be said that Hawks pictures made money, reliably, without a hint of shame.

To Have and Have Not earned $5.25 million worldwide on costs of $1.6 million. *The Big Sleep* picked up nearly $5 million on the same budgetary amount. *Red River* had box office of $9 million on expenditure of $2.7 million. Howard and Slim did not profit much from that for reasons already stated. But the business loved the picture and saw it as a landmark in the postwar Western tradition. *Bringing Up Baby* is one of Hawks's few flops: it barely covered its budget. That may have been because Katharine Hepburn was not popular yet, or because there is a turmoil in that picture over madness being more viable than sanity. It's what makes the picture mysterious and disconcerting—and a treasure in a retrospective of Hawks. *Only Angels Have Wings* was the third-highest-grossing film of 1939. *I Was a Male War Bride* grossed $4.5 million.

But he did not set out to disturb—or no more than suggesting that your beloved might be as mercurial, argumentative, and independent as Angie Dickinson in *Rio Bravo*. For a womanizer, Howard gave great leeway to his female characters along with the larger warning that fellows better watch out. He may still be revered for adventure films—like *Air Force, The Big Sky,* and *Only Angels Have Wings*—but if you examine those films closely, their "danger" falls apart. In *Rio Bravo,* it is inconceivable that the routine Burdette gang is actually going to defeat Chance and his pals. The jailhouse boys are serene and unstoppable, just as Bogart's characters are odds-on favorites. There is a scene in Chandler's *Big Sleep* where Marlowe cracks up over the depravity of Carmen and her invasion of his humble room—he finds her waiting in his fold-away bed, wearing nothing but pearls. He throws her out and is left a shuddering wreck. Hawks would never have condoned that much weakness. His Marlowe was immaculate and Carmen was just a warped cutie you could make jokes with. No wonder that he took on *Rio Bravo* as a rebuke to the social analysis in *High Noon.*

Put like that, Howard Hawks can seem like an obedient businessman, and a seeming tough guy hiding behind rose-colored spectacles. In the end, all his pictures lean toward comedy: Is *Rio Bravo* really a suspenseful Western, or an idyll for a few actors dressing up in cowboy clothes, flirting with danger and with each other? The vein of comedy is far-reaching. It includes two underrated films, *I Was a Male War Bride,* with Cary Grant and Ann Sheridan, and *Man's Favorite Sport,* with Rock Hudson and Paula Prentiss.

Hawks wanted people to have fun in an age when that was the crucial purpose of movies (art was yet to come). He was sardonic but not gloomy. He believed he was a realist, but his pictures had the airy élan of musicals. Of course, he did go into that genre once with *Gentlemen Prefer Blondes,* which is rowdy yet exquisite, and in putting Marilyn Monroe with the grave child George Winslow, he did the greatest kindness to the love goddess that pictures would ever offer her. Under cover of that, Howard had his eye on Jane Russell.

Decades later, Hawks can seem archaic, as well as sexually compromised. So it's important to say that his dreams stand up as well as those of Luis Buñuel. Both men went along with the flow, and knocked the lobs offered them out of the park. They liked life but were wary of people. They carried themselves with an insouciance that seemed to say they were only making movies to pass the time. It's not as if in justice anyone could claim that they mattered. Hawks was taken very seriously in the end with a lot of talk about how he was devoted to men doing tough jobs—when all he cared about was ease. Books were written about him, most of them too solemn or too alarmed by the thought that flirting could be one of the pinnacles of Western civilization—as long as you did it quickly and cleanly and never bothered about the Oscars. Hawks did get one of those lifetime achievement Oscars in 1975. But he was eternally cool. When he died, he contrived to do it the day after Chaplin passed away. No, of course, that wasn't scripted, but it felt Hawksian, a sly improv, and a way of getting off quietly.

Suppose he was the best professional, American-born director of the Golden Age. His work responded to that optimistic moment even if many of the movies are still alive and fun today. The culture of Hollywood has changed, but Hawks was a lifestyle model for succeeding generations and for people like John Carpenter, William Friedkin, Peter Bogdanovich, and Quentin Tarantino. I don't know how close *Ford vs. Ferrari* is to real motor racing, but it is 100 percent and at 7,000 rpm a Hawks picture.

Timing was everything in American movie narratives, and it's not incidental that Hawks's pictures are edited as if they are race-car engines. Christian Nyby cut *To Have and Have Not, The Big Sleep, Red River,* and *The Big Sky,* and did so well that Hawks let him have the directing credit on *The Thing* (after he had directed it himself). That smack of timing affected the audience: I was lucky to be eight in south London ready for keeping up with *Red River.* Going to the pictures then, awed by the crowd, the smoke, and the allegiance, contributed to the authority of the medium. I wonder whether there are equivalent openings for kids like that now. The cinema was always a child's medium. And Howard Hawks was able to walk around in tailored clothes and his aloof way, pretending to be a grown-up.

6

THE MAN WHO WATCHED TOO MUCH:
ALFRED HITCHCOCK

Hawks and Hitchcock were virtual contemporaries, and they were often put side-by-side. In the first issue of the insurrectionary *Movie* magazine (1962), they were alone together in its elite category. But you can't imagine them chatting. Howard played the game of being one of the boys while Hitch was desperate to be unique. Voyeurs like to be alone.

Forty years after his death, Alfred Hitchcock is still the best known film director there ever was, or perhaps will ever be. A time may come when he stands for Movies in the way Attila the Hun bestrides the Dark Ages or Cleopatra signifies Ancient Egypt.

People do imitations of Hitch's lugubrious voice, with the East Ender trying to sound respectable while knowing what a tease he was. No one wants to imitate his shape or his weight, but everyone knows he was as physically ponderous as he was dainty or precise with a shot and a cut. That contrast is so discerning of his contradictions. He was the most sedentary of film directors, or the least athletic, and he thrived in an age when several Hollywood directors prided themselves as sportsmen—Hawks, John Huston, Raoul Walsh, Victor Fleming, Wild Bill Wellman, Henry Hathaway, Budd Boetticher. Those guys were striking enough to appear on screen. Huston, for one, had remarkable moments as an actor. His Noah Cross in *Chinatown* is as good as anything he ever did, and so seductive a monster he could have been in a Hitchcock picture. But the idea of Hitch on a horse is comical.

Hitch never dared take such a part, yet he released few films without one of his cameo appearances. They could make fun of him or be deflating; they might be random, hardly noticeable. But they were a signature, a way of saying, *Look, this is me, Hitchcock—I'm doing this.* He was directing in an age when the general public did not yet care who a director was. The cameos were self-promotional reminders that in a dense, absorbing story he was in charge: there he is in a Stetson in *Psycho,* like a sentry outside the Phoenix real estate office as Janet Leigh enters after her lunchtime session. We don't know what's going to happen yet, but Hitch is telling us *he* knows. He seems foreboding. And as he grew to enjoy appearing on his TV show in the 1950s, a deadpan master of intrigue and fate who took no responsibility for either, so he reached out in the trailer for *Psycho,* where he is a mock agent trying to sell the Bates Motel. It was as if he didn't take his own picture too seriously, or as if to hide its being the most devastating he had made. Or as if being a director was a trick of personality. He was vain, or self-glorious, but he was furtive, too.

That was a signal of how regularly Hitch stayed in hiding. He took his art (or whatever) very seriously, but he hated to seem naked for praise or understanding. Yes, *it was him doing it*—but who was *he*? Even when he consented to the book-length interview with François Truffaut—a key step in the cult of the director—he chose to stay matter-of-fact or anecdotal. He was happy to seem like an imperious technician and manipulator, but perish the thought of disclosing an artist, a soul, or why he needed such power. He hardly referred to how much fear meant to him.

Still, it is startling that—like Howard Hawks—he never won an Oscar as best director. The response to Hawks may be written off as short-sighted, spurred by his trademark superiority and his reluctance to go in for unrelieved melodrama. But the situation with Hitchcock is perverse, as if the Academy never understood what its own trade or magic was about. It is true that his first film in America, *Rebecca,* won best picture, and he was at least nominated for best director for that, and then for *Lifeboat, Spellbound, Rear Window,* and *Psycho.* But that leaves us wondering whether anyone noticed *Suspicion, Shadow of a Doubt, Notorious, Strangers on a Train, The Wrong Man, Vertigo, North by Northwest,* or *The Birds.* Any of those films is more interesting than *Lifeboat* or *Spellbound,* two foolish show-off pictures.

As with Hawks, so many of Hitchcock's movies flourished at the box office. He was in demand and in the 1950s he had an unrivaled reputation for mystery and suspense. Even so, *Psycho* took everyone by surprise—though it played with a life-size cardboard cutout of the director in theatre lobbies warning that there would be no admission after the film had begun. That was asserting control, and the proper concentration in seeing a picture. We were put on the spot—there was no more carefree moviegoing. In its opening up of horror *Psycho* foresaw so much about where cinema was going, and it let us know how sinister Hitch had always been. A knowing cinema of cruelty—beyond mere exploitation—had been ordained.

Psycho coincided with a new kind of criticism and film history. It was exactly the film to demonstrate that Hitchcock the cunning entertainer might be a genius. He was admired by the directors of the French New Wave, and that led to his reappraisal in English-speaking countries and his figurehead role in the spread of film studies in colleges and universities.

The sedentary personality of Alfred Hitchcock suited the academic study of film—truly he identified with filmgoers (agitated yet still sitting), even if he had a way of telling audiences that he wanted to "put them through it" in the dark. It was the essence of his work that every shot, angle, and gesture had been premeditated and aimed, and the easiest way of teaching film is through directorial choices. Famously, he had his films planned out in advance so that the blueprints or storyboards could then be faithfully executed. He murmured that the shooting was often boring, but he took a week on the shower scene in *Psycho*.

Whether or not they liked Hitch's tone and meanings, so many teachers discovered that his work was a treasury for education. In turn, that cultivated the feeling that a director could be a calculating mastermind who controlled every last detail. That wasn't always true, but it was the way Hitchcock excelled. He was claustrophobic in his choosing, but that masked how his intensity left so many questions about life unasked. It was with *The Wrong Man,* so pointed and inescapable, that one had a glimpse of how close Hitchcock the Catholic was to despair in the cold universe. There comes a moment in that film where the wronged Manny Balestrero (Henry Fonda) is going to be redeemed—but his wife is already losing her mind. There are so few comforting bargains in Hitchcock.

It matched the fascination teachers and students found in deconstructing Hitchcock that a library of books came into being. As early as 1957, in France (before *Vertigo* had been seen), future directors Claude Chabrol and Éric Rohmer collaborated on a Hitchcock book that stressed his Catholicism and his attention to guilt and redemption. Robin Wood's short book, *Hitchcock's Films,* appeared in 1965. It dealt with only a few of the most recent films, but it was a model of insight. Biographies came along, by Donald Spoto, John Russell Taylor, and Patrick McGilligan's definitive book, *A Life in Darkness and Light,* in 2003. There have been studies on *Psycho.* There is Dan Auiler's examination of *Vertigo.* Camille Paglia wrote about *The Birds.* There are so many other scholarly volumes. But the shelf of Hitchcock books has to include *Hitchcock et L'Art: Coincidences Fatales.* That is the book of the exhibition created by Dominique Paini and Guy Cogeval that played in Montreal first in 2001 and then in Paris at the Pompidou, which is such a stimulating and yet suitably secretive tribute to film itself.

What more could one ask for? The films are all available now in meticulous, finished, unequivocal versions. Hitch never stooped to belated director's cuts. When he delivered a film it was done; there were no loose ends. If there were remaining mysteries, they were part of his plan. There would be sequels to *Psycho,* with Anthony Perkins becoming harrowed by the indignity as we watched. There was an alleged shot-for-shot remake of *Psycho* by the misguided Gus Van Sant, that only showed what tone, nuance, the texture of sound and light, and the desperate apprehension in faces meant to Hitchcock.

So many of the films that won best director in his time have gone stale and tedious—*Going My Way, Gentleman's Agreement, A Letter to Three Wives, The Quiet Man, Marty, The Bridge on the River Kwai, Gigi, Ben-Hur*—films with minds as made up as hospital beds or plastic coffins. In contrast, so many movies by Hitch still feel dangerous. After all, *Vertigo* in 2012 was elected by the *Sight & Sound* critics' poll as the best film ever made. That's a silly label, but *Vertigo*'s stature is understandable. Not only was it a serious flop when it opened—let's add that it is warped in its self-pity, its indulged neurotic behavior, its entirely implausible plot, and its ravishing beauty. It is also the thing that Hitch yearned for, but was always held back from—a sexual film. There may be no more erotic moment in American film than the apparent realization by the Kim Novak character that her rescuer, our Jimmy Stewart, has undressed her—just to get her out of her wet clothes—*and seen her.* And in her pretend unconsciousness she has known and felt him watching her and sighed at the tenderness of his shy hands. So much of *Vertigo* is comically farfetched, but when it works it is perhaps the most insinuating film we have.

And the public disdained that film in 1958. No wonder the impassive Hitch thought we deserved some chastising or torture. There has never been another director who has lain in wait for us with the same wrath or disgust. He is so complicated that finally he became the very thing he was nervous of admitting, a true artist best measured in the company of Patrick Hamilton, Francis Bacon, or Harold Pinter. He saw no reason to like us or himself.

———

It was not much of a life. But I think Hitchcock wanted nothing more than to make movies, and to channel the pent-up emotional energy of a voyeur into that craft. There is the English Hitchcock, a greengrocer's son, born in Leytonstone, a humble and fearful kid who wanted to be dutiful, accepted, and allowed to stay private or secretive. With a modest education, he developed an obsessive interest in drawing plans and creative design. He would be the eventual leader of film crews, handing out orders, riding herd on screenwriters, and expecting to be obeyed, but he had begun alone at his desk or his drawing board, sketching out a world as yet unrealized. As such, he edged into films as a designer and a storyboard man.

He met Alma Reville, a writer and continuity person who was a little ahead of him in the business. They married, and it is possible that Hitch never had sexual relations with another woman. But that can be an inducement to imagined sex with nearly every woman a man sees. Hitch was not alone in going into pictures on that impulse. Human beings were shapes in his dreams, and his concentration on a lovely actress was filled with a repressed desire that could be unkind. His rapture with women often found an urge to punish them—that happens to Bergman in *Notorious,* to Novak in *Vertigo,* and it is what Mother feels in *Psycho.* He put the screws on screen women, as if that was the best option a fat man could find. So the pitch of suspense in his films is tied to his smothered lust. It's not clear how fully Hitch grasped this, but the repeated undressing of Janet Leigh in *Psycho* is a pressure on the fate that awaits her. *Psycho,* in so many things, was Hitch breaking free, letting his savage id out, but that pressure had been there since Robert Donat and Madeleine Carroll were handcuffed together in *The 39 Steps* so that his hands went up and down with hers as she took off her stockings. (That scene does not figure in the John Buchan novel—indeed, the Carroll part does not exist in the book.) Hitchcock's English films are engaging and sprightly, hovering between menace and comedy, growing in confidence and nastiness, but somehow contained by English feelings that their cinema was not a serious medium or a genuine rival to Hollywood.

Hitch took his wife and daughter off to David Selznick's Hollywood in part to escape the perils of a war descending on London. (He did advise on a British documentary about the Holocaust that was never released because it might have undermined postwar reconciliation!) He always admitted, in a joking way, how much fear motivated him. But Hollywood also offered more sophisticated technology: the sound on English films was a disaster in a hollow box. American studios and budgets made richer allowance for decor or what would be called art direction. The studios provided true star personalities. The pictures and their makers made more money there. Above all, in America, movies were recognized by 1939 as maybe the central amalgam of entertainment and imagination. Americans took fantasy for granted: it was their idea of a new chance in life. Whereas in Britain people were ashamed of that impulse and its promise of disorder. Maybe with reason.

These advantages are immediately apparent in *Rebecca*. It is a film about a haunted house, the Manderley still presided over by the ghost of Rebecca de Winter, just as her dark legacy is crushing Maxim, her husband, no matter that he has a new, appealing wife. That this wife goes unnamed is a measure of Maxim's stunted emotional existence. He is named after a big gun, but he has no ammunition. Rebecca made a stooge of him; we know that from the trancelike way Mrs. Danvers handles Rebecca's abandoned silk underwear—and the way we are allowed to see an emotional candor that would have made Hitch sheepish in London. At the end of *Rebecca*, we can presume that Maxim and "I" are going to be free and happy now. But I'm never persuaded. Rebecca may abide in Maxim's head just as Mother takes over Norman's in *Psycho*.

In both films, notice how the house—as much a tomb as a home—weighs in the pressure. Hitch had found production design as an emotional manifestation. He was on his way to his obsession with back projection and the culture of screens as prisons, as opposed to proof of location and the open road. When Marion Crain drives up to Fairvale in *Psycho*, she is trapped in the shell of her car and the tormenting lifelike unspooling of back projection. There is no escape or liberty in Hitchcock, and his resolutions or happy endings come with decreasing confidence.

But in Hollywood, he confronted the question of his own identity: was he to be a conventional entertainer (as he had managed in England with *The Man Who Knew Too Much, The 39 Steps,* and *The Lady Vanishes*), or might he be something extra? Starting with a best picture Oscar and the elaborate tedium of Selznick productions, he was in a new trap at the outset. On *Rebecca*, Hitch followed his proven course—of shooting exactly what he knew he needed, nothing more—only to be confronted by Selznick's vague yet stubborn aspiration to shoot everything and any angle that might be useful in postproduction. Hitch had a picture and a style in his head complete before he started shooting, but Selznick felt that was absurd or unsporting. He made his pictures in the cutting room, with an endless second-guessing that would prove his ruin. Somehow Hitch had to get away from the mogul who had brought him to Hollywood. He had to make it clear that he was in charge.

He was blessed: in the aftermath of *Rebecca* he was able to make *Suspicion*. That neglected gem decides that Cary Grant's scoundrel was a good guy really, just misunderstood, when the bulk of the picture has revealed him as a charming, unstable risk-factor. He is Hitch's first disturbed hero, and one of Grant's most mercurial performances, unsettling but riveting. The lesson: everyone should be suspicious about everyone. That is the pulse in Hitchcock's anxiety.

More than that, on loan, he made *Shadow of a Doubt,* one of his few American films that recognizes a true America—*The Wrong Man* is another. *Shadow* plunges into the preoccupation with murder in the prim, law-abiding Santa Rosa, north of San Francisco. The affinity between the film's two Charlies, uncle and niece, is not fully explored—I think censorship held him back from any hint of incest—but here was a film in which we had very mixed feelings about the lure of murder for unhappy or unresolved people.

Then again, because Selznick was preoccupied with *Duel in the Sun* (its inadvertent benefit to us), Hitch was relatively free to do *Notorious* as a perverted love story in which Devlin (Cary Grant) is in love with Alicia (Ingrid Bergman) but full of mistrust and contempt, too. He is a step forward in Hitch's neurotic heroes, at odds with himself. *Notorious* ends on a grand rescue—the staircase escape from Claude Rains's house—but we wonder whether these wary lovers can stay together with all the flaws they have discovered in each other. Indeed, Hitch sometimes regarded his happy-ending scenes with the exasperated ennui of a connoisseur laboring through a final chapter where Hercule Poirot explains it all. There was a part of Hitch that felt an urbane, inventive villain had earned the right to escape: think of the Gavin Elster character in *Vertigo*.

Hitchcock was drawn to experiment with the language of film narrative. He had the open mind of a man who loved making diagrams. So it was that he attempted the ten-minute take, letting a camera roll for the time it took a magazine of film to be used up. This was against his grain, for Hitch had become a master of fragmented, precise, mannered shots cut together in a kind of surgery for the eye's path into inner sensibility. He was affected in this by the example of German and even Russian cinema, but it was the accomplishment of a man who thought of himself as an armchair assembler of movies. So the long takes in *Rope* are ponderous and often ridiculous, and they make it harder still to follow or be interested in the Patrick Hamilton play the film is based on, and the example of the Leopold-Loeb killing of a teenager in Chicago in 1924 and its wish to be a perfect crime.

Hitch seemed to learn the lesson: the long takes in *Under Capricorn* are moderated and more fully embedded in the melodrama where Ingrid Bergman has one of her most anguished roles. There are even moments in *Under Capricorn* where one feels the open, fluent mise en scène of a Renoir. As if he saw that, too, Hitch flinched and never went back to that style. But the fact that he had tried helps us see how much he was musing on the nature of film as a mechanism for our involvement. The secret to his style was to achieve a conscience-free voyeurism so that those in the dark could worship and aspire to the naughty light. Long before film studies chose Hitchcock as its obvious subject, he was teaching himself how his medium worked.

He was in his worst Hollywood position around 1950: the ten-minute take had drained away suspense—continued observation of people in a place could be a glory for Renoir, Max Ophüls, and Kenji Mizoguchi, but it devitalized Hitchcock. *Stage Fright* was one of his poorest films, and a travesty of fright. Then he bounced back with *Strangers on a Train,* having discovered a kindred spirit in novelist Patricia Highsmith and seizing upon Robert Walker (near the end of his life) to play Bruno Anthony, the indolent playboy who turns decisive with his notion of swapping murders. Criss-cross, he says, and Hitchcock the editor was back in business. Hopeless at life, Bruno strolls off with the picture.

Some reviewers felt *Strangers* was as farfetched as Farley Granger playing top-class tennis, but audiences responded to the wicked idea of a nice guy and a crazy sharing murders. In fact, censorship kept everything in line, but in the dark— begging the screen to act out our forbidden impulses—it seemed natural and even smart if ingenious Bruno was giving dull Guy a helping hand, and dropping the still-warm body of Guy's toxic wife into our laps like a retrieved duck. *Strangers* cottoned onto the dramatic fulcrum of acted-out fantasy, just as it half-guessed that Bruno might be . . . other than straight? Nine years later, Hitch was still ahead of that Hollywood curve in intuiting that Anthony Perkins was much more and much less than an amiable American male ideal.

The 1950s are Hitchcock's heyday, even if *The Trouble with Harry* is too fall-foliage pretty for its own good, and if the remake of *The Man Who Knew Too Much* was old-fashioned in 1957 and gave us a Doris Day who lacked the guilty moral nature that Hitch preferred in his women. *Dial M for Murder* is a stagy concoction: you can go mad working out the infernal life of its door keys. But nothing matters next to the discovery of Grace Kelly as a wan beauty and an adulterous heroine. When she came to the phone drowsy in her nightdress, suffered a strangling attempt, and then reached out for a pair of scissors (the film was originally in 3D) Hitch was making a Hitchcock film, and discovering his greatest stifled rapport with an actress.

Kelly is the paragon fashion plate in *Rear Window* (again, there had been no woman in the Cornell Woolrich story that inspired the film), but as vivacious as Carole Lombard. This was a gripping thriller with authentic suspense because Raymond Burr's husband was a shabby bear seen from afar and speculated over as a wife-killer. You can say the picture is a cross section of life around a Greenwich Village courtyard, and a defense of willful, independent investigators. More intriguingly, it is a theory on voyeuristic participation, and a sour panorama of marriage, the goal Kelly's character wishes for Jimmy Stewart's character and herself. It's a neurotic film with Stewart's chronic nomad not wanting to be tied down with the pitch-perfect Lisa, who travels with cuisine skills, courage in a crisis, and her frothy nightdress. That promise has to overlook the satiric cast on Stewart's leg, and it may even prompt outtakes of a scene where the photographer and his girl are necking intently—until in the corner of his eye he spies action in a window across the way. He's like a kid at dinner, fingering his phone under the table and ignoring family life.

Earning $5.3 million on a budget of $1 million, *Rear Window* was Hitchcock's greatest hit so far and it helped set up *Alfred Hitchcock Presents,* which played for ten years on television. It is also a film in which bravery and good humor rise above darker things, like the forlorn or mocking views of marriage seen in so many of the courtyard windows. But it is one of the supreme studies in the compulsion of looking and the attendant temptation to see and understand.

To Catch a Thief turned out a calamity, which hardly seems appropriate for such a merry, inventive thriller, full of blithe erotic wonderings. But it permitted one incidental mishap: Kelly fell in love with Prince Rainier, or the prospect of running a small, Catholic principality on the Mediterranean for which she had to quit acting. Without that meeting, I daresay Kelly could have been Madeleine/Judy in *Vertigo,* Eve Kendall in *North by Northwest,* and even Marion Crane in *Psycho.* That thought is unfair to Kim Novak, Eva Marie Saint, and Janet Leigh, all of whom became iconic in their Hitchcock films. And Hitchcock understood those ladies: Novak's shyness makes *Vertigo* more moving; Saint's chill is exactly suited to the callous game in *North by Northwest;* and Janet Leigh is a mainstream honey who has gone off the tracks—something Kelly's class might have found hard to negotiate.

Vertigo never asked to be the best film ever made, though Hitch was hurt by the way its first audiences didn't like it. He had delivered a testament; he was never more exposed than in this declaration of a director figure needing to groom a woman to fit his dream. This worked out very badly in the harsh tragedy of the story, but that grief is more complicated now that we feel guilt over the male gaze ordering women how to be, on screen and in life. I doubt that *Vertigo* will remain number one in 2022. I just hope it is not pushed aside out of social correctness, for it is an agonized account of passion in film-making, a sonata on San Francisco, Novak's greatest part, and a high point in the music of Bernard Herrmann. Of course, no one suffering from vertigo should live in San Francisco—but Hitch was a slave to perversity and self-destruction. Beneath the veil of entertaining movies, his view of life was becoming more wounded. If it had been his one wish in life to make films, somehow the commitment had served him badly. If Hawks is the undying optimist of his era, Hitchcock is the hushed pessimist, the man who knows we all live in our own traps—notably the dark at the movies.

For *North by Northwest,* Hitchcock seemed willing to make a retrospective of his own pleasures. It would be a thriller lit up with laughter. He had strangers on a train, engaged in some of the most provocative conversations in American film (Ernest Lehman was the scenarist), in which no line is used unless it has a double meaning, with Eva Marie Saint, calm and daring. It had the outline of a ridiculous (and unexplained) adventure reaching across the country on a mad diagonal, and amused by the proposition of a prairie cornfield and the surreal apparition known as Mount Rushmore, while quickly bringing them home to the church of back projection where nature and life could be forgotten.

It had a fastidious suave villain in James Mason; it had another thrilling score by Bernard Herrmann; it had Jessie

Royce Landis as Cary Grant's mother when she was his senior by only eight years. It had Grant with a good suit, a suntan, and his ineffable ambiguity—it was one of the last unadulterated star turns in film. *NNW* may be the happiest animated diagram Hitch ever made, and it earned nearly $10 million. It has an authority that is content to exercise the machinery of film and let all else go to hell. It is as insouciant and airy as a Marx Brothers film, as effortless as "Begin the Beguine," with Astaire and Eleanor Powell, all in white against a glowing black background, in *Broadway Melody of 1940.* But somehow it was not enough for Hitch.

What immediately followed was a piece of daring in which Hitch put himself up against the staid business. For all its panache, *Psycho* was made in doubt and trepidation, in black-and-white, with a cheap crew from his television show. It cost less than a million dollars, or about a quarter the budget of *North by Northwest.* Paramount was queasy over it, so the project was moved over to Universal, where it grossed $50 million. The fusion of sexuality and violence, and the strange respect for disturbed personality and for dread itself were weather systems that would alter the cultural place of cinema.

Meanwhile, Hitchcock was sixty and thrust into a level of fame he had not known before, and which could feel unseemly to a career Englishman who clung to his fusspot shyness. The man who had watched women in longing and shame was drawn into the open. On *The Birds* and *Marnie* he tried to mount an affair with Tippi Hedren. She rebuffed him, and in a few years he was a celebrity struggling in his own obese solitude, increasingly out of touch with the changing possibilities for cinema, changes that in so many ways he had inaugurated.

Frenzy seemed to hark back to his old London, and his

tongue-in-cheek murder stories of the 1930s. But it was a mis-calculation, and his most disconcerting film. The gap between *Frenzy* (1972) and *North by Northwest* (1959) is a short lesson in what was happening to cinema. *North by Northwest* is a lovely screwball thriller; *Frenzy* is an awkward flirtation with ugliness. It was as if his success had so astonished Hitch that he was exposed as a trapped voyeur and a strange prophet for that new type of alluring American, the serial or connoisseur killer. Some cineastes could now recite the anthology of his mayhem—an eerie projection of those timid murder-buffs, Henry Travers and Hume Cronyn, from *Shadow of a Doubt*.

He was an enormous influence, not just on Brian De Palma, David Fincher, Scorsese, Tarantino, Kubrick, and Polanski, but also on movie's increasingly facetious treatment of blood, cruelty, and unprecedented violence. *Psycho* gained an intellectual respectability for cloaked genres known for exploitation and pushing the envelope of censorship. The earlier principle of show-me-life was supplanted by the craze for something we'd never seen before, and something that had so recently seemed forbidden.

In the onset of pornography, it became easier to see that other directors under Hitch's sway had been edging toward a more candid treatment of sexual aggression. In his acclaimed mastery, he ushered in a tradition of fear, lust, and shame that became an overcast in cinema. So the eagerness to show and celebrate slaughter in, say, *The Godfather,* wiped away any thought that its story required a moral attitude. Even popular cinema (an increasingly uncertain tradition) had become a forum for lavishly portrayed fantasy. In *Marnie,* the thought of emotional rescue—of Hedren's sickly thief being saved—

was a mockery because she had given up one imprisoning state of mind for another. "I don't want to go to jail," she tells her husband (Sean Connery), "I'd rather stay with you." As never before, we felt Hitch's horror of men, and his despair over marriage or any other bond.

In *The Birds,* the family home in Bodega Bay is surrendered to the congregation of muttering birds, and human uneasiness retreats—to San Francisco, or to where? *The Birds* could seem like a clever new scare picture in 1963, but in hindsight it is a foreshadowing of ecological disaster, and an oblique study in the rivalry between mother and lover (Jessica Tandy and Hedren, with the same hairstyle) for an enfeebled man. The last impressive male in Hitchcock's work is Norman Bates— and he is not quite himself.

For close to twenty years, sound pictures had been a display of irrational hope during depression and war. Against the odds, that culture had produced the screwball comedies and the musicals, Fred Astaire and Margaret Sullavan, King Kong and Groucho and Mickey Mouse. But by 1960 it was clearer that our old restraints on fantasy (its desire and its vengefulness) were breaking down so that the movie house had become haunted by its betrayal of humanism or optimism. That trend encompasses much more than Alfred Hitchcock's films, yet he was supreme in his cinematic command and commercial instinct. He had established the model of a film director as a cold, taunting genius who knew so little about the world because he was afraid of it and preferred his lurking role as voyeur and surveillant. The celebrant had become our mortician.

This influence has not faded. But that is problematic just because subsequent adherents do not have Hitchcock's talent or his coldness. Something else has to be said: as a commercial storyteller, and as a neurotic controller, Hitch was desperate to be tidy. This can be a shortcoming: the longwinded psychiatric explanation to *Psycho* is a bore; the happy endings to *Notorious* and *Rear Window* do not live up to the complex characters we have encountered. The tidiness can be a dead end. Its exclusion of life and liveliness is oppressive.

By chance, Hitch's mastery had arrived in Hollywood and bloomed there at almost the same time as a boy genius, beyond mastery, yet so obtrusive he had no chance of sustaining a directorial career. But as Orson Welles would say, he could never stand Hitchcock's "icy calculation."

7

GOD? ORSON WELLES

Hitchcock was content to be a kind of devil: Satan as played by Jeeves, perhaps. But Orson Welles always went for broke—God was his natural role. So, at a time when Hollywood was most assured about what a director could and could not do, along came this large kid whose every instinct was to cut across any grain he noticed. Nothing in Orson caused more upset in the picture business than his self-glorification. But *Citizen Kane* is a story of achievement that goes up in smoke.

He was born in Kenosha, Wisconsin, in 1915. His father was an indolent inventor, gloomy and alcoholic. His mother was erratic, intense, and creative. His older brother was on a course toward mental illness. But Orson was glaringly talented—not just precocious but someone who seemed to have done without childhood, or being ordinary. He was indulged by awed teachers. The mother died when he was eight. He was taken by his father to Europe and to China. Then the father died. By sixteen, Orson was away from his Midwest, in Ireland, in a caravan with a horse (or a donkey), painting the scenery and the girls. Where was he going? In ten years, he was world famous.

I doubt Orson Welles ever thought of being or *remaining* a Hollywood film director. Perhaps he felt the "director" credit was too mere and restricting. Yet he functioned in a time when everyone accepted that studios made pictures, when movies could not be done without a studio's funding and its shackles. But in his own head Orson intended to be much more, even a force and a will breathing life into the theatre and the culture as if they were his balloons. Isn't that the possibility in the great sigh that blows "Rosebud" into our dark?

He got the opportunity of being a routine Hollywood functionary out of the way as quickly as possible. In doing that, he sailed on his unprecedented liberty and his dire public reputation as a spoiled child who would not play the game by its rules—because he was a genius. In the factory system, "genius" was a more damaging label than "loser" because it implied that the edifice of money and business was a sham and a distraction from the ineffable thing; call it art.

So, by twenty-six he had made the best American movie ever, the most beautiful and profound, with an armored perfection that daunted everyone but left him on the brink of boredom. As a true spoiled child, he had spoiled the game for anyone else. Alert to the new groundswell of celebrity, he had contrived (at twenty-three!) a surreal contract to do a movie of *his* choosing and as *he* liked (granted he honored mundane budgetary limits). The finished picture could not be interfered with, not even by its helpless owners. The studio could not see the rushes. Before he shot a foot of film he had exposed the slave deal in filmmaking and the humiliation of anyone abiding by it. No wonder he was hated. No wonder the system was lusting for revenge long before *Citizen Kane* opened.

He had achieved this by his looming, eerie beauty (childlike and feminine, but a sultry bully, too), and his two-card switch of charm and temper. He was so articulate and knew that no experience or expertise could outtalk him. It was said of him, in a spirit of weary mockery, "There but for the grace of God goes God," and if it was unclear who had coined that term, don't rule out the possibility that Orson had supplied it himself. He was everywhere in the late 1930s, commanding, a great creative leader yet sometimes insufferable. He had triumphed on stage and on radio. He was on the cover of *Time.* He did twenty-hour days on adrenaline and arrogance. In the culmination of this arc, for Halloween 1938 he dramatized H. G. Wells's *The War of the Worlds* on radio (as if it was breaking news) and goosed the nation. He had declared himself a wicked magician, or an exuberant fake. So he got his deal with RKO—though biographies are still short on how that absurd contract was arrived at.

He swooped down on Hollywood, enlisted a veteran writer, Herman J. Mankiewicz, and a crack cinematographer, Gregg Toland, and hired newcomer actors he had found in New York: Joseph Cotten, Agnes Moorehead, Everett Sloane, Ray Collins, and his composer, Bernard Herrmann. Toland told him he could learn the camera fast. After all, Orson had been looking and seeing all his life. He was uncompromisingly talented; he did nothing in an ordinary way. *Kane*'s shoot went easily—the most problem-free of his life—and he knew how to put the shots together because he had foreseen his film as a single stream. He really was so good, a natural.

I'm not hesitant about calling it the best American film

ever, and that's not because of its array of novel or semi-novel things—like deep focus, extra-wide-angle lenses, ceilings, riotous overlapping sound, and languid dissolves. It's because this is a film (as its working title warned) that is *American*. It's a study in the futility and the addiction of trying to be great at the expense of life, a virus that has hurried on since 1941. This is a picture aching to sustain ambition and meaning—for "Rosebud" being an answer instead of a forlorn abracadabra in the middle of your last night alive.

Pauline Kael called *Kane* "a shallow masterpiece," and that is a useful idea. Movies always offered the prospect of quick, penetrating shows to stir a great mass of people. So one can say that *Birth of a Nation, King Kong, Gone With the Wind, Casablanca, Psycho, The Godfather,* and *Jaws* are all shallow triumphs, brilliant but glib, in that they are accessible to millions of us at a single viewing. We still like that promise. The point of cinema as a mass medium was: give it to me now, *sock it to me. Kane* does not fit that bill: it is complicated in structure and points of view and tentative in its meanings. We do not like Charlie Kane—in part because he is so needy a tyrant.

Still, *Kane* is ravishing: you may not believe you have seen a masterpiece, but a train has hurtled by, leaving you shaken in the slipstream, not quite sure whether you have succumbed to Charlie or to cinema.

There are hallowed American masterpieces, novels such as *Moby-Dick, The Portrait of a Lady,* the play *Long Day's Journey into Night,* the music of Charles Ives and Charlie Parker, and the paintings of Edward Hopper. *Kane* is somewhere in that mix, beautiful but obscure, satirical, and pessimistic. It warns us, well, if you don't get it, the worse for you. The film demanded to be seen more than once; America had not dared that before. Then RKO released this insolence, despite its "difficulty" and the mounting realization that Orson had poked William Randolph Hearst in the eye and challenged Hearst papers to take vengeance on the film.

As if Welles didn't foresee that—he was hardly blind to the dynamic of promotion, or to his own perversity. He had challenged Hearst just as, in the movie, Kane defies Boss Jim Gettys and so incurs his own political ruin. That suggests two things: first, that Orson was so opposed to Hollywood decorum that he was indifferent to *Kane*'s failing at the box office (if you study his work, you feel he believed in failure and was moved by it). And second, that Hearst was always a feint, for Welles trusted the screenwriting conspiracy between Mankiewicz and John Houseman to create a portrait of egomaniacal talent and childishness that fit no one as much as Orson Welles.

George Orson Welles: Charles Foster Kane. Welles was no novice with aural rhythms; he could improvise Shakespearean verse or the cadences of the King James Bible as if pulling a rabbit out of his sleeve.

I doubt Welles could have tolerated anything as vulgar as Hollywood success. A rueful streak in him wanted downfall as a counter to trite Hollywood well-being. Even if *Kane* is meticulous, made with a concentration that may have exhausted a twenty-five-year-old, Welles was prepared for it to become a warren of dispute and rumor. (Borges would call it a labyrinth without a center.) I won't say he was so far-seeing that he planned what would happen. But by 1972, when his picture was already hailed as the best ever made, it became the subject of fierce controversy. Wellesians deplored Kael's brash exposé of the film's production (in a *New Yorker* essay, "Raising Kane"), but the Welles defenders were naive. There was a ferment in the man that could have provoked the argument over who wrote the film—Mankiewicz or Welles—when a deeper truth was that Welles had instigated it himself by being the secret model of the character. Remember how Kane finishes the review that attacks his own wife after Leland has fallen asleep at the typewriter. How little Kane ever loved Susan. How much she was a surrogate in his desire for public affection. Better that such a man has a hit show than becomes president.

So when *Kane* came to life properly it was in a new age of film in colleges, of important film critics and even books about the movies. An argument raged: was Welles an opportunist and slick shit (more or less Kael's view), or was he a wounded saint of independent film artistry such as Peter Bogdanovich and other supporters aspired to for themselves?

Hold on to both possibilities. I wonder if deep down Welles wasn't willing to have *The Magnificent Ambersons* turn out to be a lost film. On arriving in Hollywood, Welles had warned that the system would never let him make a second film. A part of him saw how the Booth Tarkington novel was set to be a tidy 1940s melodrama (like *The Letter* or *The Little Foxes*), a composed lesson in personal and societal decisions, with bows to history, class, costume, houses, and their archaic values. This was a world Orson had heard of in his childhood. That's how enough remains of *Ambersons* to think it could have been a Hallmark masterpiece, the crowd-pleaser that a careerist Welles needed to establish himself as a William Wyler or a David Lean. As if an ego that lonesome and wild could honor any establishment.

Thus it happened that Welles left his second picture at its crucial stage (as his editing confronted RKO with a 131-minute cut). He went off to Rio, to mount a fanciful government-led movie meant to improve U.S.–South American relations. You have to be high-minded to believe in this and very loyal not to see how Welles fell in love with Rio and its Carnival and its girls, and shot some lofty, pretentious footage, lacking in his sharp, sardonic gaze, and so allowed *Ambersons* to slip away.

You may find that interpretation unfair, because poor Orson was betrayed. As if he had not known how treacherous the Hollywood system was. He could have cultivated relations with RKO, though as some Welles allies admitted, it was perilous to ever let him sit down with money people. He was so intolerant of them, and so much his own angry worst enemy. *Kane* had been a landmark aberration in Hollywood history, immaculate yet independent, but *Ambersons* would be a different model, a "masterpiece" left in ruin. Of course, there is a precedent for that, the hours of *Greed* thrown out to turn Erich von Stroheim's epic on self-destruction into a more comfortable two-hour movie. Welles would say that what happened to *Ambersons* had broken his heart—and all you need to digest that sentiment is to believe that Harry Lime had a heart as opposed to a chronic lust for limelight. Welles held his heart secret.

As it is, *Ambersons* is a sentimental archeological site: it has lovely finished scenes—the ball with groups of conversations mingling together; Uncle Jack going off to get a job at his advanced age; the Major staring into the fire; Georgie devouring strawberry shortcake while Aunt Fanny (Moorehead) has a breakdown beside him; the competition of automobile and horse-drawn sled in the pretty studio snowscape (as contained as the snow globe in *Kane*). Plus there is the loving voice-over that describes George's comeuppance while we see the city succumbing to the harsh grid of progress. That narration was a part of Orson that he cherished, his voice as melancholy chorus. It wasn't just that he was raised on radio; he was deeply moved by his marinated baritone (it was destined to do commercials).

So in cinephilia's archival pipe dream the search goes on for the missing *Ambersons* footage—there is a script and some stills to let us imagine Fanny stranded in a shabby boardinghouse with the family magnificence eroded. Wellesians can live on the thought that with its three lost reels the film might have been greater than *Kane*. It was more conventional in its slower, cozy pace; it had a *Masterpiece Theatre* regret over the decline of white, moneyed ownership in Orson's Midwest. But instead of going back to Los Angeles to defend his threatened picture, Orson stayed in Rio, pretending that he would make his vainglorious South American promotional panorama— *It's All True* (1993) was the salvage job done eventually on it, exotic but shallow in its politics. Welles couldn't stand studio control, so why kid ourselves that he would accommodate a government?

There are ways in which Welles retired after *Ambersons*. He was hurt; he had demonstrated the barbaric state of the system; and he went away, rather as Kane retreated to Xanadu, instead of staying to fight it out in the hurlyburly of political life. That was no loss for Kane because he had no serious political beliefs beyond winning power and attention. So Welles started to do all manner of things to illustrate his genius for doing anything. He adopted causes; he wrote journalism; he hobnobbed with FDR (so he said); and no doubt he entertained notions that he might be president, though he would have been too prey to boredom to go through the slog that required. He acted on radio. He threw together a chaotic stage production of *Around the World in Eighty Days* (1946) as a vindication of disorder and doing far-fetched things casually. He acted in several dull, conventional movies and abandoned the notion that he might be a heartfelt or dedicated actor. He would be a show-off, doing his scenes on arrival, without care or preparation. Along with parts in the silly films there was one gem, the perfect part for him, Harry Lime in *The Third Man,* that overcoated bogus charmer, writing his own cynical lines, transcending Graham Greene's bleak view of Lime as evil.

I don't minimize these years, or mean to attack Welles. He was a genius at taking on so many things that hardly anything was ever complete or satisfactory. He kept moving, and he was still young and agile enough to have fun. He had love affairs and he wooed Rita Hayworth, not quite because he bothered to know or like her but because she was an ideal consort of the moment in the mid-1940s. Their marriage did not work out, but I don't think Orson had the stamina for a lasting relationship, or for the parenting that came out of his three marriages. It was not that he was unfaithful so much as he was not fully interested. He was totally creative, but life tries to be foundational and pledged to compromise. It bored him.

He made *The Stranger:* he directed it and acted in it, and it is a gesture toward a serious study of the Nazi spirit. But it doesn't engage its director or its viewers. It's seductive but hollow. Much the same has to be said for the more spectacular *The Lady from Shanghai,* in which his indifference to a thriller story takes him into several versions of bogusness, or heartlessness, as a motif in acting. Because he never took his own roles seriously, he was on the verge of seeing that most acting was metaphysical fakery. That may be his most profound and disconcerting subject. We are taught to shun fakery, but it tempted Welles and seemed alluring and tasty.

Everyone in *The Lady from Shanghai* is pretending to be something as a cover for their lack of identity. The chance of reality, or of secure emotional being, had burned off in the brightness of the nuclear age. The film is funny at times, showy and full of arresting situations that go nowhere. It is made on the run, in a desperation masked as gaiety. It has Rita Hayworth, but only as a studio pinup, bereft of affection or understanding—or even the attempt at such things. It is what a cold-blooded genius might have done on a bored afternoon, and forgotten the next day.

His odd habit of leaving his own pictures stems from the way he was not always quite there. Already, he was telling himself that he had done his observance of cinematic craft and diligence in *Kane*. He had made the best film—so why try to repeat that? This is a frightening glimpse into his lack of thematic depth or originality. Welles had the facility to shoot any script he picked up and to do it with panache and knock-out scenes. But he had trouble generating or feeling scripts or dramatic ideas of his own. There was something heartless in his brilliance, and it had to do with the missing writer in him. It was Mankiewicz and Houseman who had schemed out the idea within *Kane,* the pulse that outlasts all its gimmicks, the mixed feelings about superb loneliness, the natural plight of a boy genius.

He went away. As if pained by America, or worried that his taxes and his support of radical causes might get him into trouble, he became vibrantly nomadic or European. Shakespeare was the first excuse. In 1948, at Republic—one of the least welcoming places in Hollywood—for peanuts and in twenty-three days he had done a vivid, coherent *Macbeth,* as if to say, Look, I can do one of your foolish organized productions. It's not hard. The result is taut, sinister, and impressive. But it was deemed cheap and common compared with Olivier's lush, moody *Hamlet* done in the same year and blessed at the Oscars. Shakespeare's savage Scottish story and the modest money made Welles think he was doing one of his underfunded but ingenious Mercury productions. In the same energy, he might have made a classic film noir, but that would have been too sensible or obedient. Instead he took off for Europe, his ambition soaring on the idea of an *Othello,* done as richly as his *Macbeth* had been cut-rate. Except that he lacked the riches. It took him years, stopping and starting as he earned a little more money from acting in poor films. *Othello* came together, at last, in 1952, and it is muddled, florid, nearly unaware of Desdemona, and fascinated by Iago (Micheál MacLiammóir) as a man driven by envy, malice, and an unspoken homosexual attraction to an Orson in blackface. MacLiammóir was an old friend. He had been part of the gay team that gave Orson his first professional roles at the Gate Theatre in Dublin in 1931–32 when he was sixteen.

The church of Welles treated *Othello* as an audacious adventure that survived all its vicissitudes. Another possibility exists: that this *Othello* was done in defiance of tidy Shakespeare translations. Welles was acting out of a reckless barnstorming attitude to doing theatre and a growing amusement at the artifice of film and its labored attempts to be persuasively real. The story of the chaos behind *Othello* is more intriguing than the film itself. Years later (in 1978, for West German television) Welles seemed to understand this by doing a documentary, *Filming Othello*. By then, it was clear that his early taste for fluent narrative and the illusion of spatial reality (key elements in *Ambersons* and *Kane*) had been supplanted by the intrigue of deconstruction at an editing table, playing with the filmed elements and musing over what had really happened. Welles became a pioneer in seeing how editing could again be the engine of films, and an education in the illusions of fantasy allied to the technological defeat of fact. Of other contemporary directors, only Godard made that same journey.

That's the spirit in which one needs to approach *Mr. Arkadin,* or *Confidential Report,* released in 1955, but eventually the basis for many variants (the Criterion complete offering has three versions of the film, with elaborate commentary that ignores how poor all the versions are). Welles had made a pastiche thriller (maybe in mind of *The Third Man*) that lacked foundation in character, place, or suspense. In writing it himself, he proved his shortcomings. *Mr. Arkadin* seems deliberate but disdainful pulp trash—the dream of a wealthy, powerful man who hires an agent to investigate his own past and then starts killing off the witnesses the agent has uncovered.

It was alleged that the film was based on a novel published under Welles's name. That book exists, though Welles was nonchalant about never having read it, let alone written it. It's evident now that an acolyte, Maurice Bessy, had written it. Welles had scrambled it together as a film, the parts of which never found narrative resonance. He hired an unappealing actor to play the investigator, and he let his third wife, Paola Mori, be photographed as the female lead. Those casting decisions were perverse dead-ends, but suppose that was Welles's design. Did he want to make a broken film with himself as a pantomime Arkadin in cloaks, a spade-like beard, and glittering eyes? It's the film where he exults in the story of the scorpion and the frog—the best reason for seeking it out.

There's more to be said, for *Arkadin* is a lampooning of the revered *Citizen Kane*. In this 1955 remake, the man of power employs a process of search and inquiry to obliterate his own past. It's a nihilist obverse of Thompson's search for testimony that introduces the flashbacks in *Kane*. Indeed, Arkadin vanishes at the end of the film: his plane is seen flying, but it's empty. It's as if fourteen years after *Kane*—and in advance of its being reclaimed by critics and historians—Welles was so unimpressed with his perfect film that he was mocking it. Maybe he was a perfectionist who loathed his own meticulous craft, and a philosopher who had lost faith in meaning. This is a pattern in manic depression, so the contradictions in Orson's personal psychology become clearer, and sadder. He was a beauty who turned helplessly obese. A father who barely knew his children. He was a genius who would eventually be reduced to commercials for garden peas, mashed potatoes, and jug wine. Not that he spurned that chore. On the contrary, he reveled in it and its contempt for humanist meaning. You can say he *had* to do the commercials, but perhaps he relished the ignominy.

Thus, at the age of forty-three, Welles came back to America to be Hank Quinlan, the corrupt border police chief in *Touch of Evil*. Has an actor his age ever been so eager to be odious, enormous, and unwholesome? The make-up says something about his torture. This happened because of a chance remark from Charlton Heston, the star of the project. Welles pounced on it, ponderous as Quinlan, but swift and penetrating as the director. As if by magic, he came "home" to make a true noir with an instinct for Mexican-American border tensions that seem obvious now but were daring then. He had picked up a promising script by Paul Monash, but flipped it so that the original novel's marriage of American cop and Mexican woman became the far riskier Mexican man and American woman. We admit, Heston was not Mexican (though he takes a Hollywood-esque shot at it), but Janet Leigh's wife is very white and sexually vulnerable when she goes to that motel on the edge of town. Even today, sixty years later, try thinking of an American movie in which a Mexican man is ready to fulfill his honeymoon duties with a white bride. Welles the multicultural liberal is on full view, and he shifted location from a southern Californian town to the border itself (filming in what was then the wasteland of Venice Beach, in Los Angeles). Then he had the wit and the flourish to deliver that serpentine opening shot in which a car goes over the border before exploding.

Quinlan and Arkadin are grotesque portraits of aggrandizement and self-hatred vying in Welles the man. That helps us see how steadily he was drawn to "great" men on the point of extinction, or vanishing. Quinlan encounters an old flame, Tanya (Marlene Dietrich, herself at a point of self-parody), who hardly recognizes him and tells him he hasn't got any future. Then untidiness or indiscipline intervened again. *Touch of Evil* was always an effective, dark thriller, but Welles apparently walked away from it rather than shepherd it through postproduction. So he would complain that Universal had spoiled his film, and once more there were stories of different versions. Years later, Walter Murch tried to get back to Welles's intentions, but I'm not sure his careful restoration is better than the original. Welles's unquestioned creativity was tumbling into confusion. He was so inventive that his head was full of other ways of doing things. This was in the dawn of the French New Wave and the Godardian sense of every film being a reconstruction of its initial impulse. More than other American directors, Welles understood that movies could not be made in the old ways any longer. In improvisation, and lightweight filming equipment, he found a way of adhering to imaginative flux.

Touch of Evil won prizes at the Brussels World Film Festival, though Universal had been reluctant to enter that competition. So much of it was a tour de force—thus the intricate, long set-up in the motel where Quinlan plants and "finds" the sticks of dynamite, and the gallery of lurid cameos, not just Dietrich but also Mercedes McCambridge, Akim Tamiroff, Joseph Calleia, Zsa Zsa Gabor, and Dennis Weaver as the jittery nightman at the motel where Janet Leigh's Susie goes for "a rest" instead of her honeymoon. That nightman was a crazy not seen in American pictures at that time. The motel sequence has a sexual threat that was then new and is still disturbing today (and it came before *Psycho*). But for all the swagger of its old-fashioned "success," this was the last picture Welles would make in America.

He became European again, living in Spain, and coming back to Hollywood only for increasingly cynical performances as an actor—*The Long Hot Summer, The Roots of Heaven, Crack in the Mirror, The VIPs, Is Paris Burning?, A Man for All Seasons.* Those show-off turns need to be seen against the soundtrack of his voice-over commercials, resonant with unreliability.

It seems like a model of creative disaster. But in those same years, very much on the run from stability or being organized, Welles delivered a series of films all unlikely but possessed by a strange assurance, even serenity: I mean *The Trial* (from Kafka), *Chimes at Midnight* (from Shakespeare), *The Immortal Story* (from Isak Dinesen), and then *F for Fake* (his last masterpiece?), from his own inventive and evasive soul.

These late films are still neglected. They appeared in unexpected ways and were shot on the edge of failure, as if Welles needed crisis to be inspired. *The Trial* came to life once it had to make do with the abandoned Gare d'Orsay in Paris for its improvised sets so suited to Kafka's authoritarian desolation. As if he had seen *Psycho*, Welles seized Anthony Perkins for his Joseph K, and brought in another gallery of arbitrary presences (Jeanne Moreau, Romy Schneider, Tamiroff again). It is not just revelatory Kafka, it is a haunting rendering of mythic paranoia. If it was the only film Orson ever made, we would be in awe of its spiffy unease. It helps, perhaps, that Welles the actor has no more than a cameo in the role of the advocate (he was a late replacement for his first choice, Jackie Gleason). Even so, he was tempted to make his role a fraudulent authority figure, Quinlan as a fussy bureaucrat. Welles was always battling with his own ego, a thing he both fed and rebelled against. In the same way he never tamed his raw appetite. So beautiful once, he had become a notorious hulk.

Chimes at Midnight was the Falstaff story gathered together from several plays—a character he had loved since he played the part on stage in 1939, with Burgess Meredith as his Hal, when Meredith was eight years his senior. The shooting (on Spanish plains, not in Olde England) was beset with budgetary problems. The sound was and remains miasmic. The attempt to catch the fifteenth century is often at odds with film's modernity, though there is an awesome battle, a triumph of montage, mud, and brutalism. The illustrious actors come in and out (Moreau and Margaret Rutherford, John Gielgud and Keith Baxter), less real people than star turns, and yet it is one of the most touching films of Shakespeare ever made. It is also the most naked acting Welles would ever do, the plea of an unreformed boy who longed to be an old man.

The Immortal Story is fifty-eight minutes long (and his debut in color), made for French television, with Moreau exquisite if too old as the woman in a fable about the eternal value of fiction, in which Welles gives a simple but somber performance as a seated Mr. Clay, the rich man who wants to own and control the process (like a movie mogul?). As TV, it needs to be taken in with the attempt he made at a seventy-three-minute *King Lear* in 1953 for CBS's *Omnibus* (directed by Peter Brook), when he had to play the lead in a wheelchair because of an accident—he thrived on mishaps—and *The Fountain of Youth*, a John Collier story he adapted in 1958 for the *Colgate Theatre* show.

Then there is his attempt to make a film from his *Moby Dick Rehearsed* stage venture in London in 1955, with a cast that included Patrick McGoohan, Joan Plowright, Gordon Jackson, and Kenneth Williams. I am not making this up. Welles made it up. It is still possible that fragments of that filming exist somewhere. The mystery lives—and the regret. This is the ending of *Kane* over and over again with the sled tossed into the furnace.

It was as if he could only work in hostile settings. He resisted success or regularity but was a magician of the disorganized moment. That may be why he was giving so much time to prolonged interviews for television. He was a great talker (as spontaneous when himself as he was off-putting when acting). He was in his element, as at a dinner table of his admirers, where he would tell droll anecdotes about himself and his brilliant but unlucky career. His genius made gold out of misfortune.

That defines the setup for *F for Fake,* an essay about art and dishonesty that employs Clifford Irving (who hoaxed the autobiography of Howard Hughes), the art forger Elmyr de Hory, the statuesque strolling of Welles's mistress, Oja Kodar, and Orson himself as a genius but also a fairground charlatan pulling the wool over our eyes and turning it into a coat of many colors (or the emperor's nakedness). Years ahead of popular understanding, *F for Fake* grasps that a bold but disenchanted filmmaker by 1970 might make an essay about filmmaking, a shaggy-dog story, and a philosophical rumination all in one. It is one more picture that would justify descriptions of mastery if it was the only thing this one-man orchestra had ever done. It anticipated the dissembling life yet to come in which we would all exist on screens. Welles would die ahead of the Internet, but in a way he was a Moby Dick wrestling with the net.

There were so many other projects started and then dropped, interrupted or mislaid, from a version of *Don Quixote* to . . . *The Other Side of the Wind* (was that title always a tease?), which became his profligate, endlessly unsettled obituary. In the early 1970s, he had thought to make a movie about an aging film director (played by a long-suffering John Huston) who is at an *8½* moment in his life, uncertain what or whether to do anything next. Crowded out with friends, acolytes, and hangers-on, and with Oja Kodar taking a more significant and dubious creative role, it was a satire on the film business but on cine-philia, too. At its best, it might have been Kafka done through the voice of Nabokov. But when Welles died, in 1985 (still only seventy), the film was unfinished, in the ownership or posses-sion of others, and in a frenzy of rumor, for Welles was still being voted director of the best film ever made. So *The Other Side of the Wind* had to be the greatest inaccessible movie. Was that chaos intended by Welles? Or had he reached dismay or stasis, like Kane in Xanadu? It's impossible to decide, unless you respect his phenomenal marriage of disorder, vision, and a fatalism not normally allowed to direct movies.

At last, in 2018, *Wind* was "finished" and released. It's up to us to judge whether it is a swan song or an unholy mess. Any-one is allowed a disaster, or something better lost: if it was the only film he never finished, you would wonder, Who the hell did that? It might be regarded as a ruined monument, a film by Ozymandias. It doesn't matter: you fade out with a profusion like *The Other Side of the Wind*, or a single word, your "Rose-bud." Just so long as you stay an *enfant terrible*. Welles died after an afternoon doing card tricks on TV's *The Merv Griffin Show*. An error in destiny? Suppose he took on that gig as seri-ously as he ever did a movie. On the show, he told Merv, "I am not essentially a happy person, but I have all kinds of joy." And then he turned up four aces in a row.

8

GODARDIAN

Orson Welles said of Jean-Luc Godard, "He's the definitive influence if not really the first film artist of this last decade, and his gifts as a director are enormous. I just can't take him very seriously as a *thinker*—and that's where we seem to differ, because *he* does." That was about 1970. In 1967, Richard Roud had published a book, *Godard,* that began, "Jean-Luc Godard is, of all contemporary directors, the most controversial. For many, he is the most important filmmaker of his generation; for others, he is, if not the worst, then the most unbearable."

I think that was the best thing in the book (176 pages); it grasped both the precociousness of Godard and his determined transgressiveness. But the book soldiered on. After all, it was the first in an ambitious new paperback series, *Cinema One,* generated by the London publisher Secker & Warburg and the British Film Institute. Books about film directors!

Only a few years before, such a publishing venture would have been fanciful. Secker & Warburg had edged into the subject area two years earlier with Josef von Sternberg's autobiography, *Fun in a Chinese Laundry,* still one of the most daring books by a film director. The field was so new then. But as I recall, Roud's *Godard* did rather well, though I think he knew his book was a year or two late—the horse had bolted the stable and was as far away as mustangs by 1967. But young filmgoers were avid for explanations of Godard, just as they could hardly keep up with his films. Between *À Bout de Souffle* (1959) and *Weekend* (1967), he had delivered fifteen films. (Terrence Malick has made ten in forty-seven years.)

Not that "delivered" is the suitable or Godardian word: the pictures had popped out like e-mails on a busy afternoon, improper jokes or impulsive poems jotted down between three and four o'clock. If an artist was supposed to preside over an orderly career, in preparation for a lifetime achievement award or a catalogue raisonné, Godard was a rowdy needler savaging those self-important processes. His significance lay in saying it was absurd for an alive and thinking filmmaker to carry on in the measured steps that had sustained David Lean, William Wyler, and just about any other director you cared to think of. Godard was the first director to assert and then demonstrate that a whole film could be done in a flash. Or on an impulse.

Pierrot le Fou was shot in June and July of 1965, and it opened in Venice at the end of August. Two days before shooting started, "I had nothing, nothing at all," Godard admitted proudly. People weren't supposed to make pictures so swiftly or spontaneously. But *Pierrot* feels as if it was done in just one afternoon—and I mean that as praise. *Doctor Zhivago,* the Lean picture, was released at the end of 1965. At a cost of $11 million, it ran 193 minutes, after a shoot that lasted ten months. And it was archaic mush. It is no exaggeration to say that in the time it took to conceive of *Pierrot le Fou* and finish it, David Lean, a dour perfectionist, was fussing over ten minutes here or there in his grind of post-production. His perfectionism was rooted in a feeling that a movie should be monumental and measured. Millions could believe they had had a large and gratifying experience that had placed the history of the new Russia as a sad love story, with Julie Christie a Lara from South Kensington, and a relentless musical theme fit for elevators.

If you cherished *Doctor Zhivago,* and feel happy with it still, I am glad you are here, because in any diagnosis of health and aliveness a writer needs examples of the moribund. Let me just suggest that *Doctor Zhivago* was always old-fashioned, sentimental, and picturesque while posturing toward political significance. It was the Soviet Union for Surbiton or Pasadena. Whereas *Pierrot le Fou* was offhand, indelible, and a summer rapture. As far as I can tell, it cost about $300,000. That sum is not a defense on its own: $300,000 is a lot of money to most people because they do not have it. But the comparison is instructive, and a part of Godard's disruption was in the new way of working. While a David Lean strove to get his picture "right," or at least not wrong, Godard threw his fervor on the wall because he did not recognize mistakes. When the sun fell on Anna Karina's rueful face and her dark smile, that was enough. There are instants in *Pierrot le Fou* where its grasp of love and love's death are like hummingbirds on your veranda, while *Doctor Zhivago* is a pantechnicon struggling up a distant hill with a grand piano to be carried up the stairs.

I don't wish to be hostile to all of Lean, but he does illustrate a fallibility in film careers: Success comes and goes, just like hummingbirds. Directors, and others, have their moment and should be grateful for that. Lean had excelled in the postwar years in Britain, a time of austere funding, when British film flowered (the garden also contained Michael Powell, Emeric Pressburger, Carol Reed, and Robert Hamer). But Lean was the director of *Brief Encounter, Great Expectations, Oliver Twist, The Passionate Friends,* and *Madeleine.* We are used to seeing British literature made into films now, so it's easy to forget how Lean invented that genre with two black-and-white pictures that have not been surpassed for their radiant if abridged incarnation of Dickens. *Brief Encounter* is a classic (though a little staid now in its self-repression), but *The Passionate Friends* and *Madeleine* are so worthwhile it is bizarre to have them overlooked.

Lean (who had been raised a Quaker, forbidden from seeing films) burst into life in those years, on modest budgets, with exceptional craftsmen and outstanding actors—notably Alec Guinness, Robert Newton, John Mills, Jean Simmons, Martita Hunt, Kay Walsh, and so many others (including Anthony Newley and Diana Dors in small parts in *Oliver Twist*). So Lean had his glorious moment, enough to exacerbate regret at the slowness and the dismal pomp of what followed. Well, maybe, you are saying, but isn't *Lawrence of Arabia* remarkable? Yes, it is as a desert promotion, and for the uncorrected imperialism that was blithe about casting Alec Guinness and Anthony Quinn as Arabs. Going from the immediacy with Dickens to the increasing complacency of spectacle in the big epics is to see authenticity draining away. There is so much more sand in *Lawrence* than there is Lawrence the man. Peter O'Toole poses in a grand manner to divert us from the film's insecure grasp of Lawrence himself. He is hopelessly tall for the part.

I was not alone in these opinions. In 1968, when Andrew Sarris published *The American Cinema: Directors and Directions 1929–1968,* he placed Lean in the "Less Than Meets the Eye" category (this was grade 5 in his hierarchy). "By the time Lean gets around to propounding a question no one really cares about the answer," wrote Sarris. This codification of opinion was an important step in the definition of movie directing. Sarris's book became a battleground and a map for distinctions of taste. The book was the fulfillment of a 1962 essay "Notes on the Auteur Theory," an approach that shaped debate and pushed some American movie directors into intense sessions with their shrinks. For until very recently they had thought they were hacks, or pros or artisans—or plain lucky to be getting away with it. And now they were expected to be artists? Instead of just rich, spoiled, and with all the crude advantages that America reckons gather around that job and its condition.

Sarris was laying down the law on a frontier that had had no maps. This was not entirely in his nature: he was modest enough to admit that in compiling a top ten list for 1958 for *The Village Voice,* he had actually omitted *Vertigo* and *Touch of Evil.* No one is perfect. But auteurism did prompt directors to be more arrogant or pretentious, just as it encouraged *The Village Voice* and other places to hire personality film critics, while schools all over knew they now had to have film courses, publications, and tenure.

Sarris believed movie was an opportunity for personal style, as opposed to a display of material or content: "The art of the cinema is the art of an attitude, the style of a gesture. It is not so much *what* as *how*. The *what* is some aspect of reality rendered mechanically by the camera. The *how* is what the French critics designate somewhat mystically as mise-en-scène. Auteur criticism is a reaction against sociological criticism that enthroned the *what* against the *how*. However, it would be equally fallacious to enthrone the *how* against the *what*. The whole point of a meaningful style is that it unifies the *what* and the *how* into a personal statement."

Sarris was correct for the 1960s, and his final hope is amply embodied in the manner of Godard's films. But in stressing the how, some dishonesties or damage in the what of American movies got overlooked. Auteurist criticism liked to believe films were about their own style. And film now finds itself in a crisis because that approach enabled an empire of female "beauty" and male supremacy that has gone deep into our nervous system.

The auteur theory was as French as it sounded, and Sarris had spent time in Paris in the late 1950s where he had met François Truffaut and Jean-Luc Godard and observed their lyrical fury in *Cahiers du Cinéma* as they attempted to present a history of cinema founded on the principle that some directors were better than others (at least some of the time) and that that differential pointed to the assumption that directors made films, that they were creators (like Dickens or Rembrandt or Mozart—the language was lofty) whose vision and talent protected them (and us) against all the vagaries of the business, the technology, and the inescapable circumstance of collaboration.

There was nonsense and insight in this, but that hardly mattered in the 1960s as the dream of being a film director became a beacon for young people—more usually young men—not only in France but in so many other countries. Veterans in Hollywood had been fearing the game was up, but now a legend of immortality was rewriting the past. Hitchcock and Hawks were effectively over by 1970, but the 1960s and 1970s were their heyday, if only to sustain the nerve of a young generation of directors who wanted to follow them.

They had illustrious company, for in the early 1960s it was apparent that several masters were at work in cinema. In Italy, Federico Fellini and Michelangelo Antonioni became essential heroes. *La Dolce Vita* (1960) was one of the signal movie events of that time, and it was quickly followed by *8½*, which was nothing less than the vexed meditation of a famous director over what he might do next. The director had become an exemplary character like the lone rider in Westerns. Antonioni had delivered a scandal at the Cannes Film Festival of 1960, a film that was booed and cheered at the same time, and which helped to define the new cockpit atmosphere of Cannes. That film, *L'Avventura,* was curiously like *Psycho:* a picture in which the apparent heroine disappears early on, and is never recovered or explained. But in that search for her Antonioni had composed a majestic study in emotional fatigue and the feeling that advertised romantic destinies were unreliable. Moreover, *L'Avventura* was the first film in a trilogy, completed with *La Notte* and *L'Eclisse.* In three years, with a sumptuous, slow mise-en-scène, and players as forlorn and entrancing as Monica Vitti, Jeanne Moreau, and Alain Delon, Antonioni had given us a great novel for an anxious but sexy age. Many real novelists were filled with envy.

Some argued that the elegant disenchantment in Antonioni was modish and even pretentious. But any charge of humorlessness was erased by *Blow-Up* (one of the best accounts of London as fact and delusion in the 1960s), as searching an inquiry into the mechanism of film narrative as Hitchcock's *Rear Window*, twelve years earlier. At that point, Antonioni was more a wanderer than an Italian. He found himself in being "lost." In the next few years he would do *Zabriskie Point* (about the American desert) and then *The Passenger* (about the more complete existential desert in which we wander). From 1961 to 1975, Antonioni was a serene artist stepping farther forward with each new work so that it was hard to keep up with him. In concert with this, he was personally aloof or mysterious: he seemed to need Monica Vitti for a while, but so little else about him was human or celebrity-like. Was he a new Garbo, wanting to be alone? Or was he a pioneer in Asperger's? The obsession in film directing sometimes came close to going blank (like a white screen).

In India, in Bengal, Satyajit Ray had labored for several years to make what was soon called *The Apu Trilogy*. Then he was established as the Indian director every trained intellectual in the West should see. This was an inaccurate reorganizing of the profusion of Indian cinema, and a breakthrough that did not quite see that Ray was true to a tradition of tasteful human-ism reaching back to Vittorio De Sica and Jean Renoir. A similar feat of reappraisal converted Akira Kurosawa into the outstanding Japanese director. His great work was from the 1950s—*Rashomon, Seven Samurai,* and *Ikiru*—films that were easily absorbed in Western understanding. And copied: *Seven Samurai* became *The Magnificent Seven* (1960). But careers like those of Ozu, Mizoguchi, and Naruse sank in more slowly.

Still, the most esteemed and forbidding auteur was Ingmar

Bergman. It was in 1957–58 that the Swede was hailed as our genius for the apocalypse with *The Seventh Seal* and *Wild Strawberries*. There was a 1958 retrospective Bergman season at the London National Film Theatre that helped identify that screen as the place where British filmlovers had to be. Into the 1960s, Bergman defied his own reputation. It was said that he was a wreck, stumbling from one nervous breakdown to the next. It was noted that he refused invitations to come out of Sweden and into the maelstrom of commercial cinema. All he did was remain in his Swedish stronghold. He even found an island, Fårö, where he could live and work in seclusion. He made *Through a Glass Darkly* and *Winter Light,* and then in 1966, on Fårö itself, with Bibi Andersson and Liv Ullmann, both his lovers, he made *Persona,* which in its brevity and depth was immediately clear as one of the most challenging film statements on identity ever made. It was as chic as the Stones, Warhol, and Muhammad Ali. Or as in as Godard.

I am leaving out some names, but as Hollywood talked about how it was coming apart, and as veteran directors died, retired, or sank into pastiche work, and as young people awoke to the idea that cinema might belong to them, so there were these epic art house careers. In the middle 1960s, the cinema had so many triumphs—not just Antonioni's trilogy, or Fellini, Ray, and Kurosawa, or *Persona.* There was Buñuel, too. How could anyone minimize the art that delivered—in the space of a few years—*Blow-Up, Persona, Belle de Jour, 8½,* and even Joseph Losey's *The Servant* in England? So many of these films were unprecedented in their gravity and nerve—and they have lasted.

Then, in 1967, Hollywood in the form of Warner Bros. would make *Bonnie and Clyde,* and a new critic, Pauline Kael, would tell Americans to get with its glee. Here was a film that took a 1930s genre and insisted that it was alive again in the late 1960s mood of dissent. The auteurist itch was on board. Then Robin Wood did a monograph on Arthur Penn, the maker of *The Miracle Worker,* the aggressively artistic *Mickey One,* the butchered *The Chase,* and then that explosion of vitality, sex, and identity in the show of outlawry, *Bonnie and Clyde.* Wood intuited that Penn was the auteur, so he was not obliged to face the truth that, despite Penn's talent and his way of tenderizing tough action, that film was the work of its star and producer, Warren Beatty. The public had never doubted: stars made movies. Didn't *Butch Cassidy and the Sundance Kid* (1969) owe itself to Newman and Redford? Can you remember who directed it?

There was even a moment in the untidiness of striving when it looked as if Godard might have made *Bonnie and Clyde.* In hindsight that seems preposterous, but it's no stranger than Godard making one damn film after another, every one of them fanciful, or more theoretical than necessary. So many directors were weighed down by film projects that seemed awesome and grave—*and difficult* (like the bloated *Cleopatra*). Godard acted as if his projects were casual or so cheerfully unlikely as to make difficulty redundant. Of course, Beatty would not have let Godard in on his *Bonnie and Clyde.* He knew that movie had to address *his* heart and his needy identity—it was a way of proving he had significance, instead of just an opportunistic alertness and looks to die for. The young American revolutionary was actually set in old attitudes to storytelling: he really was comfortable with Warner Bros. styles from the 1930s and 1940s. But Godard was talked about as director (after Truffaut opted out) and Beatty had an instinct for fashion.

Jean-Luc Godard was born in Paris in December 1930, the

son of a Swiss doctor and a mother whose family was in bank-
ing. They were rich, or what seemed secure, and Godard all
his life had the clashing instincts of a bourgeois and a radical.
Though sometimes associated with Communist sentiments, he
was a famous money-grubber. When he was four, the family
moved to Geneva, and Godard was there through most of the
war, largely spared the test of living under occupation. He was
not a boy moviegoer. That habit set in after the war, when he
was sent to Paris for a good education.

He grew up in a time of philosophical and political ferment;
it was the age of Jean-Paul Sartre and Maurice Merleau-Ponty,
of being and nothingness, the phenomenology of perception,
the wellspring of Godard's voyeur fatalism, and a reason why
the computer speaks such sense in *Alphaville*. Godard was
well read and he tried to be a visual artist—it would not be
noticed always, but Godard has one of the great non-arty eyes
in cinema history, in which the sensuality of the visual contests
the abstraction of montage. He could be sensitive to fluent
cinema—Renoir is evoked in *Pierrot le Fou*—but his nature
lay in editing, as both argument and interruption. No fiction
director so thrived on self-generated breakdown or disruption.
He seemed like someone raised on Hitchcock (as opposed to
Renoir), but whereas Hitchcock interrupts only to find a neurotic process of suture and repair, Godard scatters the stream of
old-style cinema to grab at challenging ideas. Thus in *Pierrot*,
he gives us an action scene with a voice-over that analyzes it as
a cubist set of tropes from narrative history. Radical in 1965,
that can now be seen as the way most of us watch television,
like editors or historians—or maniacs.

He married the intensity of silent cinema and all the dialectical possibilities of editing. He knew he was a child of the age of movie, and in his education he had veered from an interest in politics and anthropology to missing classes so that he could go to the movies. In that pursuit he was as sleepless-encyclopedic as a heretic or an obsessive-compulsive. There was a fanatic and a terrorist in him. He was never popular or likeable, and any examination of his life discovers that he disdained being agreeable. He was one of the first people in the 1960s to wear dark glasses at public events, as if to deny or occlude visibility (or to pretend he was watching life as cinema?). He was also so inexperienced in life that he put on authoritarian airs—or were they entirely natural? He reminds me of Michael Corleone.

I am stressing this education of Godard because it may be the most instructive thing about him—and about us. He was, self-consciously, offsetting a humanist tradition that was being undercut by so many technologies: advertising (his love-hate obsession), television, thought control, and movies. He had violently mixed feelings about the great illusion of golden cinema, the suspension of disbelief, when skepticism was his oxygen. It had made him, yet he felt it had warped him. Unless he was born warped.

Godard is like Marshall McLuhan in that, growing up in the romantic culture of movie storytelling, he was uncannily aware of (and angry about) the way romance was a commercial-cultural construct of reality being imposed upon us. In short, there was no good reason to believe in movies anymore. They deserved structural deconstruction. And this was the kid who seemed to have seen every picture and to believe it was hardly possible to be alive without seeing everything as a potential movie. He was always framing other people.

He could seem and be intellectually brilliant, but there was a blank adolescent sensibility behind the dark glasses, accompanied by a lack of felt experience. Spending your life in the movie dark can leave you indifferent to the light of others. So the allure of being a film director, insolently in charge, was a way of bypassing the years of learning and accommodation that might have been expected in Dickens, Flaubert, or Tolstoy. See enough films and you could dispense with life: that wishful thinking has gripped so many cineastes, and it has its natural child in Quentin Tarantino, born the year Godard made *Le Mépris,* also known as *Contempt.* That general noun can apply to the feelings between the characters or the personages in that film (a few years ahead of *Persona*), but it extends to Godard's regard for the feelings summed up in that dead-end destiny for modern society, a slave-minded audience. So "a director" can kid himself that life is no problem, rather just an anthology of scenarios. This is the seedbed of a thousand abject pictures and their gloating careers.

The contempt extends to Brigitte Bardot, the actress Godard had to accept to gain the big American money to make *Contempt.* He had actually wanted Frank Sinatra and Kim Novak as the couple played by Michel Piccoli and Bardot. He knew he had to have BB naked (to qualify for the money) so he made that display the first scene of the film—get it over with. Godard talked a lot about marriage and prostitution, and the exploitation of women, but if you take in his whole career there is so much evidence of misogyny. In his script for *Contempt,* he said that the husband lived as an animal, while his wife was a vegetable.

He gave up on school, and the depressing example of people

who knew more than he did. In the 1950s in Paris Godard lived in cinemas and fell in with the group that would be the New Wave. That meant Truffaut, Claude Chabrol, Éric Rohmer, and Jacques Rivette, and many others who did not quite gain the breakthrough career of the big names. He wrote, for *Gazette du Cinéma* and then for *Cahiers du Cinéma*. He never had Truffaut's journalistic edge or Rivette's unique exploratory way of writing. But he loved words: his films are full of signs, graffiti, and the pathos of handwriting. Godard was a poet of abrupt slogans—"The cinema is truth twenty-four times a second"—and absolute assertions of insight and dogma that sneered at argument or even discourse. He tried to get work on the edges of the French film industry, and he was putting what money he could scrape together into short movies. You must realize that young filmmakers acquire a raging hatred of money so that they may steal it when necessary. He was an outlaw with all the instincts of a secret policeman.

À Bout de Souffle, or *Breathless,* was conjured together out of chaos. Truffaut and Chabrol had worked on a newspaper report of a hoodlum and his girlfriend. Godard liked the outline. He got the vague interest of a producer, Georges de Beauregard, and then he begged Truffaut and Chabrol to give him their endorsement. So the idea was launched. Godard had Jean-Paul Belmondo as his lead. They had done a short together in 1957 for which Godard had dubbed Belmondo's voice—the effrontery, as if Belmondo's voice wasn't as endearing as his lopsided grin. But the director hadn't been sure what the character should say while they were shooting. For Godard, being "in synch" was as corny as being in love.

Then he had the cunning to ask Jean Seberg to be his actress.

She had been "discovered" in America by Otto Preminger, and roundly chastised for her work in *Saint Joan* and *Bonjour Tristesse*. She was in Paris, lately married to a Frenchman, and Godard offered her $15,000 to do the picture. She had her hair cropped short from *Bonjour Tristesse* and she could speak enough French to sell the *New York Herald Tribune* on the streets. The entire budget of the film was under $100,000. It was like a student film, or an amateur enterprise. When the cut proved too long, Godard arbitrarily shortened his own shots and was thereby acclaimed as the inventor of jump cuts.

No one else would have done it, or dared to do it; but no other film-mad kid (nearly thirty) was quite so cynical or bereft about film itself. He treated the medium in the way Andy Warhol reassessed painting. *Breathless* as a title was key for the English-speaking audience. The pairing of Belmondo and Seberg had an astringent alchemy—the French love of Americana was going sour (Indochina was becoming Vietnam). They were kids poking at adult experience. And the picture was taken over as a photographed entity by Raoul Coutard, another kind of genius who would provide wings for Godard's first run of films. Just as Gregg Toland relieved Welles of cinematographic anxiety on *Citizen Kane* so Coutard's proficiency and drive (he would become a good director, too) left Godard free to push abstract constructs into the cinema verité.

Movies had invariably been meditated over, mounted, and prepared; they had scripts, budgets, and rehearsal. They were daunting tasks. Godard sidestepped those traditions. He wrote dialogue by hand on the set or he had the actors improvise; he trusted Coutard to surmount any technical difficulties imposed by the lack of money and to make those shortcomings virtues.

Then he edited the film as if he was another person and not the grim observer of its shooting. Seberg thought it was all crazy (she was a Hollywood player, raised by a great disciplinarian in Preminger) but the film established her in history.

From its first moments, where Belmondo compares himself with a poster of Humphrey Bogart (who had died two years earlier), *Breathless* is off-the-cuff yet relentlessly self-conscious, and that was the harbinger of dead-eyed modernism in movies. It was a film noir made by kids on an impulse, but so aware of everything from *Detour* to *In a Lonely Place* that *Breathless* is a kind of psychotic lecture on film history. Godard could never tell a story without referring to the library of movie stories. As he put it, "We barged into the cinema like cavemen into the Versailles of Louis XV."

The film made money; it attracted a young audience, not always would-be filmmakers but helpless inhabitants of the age of film feedback and screen urgency. When Ruby shot Oswald or when Geoff Hurst scored the fourth goal at Wembley in the 1966 World Cup we all felt *live* and alive. We were looking at ourselves already, in a cool mix of amazement and detachment, and that was Godard's essence, along with his headlong immersion in projects.

He never stopped to breathe. Often with Georges de Beauregard, and always with Coutard, he hurried through the genre gallery of films. *Le Petit Soldat* was about political guilt; *Une Femme Est une Femme* was sort of Lubitsch; *Les Carabiniers* was a war picture, brutally diagrammatic, about boys in battle; *Le Mépris* was inside film, as stark as *La Dolce Vita* had been pulpy and decadent; *Bande a Part* was kids on the loose, rebels who did not know the word "cause" but who danced the

Madison and raced through the Louvre with philistine zest; *Une Femme Mariée* was sociological analysis, Lévi-Strauss with skin; *Alphaville* was sci-fi and Fritz Lang–ish. It was in that rush that the possibility arose—after Truffaut had turned it down—that the Robert Benton–David Newman gangster script for *Bonnie and Clyde,* done in admiration for early Truffaut, was thought of as a Godardian venture.

I have held back two films in this listing, plus the most significant collaborator Godard would ever have. He had met Anna Karina in Paris in the late 1950s when she was a model in advertising. He had offered her a small part in *Breathless* but she refused because she thought she would have to be nude. But he came back to her for *Le Petit Soldat,* and by then they were in what movies called love.

In the Godardian scheme of film history, it felt as necessary to have a girl as it was to have a camera. Weren't all films in need of a girl, whether or not she would do nude? Without a she in the narrative, the guys would have to admit they were dying. It was Bonnie who kept Clyde from nihilism. Hadn't Jean Seberg set up *Breathless*? Hadn't Griffith depended on Lillian Gish and likely never touched her, just as von Sternberg needed to photograph Dietrich to seduce her, and then to have her discard him so that his gaze was clouded with humiliation and she could stare back at him in her ironic strength until this woman became his adored devil? Hadn't Bogart come back to sour sharpness with Lauren Bacall as the fresh olive in his drink? Hadn't Nick Ray fed on the melodrama of Gloria Grahame? Hadn't Louis Malle and Truffaut and Antonioni and Losey contemplated Jeanne Moreau, without admitting that her look was fickle or unattached?

Vivre Sa Vie was a complete romantic tribute: it dwells on Karina's face in awe and fondness—there she is at the movies, weeping over Falconetti in Dreyer's *The Passion of Joan of Arc;* there she is dancing around the pool table to vamp a guy, like an assistant director's girlfriend who says, "Sure, I'll be your Cyd Charisse." There she is in a café talking to philosopher Brice Parain. And then she is dead on a side street. Shot in grave black-and-white, with a harrowed score by Michel Legrand, attentive to the societal issue of prostitution, *Vivre Sa Vie* clings to the hope that to be filmed is to be alive. Some said Karina was not a trained or accomplished actress, but the film is radiant over her imprisonment. It was hard to think of a director so pledged to a female presence on film.

They were wildly in love, but then he would go missing for a few weeks, leaving her, as if to warn her. Next he wondered if she was faithful to him. She did not understand the films they were making, or the distance he maintained in directing her. There was passion, no doubt, but little complicity or mutuality. *Vivre Sa Vie* is very emotional, but its rigorous separation into chapters is part of what Godard took for granted: that he was looking at his wife on a screen, one point of which was that he could not touch her. So her character seemed doomed and alone.

Pierrot le Fou is about an old flame (thus the dream that love is our destiny). Ferdinand (she calls him Pierrot) is married with kids. He seems to be a success. He attends a party where one female guest is vacantly nude and where Sam Fuller rants about the task of a movie director: "The film is like a battleground . . . Love . . . Hate . . . Action . . . Violence . . . Death . . . In one word . . . Emotion."

Fuller was one of the American directors Godard the critic had acclaimed. At this party he wears dark glasses and looks like a toy King Kong, speaking about all that action but perilously still and posed. Already, Godard seems to understand that the talk of action is fake. But then the married couple leaves and Ferdinand agrees to drive the babysitter, Marianne, home. She and Ferdinand were lovers in the past and now they kiss again in a parked car. Love still, or loss overcome. They go off together, into an episode of unexplained violence. In summer, they plunge into the South of France, "Like spirits through a mirror."

They have an idyll on a beach somewhere. She sings and dances; he imitates Michel Simon, the actor Renoir loved, and quotes the novelist Louis-Ferdinand Céline. They have wild animals. He is writing something: we see the words like spiders on the page. She talks of boredom, not knowing what to do, and it feels like a last song. They are headed toward tragedy and betrayal, and they know it. There are scenes where Marianne stares into the camera, sunburned and half-sullen, and tries to define the jostling of feelings and thinking, words and looking, and their incompatability, the animal and the vegetable. It is plain that she is talking to Godard and that the summer is turning scorched and dishonest. *Vivre Sa Vie* and *Pierrot le Fou* are a valediction on romantic movies and the romanticization cinema inflicts on reality. With lasting bitterness, Godard saw those tropes as opioids. He and Karina broke up, and Godard embarked on his retreat from entertainment cinema, romanticism, and moving us.

Until *Weekend,* at least, he retained a following among smart young people who thought of making a movie, or being in one.

In *Weekend,* it became clear that his mordant view of society had set in with a vengeance. He went back to live in Switzerland as time went by and he became like a writer who was writing essays on the end of the world on video but who had given up on being a director. There would be remarkable, beautiful films, arresting in their ideas and subtle in their construction. These include *Tout Va Bien, Numéro Deux, Every Man for Himself, Passion, First Name: Carmen, Hail Mary.* Most impressive of all is *Histoire(s) du Cinéma,* an encompassing video essay completed in 1998, and presented as a book, too. At 266 minutes it is the most complete and intelligent description of the medium ever done, full of bleak affection and foreboding. Of course, it seems too dry for those who are dying of thirst.

Moreover, in the twenty years since it was made, "movie" has been altered by the uncatalogued collection of fragments on one's phone, all there but not connected except in blind editing. Godard will be ninety in 2020. He married again, to actress Anna Wiazemsky (she appeared in *Weekend* and a few other films, but without the resonance Karina had had); he has had a close collaborator and lover, Anne-Marie Miéville; and there was a rich and contentious partnership with Jean-Pierre Gorin, in a period of Marxist filmmaking named after the Soviet documentarian Dziga Vertov. But he is less the director now than a reclusive seer near Rolle, the endless, helpless editor of imagery, an archivist, and the worshipper who felt his church was going dead some time before the general culture realized that "movies" were a subject for nostalgia more than urgency.

Quite properly, "Godardian" is the age that succeeded "cinematic" or "movielike." It is also a forecast of confusion where once there seemed marvels fit for a Rousseau jungle. But if the best lasting subject of the facticity of movies is things that were lost—a sled in *Citizen Kane,* a last chance in *La Règle du Jeu,* an entire woman in *L'Avventura*—then *Pierrot le Fou* is one of the most intense imprints of lost feelings, including the cult of cinema itself.

9

THE GHOST OF NICK RAY

Once upon a time, Hollywood people had no interest in what was being made in Spain or Mexico. But in the 1960s, at film festivals, strangers began to meet and talk about different ways of doing movies. "Godardian" was an excitement that swept over frontiers: *Alphaville* was shot in Paris but it understood every modern city. When it was appreciated that the French New Wave was crazy about American pictures it became easier for young Americans—the film student, a new character—to rediscover their own archive.

One day in 1961, two directors shared a meal in Madrid. Without believing in any deity, it turned out they were both making films about God. That was something to chat over. They could hardly have been more different. Nicholas Ray was fifty, tall, handsome, American, and unquestionably a big man in town. He seemed seasoned, even if he sometimes behaved like a kid.

He had asked Luis Buñuel for a meeting. Ray had just made

King of Kings, from a base outside Madrid. This was a big picture; it had to be, not out of any faith in its lead character, but because Hollywood money was still loyal to biblical epics rooted in what was supposed to be a widespread public allegiance. In 1959, *Ben-Hur* had won eleven Oscars plus a box office of $150 million. *King of Kings* had cost $5 million, and it would earn over $13 million.

Luis Buñuel was sixty-one, Spanish, hunched, reserved in his fatalism, going bald and deaf. He had come back to Franco's Spain to make *Viridiana,* a transgressive parable that scorned the cultural cliché that had cast Jeffrey Hunter (a blue-eyed Catholic of Irish descent) as Jesus Christ, or Jesus of Nazareth, the K of Ks. On the cross, Hunter's armpits had been shaved, so that the crucifixion should be wholesome. You likely have no reliable idea now who Jeffrey Hunter was. The legend of Jesus Christ himself is slipping. It's hard to ascertain what *Viridiana* cost, because its budget was so modest. But it shared the Palme d'Or at Cannes and became a distinguished, heretical "outrage." *King of Kings* won nothing, but it sustained the economy of Samuel Bronston Productions and Nicholas Ray for another year.

As Buñuel described the meeting, Nick Ray was perplexed. He "asked how I'd managed to make such interesting movies on such small budgets." Ray did not know that Luis's mother had paid for *Un Chien Andalou.* Buñuel said money had never been a problem for him. "What I'd had, I'd had. It was either that or nothing at all." In other words, if you had $5 million for a *King of Kings,* you would have proceeded. But if you had just $50,000, well . . . make do with that. Wasn't there a story about a few loaves and fishes feeding a multitude?

"You're a famous director," Buñuel said to Ray. "Why not try an experiment? You've just finished a picture that cost five million dollars. Why not try one for four hundred thousand dollars and see for yourself how much freer you are?"

Ray tried to be sophisticated in his answer. "But you don't understand. If I did that in Hollywood everyone would think I was going to pieces. They'd say I was on the skids, and I'd never make another movie!"

Money was as potent as any storyline and as perilous as infatuation. Think of it as "Other People's Money," a joke but a barb that can pierce directorial balloons. As the studio system broke down, so directors might have to search for their funding, and they could be undone by that challenge. The appropriation and spending of OPM can approach theft and fraud, self-deception as well as the tricking of others. This needs to be kept in mind with the proud defense of integrity in film directors' search for truth. Every movie, good and bad, is a snaky treasure map, but "auteurship" was generally spared the pitiless examination of accountants and lawyers in the ardent pages of *Cahiers du Cinéma* or *Sight and Sound*.

Beginners say they want to make a movie so badly they'd do it for nothing—until nothing turns as practical as petty cash. You'll need a screenplay, a camera, a few new faces, and $50,000—then add a zero or three. And a lot of the money ready to get into movies can be testing: it may be dirty or compromised, anxious to meet the actresses and go to Cannes. It isn't straight money, free from laundering and skimming. *But never do this job with your own money.* Ideally, you should have none of your own as protection.

Alas, a first $1 million payday can weaken so much resolve. It leads to a house in the hills, a small but startling Lucian Freud, a couple of cars, then wives, with entourage, just to keep up appearances. With that schedule of payments, for the next job you'll need $5 million. You might as well go for a smash hit for Marvel if you want to sleep at night. So much for the trans love story set in Idaho and that new face from Boise.

Nick Ray was out in the wild open of being independent, and it was more than he would survive. *King of Kings* is not as foolish as its concept or its promotion in which the title words were carved out of some towering rock in an epic desert. Robert Ryan is impressive as John the Baptist (it was his fourth film for Ray). Hurd Hatfield makes a dry, enervated Pontius Pilate. Orson Welles read the gravity-heavy narration, without credit, for cash in hand. The Sermon on the Mount scene is very creatively done, with a moving camera and Jesus walking in the crowd. You feel you are there, alive, in the moment. It is the kind of scene Nick Ray could do so well, like the gang at the chicken run sequence in *Rebel Without a Cause,* or Cyd Charisse dancing in front of Robert Taylor in *Party Girl.* But *King of Kings* hardly plays now, except at Easter, for the shrinking congregation that remembers what Easter was.

In fact, Ray's next film was the onset of his disaster. In Spain once more, and for Bronston Productions again, he directed *55 Days at Peking,* with Charlton Heston, David Niven, and Ava Gardner. It's about the Boxer Rebellion (it says). It had some fine action scenes as well as a vague feeling for a United Nations approach to troubles in the world—along with a complete lack of interest in those troublesome Chinese and why they might be angry in 1900. British actress Flora Robson played the evil Dowager Empress Tzu Hsi with narrowed eyes, long fingernails, and lisping English. Bronston was ambitious after doing Jesus. This new film cost $9 million but then it only earned back $10 million—which means it was a business failure: on $9 million it needed to earn over $20 million. And truly, it had no other end in view but revenue.

The experience was worse for Ray. His health broke down during the shooting and maybe his creative morale suffered too. Call it his spirit or his conscience. He was drinking too much; he was taking drugs again; and he could not stop gambling. Some saw him as a big shot burning out. He had to be replaced to have the film finished. It was the last commercial picture he would ever make; he was fifty-three. Buñuel had *Belle de Jour, The Discreet Charm of the Bourgeoisie,* and *That Obscure Object of Desire* ahead of him. It's hard to pin down what *Belle de Jour* cost: with Catherine Deneuve in and out of Yves Saint Laurent clothes, and its excellent cast, its budget may have risen to $1 million. But the picture earned over $20 million, and it has a lucidity, a sensuality, and a deadpan humor that Nick Ray could only have dreamed of, even when Hollywood was not laughing at him.

They did laugh, in part because Ray had talked so much about being a rebel, true to his art, and someone who needed to break away from Hollywood—yet on American expense accounts. In doing that, he had signed a $1 million contract with Bronston and then boasted of being the highest paid director in the world.

That meeting in Madrid is emblematic. Nicholas Ray had authentic, romantic ambitions to be a great artist, and even in his unstable Hollywood career he had been accused of that greatness. In 1958, Jean-Luc Godard, talking about *Bitter Vic-*

tory, had declared, "The cinema is Nicholas Ray." This was not mere hero-worship, even if Godard felt an emotional desire to praise a kind of directing that appealed to him for his own career. For those French critics (including François Truffaut and Jacques Rivette), Ray was brimming with a daring cinematic energy that wanted to break free of Hollywood restraints, and which was capable of filling the screen with form, color, danger, and intense feelings. If there was not one perfect Ray film, his fractured quality was in itself romantic. And so *They Live by Night, In a Lonely Place, On Dangerous Ground, The Lusty Men, Johnny Guitar, Bigger Than Life, Bitter Victory,* and above all *Rebel Without a Cause* were worshipped by the French.

And by me. The startling opening shots of an escaping car filmed from a helicopter in *They Live by Night,* the view of Robert Mitchum's broken-down rodeo rider limping across a windswept arena in *The Lusty Men,* a CinemaScope screen suddenly ablaze with yellow cabs in *Bigger Than Life,* Dean's red windbreaker and the white milk in *Rebel*—the shots and the fragments are piercing, even if sometimes those films lapse into awkwardness. Godard was not wrong: Nick Ray could show us that formulaic entertainment might have glimpses of poetry and personality for a few minutes that were beyond amusement or diversion.

Ray was ardent and gloomy, creative and self-destructive, and he was a test case at a crucial moment of turmoil in the status of the film director. The American studio system was breaking down and *Rebel Without a Cause* was forerunner of the wave of *Easy Rider:* films about young mavericks at odds with American prosperity and conservatism, movies prepared to say that America was far from an okay empire or an easy place to be. The lonely place in Ray's fevered imagination was the Los Angeles he might triumph in. He wanted new subject matter: *Bigger Than Life* was a melodrama about how easily so-called miracle drugs could bring crisis and tragedy. *Bitter Victory* doubted the settled role of heroism in war. Ray was pushing the limits of genre, yet he craved success and was vulnerable to its rewards. He wanted to be an auteur and an artist, a rebel but an insider, too. And he disapproved of common sense.

Like Walt Whitman, he was proud of contradicting himself, and all others. He was a womanizer: on *Rebel,* he had an affair with the underage Natalie Wood (she was also involved with Dennis Hopper, who was acting in the film). Such action today would shut a career down. At the same time, Ray had some homosexual relationships. When he looks at Dean and Sal Mineo in that film, you cannot miss the yearning. Later on, when his mainstream career was over, Ray became interested in pornography and he considered doing a film with the adult actress Marilyn Chambers. He had an instinct for the psychic undergrowth in human behavior that entranced Buñuel.

When he talked to the Spaniard, it wasn't just that he was fearful of being mocked by the business. He wanted to be rich *and* to be honored by a system he despised. His screenwriter hero in *In a Lonely Place* (Dixon Steele, played by Humphrey Bogart) is turning murderous over these contradictions. Ray never quite realized that Godard—and the American knew of the praise Godard had given him—was ready to make a movie (like *Pierrot le Fou,* full of Ray's vibrant dismay) for a ridiculously un-American sum, no more than $300,000 in 1965. There's a scene in that film where the Jean-Paul Belmondo character drives his car into the Mediterranean on a romantic existential impulse. Because he could not afford to buy a car for the shot, Godard sacrificed his own Ford Galaxie. But when Ray shot the chicken-run sequence in *Rebel,* he had a fleet of custom cars and stunt drivers.

In the 1960s, Godard was unstoppable: he had made fifteen feature films by 1968. Ray became a nomad in those years, more and more affected by his own excesses and his lack of money. After *55 Days,* there was only his attempt at Harpur College in upstate New York to conjure a new kind of film from the adoration and sacrifice of his students and equipment or facilities that he could beg or steal from old associates. This would be called *We Can't Go Home Again,* released only in 2011, thanks to the persistence of Susan, his last wife or companion, who had collaborated on the screenplay—if anyone could ever locate such a plan. The film is passionate but incoherent, a montage of changes in direction. Some said it was an exploration of creative variety; others saw it as unwatchable and painful, but more films like that are finding screens today. Its homelessness asserted that anyone could make a movie by the 1970s: the mechanics of filming, or shooting, were breaking open, though the iPhone was still to come. Ray had an instinct for that future, and no way of knowing why anyone would watch such a product.

I met Ray in 1978 when he visited Dartmouth College, where I was teaching. He was just out of hospital after cancer surgery. That he was on his feet, a spectral figure, testified to his courage and his resolve to go on. I had loved his films for twenty-five years, since seeing Dean in *Rebel,* and it was impossible to resist the appeal of the ruined romantic. I was prepared to give him some money (he had come to Dartmouth for the "honorarium") but Susan Ray took me aside in patient kindness and absolute loyalty and urged me to do no such thing, because if he had any money he would spend it immediately, and badly. So I became friends with the Rays. I helped Nick eat scrambled eggs for breakfast, then I saw him at his last birthday in New York. He looked stronger then. His white hair had come back like fire after the cancer. That's where I met Tom Luddy for the first time (the great Connection, Octave of the American film world—that's Renoir in *La Règle du Jeu*). Wim Wenders was there, too, and his affection for Nick did not smother opportunism. So Wenders made a film, *Lightning Over Water*, a rueful study of a dying director. It's a documentary, I suppose, but it's a lyrical Götterdämmerung, too, beautiful at times but painful to behold. It's a sonata about a man who had given up fact for dreaming. Thus, it is true and close to Nick, yet it is an ominous valediction and warning on being a movie director. It was released in 1980, but somehow it seems from much longer ago.

Nick died on June 16, 1979; he was sixty-seven. Buñuel took his last sigh in Mexico City, July 29, 1983. Nick was a wreck to the end; Luis existed in a somber mastery that knew glory was a trick, and reveled quietly in how his body was letting him down. I don't mean to sentimentalize Buñuel by suggesting that he did not also work for money, prizes, and friendship with actresses. But those things impressed him no more than a good cigar, a fine brandy, and any pretty woman. He ended his memoir with a cool, laconic estimate of death and how to do it, and I think Nick would have loved that prose and wanted to make a film out of it, just as Wenders had been drawn to show the last glimpse of Nick, like the tattered flag on a pirate ship.

Nick and Luis were both heroes in a cultural moment when it seemed a swell thing to be a movie director.

When I speak of the ghost of Nick Ray, I am trying to convey a shifting presence or example—a haunting—that never achieved coherence, let alone a solid career. But Ray was a light to the generation of young American directors that believed they could force passion and reality into the moribund narrative codes of old Hollywood. If you loved *Bonnie and Clyde* in 1967, and if you recalled Nick's debut picture, *They Live by Night* (1948), you had to appreciate how far Arthur Penn and Warren Beatty had fulfilled an idea that Nick had launched, that sweet, lost kids on the wasteland prairie might take up cars and guns, love and danger, just to prove they were alive.

Nick never made a whole film, or one without flaws or wounds and his unique desperate awkwardness. He was the saint of the religion that knew regular American movies (like those by Hawks and Hitchcock) were too damn hard to do if you wanted to change your mind while you were working, if you were going to break free from the factory plan. When Truffaut wrote about "the great crippled films" of Nicholas Ray, he was talking about that perilous hope more than an Oscar-winning achievement.

If only Nick had had some wise film producer to look after him—someone like Stephen Frears.

A VERY ENGLISH PROFESSIONAL:
STEPHEN FREARS

The intensity of being Nick Ray, or Godardian, could be suf-focating and not easy on family, lovers, or dependents. So this is the place to defend the steadfast and invaluable role of pro-fessionalism—or doing a job—in film directing in the manner of a conscientious tailor or a doctor.

Stephen Frears is persistent and even cunning about not regarding himself as seriously as lofty directors have been trained to do. Should we take him at his own estimate?

His record is exceptional in its variety and skill. So many of his films are as entertaining as ever. He is warm, funny, and aware. I was going to say he is "very good," but that's not adequate. You know something about him straightaway by seeing how he will try anything. It's as if he's saying, Well, really filmmaking is just aptitude or willingness, a certain kind of optimism, instead of that bigger thing, art or auteurship. I can see his face wrinkle with skepticism if you asked him to claim "auteurship."

Frears makes me think of William Wyler (1902–81), a director of high success rate and reputation who felt it was his role to be of service in rendering intelligent versions of Sinclair Lewis's *Dodsworth;* Somerset Maugham's *The Letter;* the novel that made *Mrs. Miniver;* Henry James's *Washington Square,* which became *The Heiress;* Theodore Dreiser's *Sister Carrie;* delivering Audrey Hepburn in *Roman Holiday;* and containing Lew Wallace's *Ben-Hur.* We can say now that *Dodsworth* and *The Letter* are better than *Ben-Hur.* So be it. The point is that Wyler measured himself for consistency and care. He won three best director Oscars, he had three best pictures, and he helped get nominations for thirty-six performances (though not Olivier in *Carrie,* which may be the actor's best movie work). Wyler was never willing to say, This one is for me! He didn't let his *me* get noticed.

I like Frears, and I do know him. We are nearly the same age and I've met him and e-mailed him over the years. We did an event together at the Berlin Film Festival in 2010. I had chosen his *Mary Reilly* in a fifty-year retrospective of films to play at the festival, but he regretted that attention. So we had a public conversation in Berlin where I tried to praise *Mary Reilly,* and he said, No, really, it wasn't very good. I'll come to that discussion, without hope of settling it, but I think those there enjoyed the reversal of roles and his good humor. It might be useful for directors to explain in public why some of their films are not good enough—if such films have ever existed.

Let me try to convey the variety of Frears quickly. If you are reading this, you are likely to have reasonable knowledge of his work. He has been at it steadily and some of his films have been talking points—like *Dangerous Liaisons, The Queen,* and *A Very English Scandal.* You know about Stephen Frears.

In which case, what do you think of *Saigon: Year of the Cat*? Please understand, there is not the least recrimination if you have not seen that one, or heard of its intriguing title.

Still, *Saigon: Year of the Cat* is a movie, 105 minutes long. It was made in 1983 for Thames Television in London as a movie or a play—it's hard sometimes to distinguish those terms in British television. But it was filmed. It's the story of an English woman, an assistant manager in a bank in Saigon, in 1974. She gets involved with a rather mysterious American who she guesses is with the CIA. So it's a love story set in that corrupt city poised to fall. It was written by David Hare. The man is Frederic Forrest, the woman Judi Dench. You don't believe me?

It's not that it's "great," though I think it's very good and as unexpected as a romance between Forrest and Dench. And it was hard to believe that given that plot situation David Hare was going to prove a poor choice. In its setup it is, as we say, "interesting," as a Stephen Frears film that came and went. I suspect he would be philosophical about that.

You might think that in the years since 1983, during which Frears became an easygoing British institution, he would have moved on from television. But in 2019, there he was doing *State of the Union* for the small screen. Once again, this was not simply work, or staying in practice, but finding a fresh approach. In the same way, in 2000, he had done a new *Fail Safe* by going back to the conditions of live TV drama from the 1950s, and now *State of the Union* was a unique ten-part series of ten-minute episodes. There was nothing quite like it.

It had a couple (Rosamund Pike and Chris O'Dowd) meeting in a pub before marital therapy sessions in some smart, leafy arbor of a privileged London. The protected air extended to their relationship: allegedly on the brink of divorce, they were as chatty and amusing as a couple from screwball comedy. Their wordplay overrode anguish but left one wondering why try this novel TV format without more substance or purpose? It seemed a ploy to suggest they were breaking apart when all they wanted was a pretext for bickering, one-upping, and flirting, like Cary Grant and Rosalind Russell in *His Girl Friday* (which is a year older than Frears).

So, to my eyes, *State of the Union* wasn't credible or open for sympathy. If I'd been overhearing that couple in a pub, I'd have moved away. The apparent originality turned precious and faintly smug. The chance of sharp writing and acting getting at a broken love seemed as calculated as the several plain but cute dresses Ms. Pike wore in every episode. But there was Frears persevering with TV, and angling to make it different and worthwhile, instead of behaving like a grand movie director doing shameless, epic rubbish. This comes from his temperament and his having set out when television was the most inviting place for uncommon stories, just as the BBC was the best movie studio Britain would ever have. Though he seemed equally at home with the companies that contributed to commercial television, Frears has handled himself in a country where many filmmakers complain about how frustrating or impossible it is to do work. He's always doing something with a charm that has never lacked for openings. Huge budgets make him nervous, but he is good at assembling just about enough. He is as old-fashioned as a contract director from the 1940s, and as accomplished. But always more unexpected than a Wyler or Michael Curtiz. In 2020, he was back on TV with *Quiz*.

Frears was born in Leicester in the middle of England, the

son of an accountant. Later in life he learned his mother was Jewish. He went to Gresham's school and then to Cambridge where he messed around in theatre. I don't say that to suggest a frivolous attitude, but putting on plays then at university was an untidy collaboration for a generation of smart, iconoclastic, and rivalrous people. Britain was changing fast and young talent seized on its chance to be subversive or cheeky, and successful. Frears did not have the personality to take charge or impose himself. He was not as radical as Ken Loach, Mike Leigh, or Alan Clarke. It was natural therefore that he would drift towards the BBC which was still learning about television, and so loosely organized that unruly talents and ideas got on screen. Some consequences of that were the commissioning of original plays and letting a whim like *Monty Python's Flying Circus* take off.

In time, Frears made fairly big, moderately "important" movies. He went to Hollywood and he worked with serious American money. But he has never had a flat-out hit apart from *The Queen*. He was twice nominated for directing Oscars but did not win; and I don't think he felt as comfortable in Los Angeles as in the pubs and resting places of north London (the world fondly viewed in *State of the Union*). All along, he kept going back to the small screen because he found its budgets and its creative freedom more manageable, and because on television in those days the writer was given pride of place, and respect. TV did not cultivate large directorial personalities, or egos— though such figures did exist in British movies, with Joseph Losey, Richard Lester, Tony Richardson, John Schlesinger, and Stanley Kubrick (three of them American). They were auteurs, or people who made *their* films. Whereas on the small box directors served the writers, the actors, and the general concept that when one job was over they'd all take another.

So, in the early 1970s, Frears made *Gumshoe* as a movie, in a friendly pastiche of American genres transposed to Liverpool. He directed *The Hit,* a deft rendering of a French *policier* or a film noir on the landscape plateaux of Spain. But his most personal work was for television and for Alan Bennett. In the quartet of *Beyond the Fringe,* Bennett had been the quietest or most recessive talent. Being part of that lively team had obscured his solitary nature. But by the 1970s he was emerging as a sad voice for values and types being lost in a rapidly changing society. As a dramatist he fixed on small actions and unobtrusive lives—ordinary situations with run-of-the-mill muffled people, averse to melodrama or starriness. This would be the thread of his *Talking Heads* series which consisted of heartfelt communions between writer and actors, chamber plays for television presenting the ghosts of Britain's lost order and archaic reticence. If you look at *Bed Among the Lentils* (1988), the soliloquy of a vicar's sad wife who at last finds pleasure, you have to remind yourself that the actress is Maggie Smith, so plain, unmannered, and appealing (so un-Dame-like, so far from Downton)—her best work? Frears didn't make that, but maybe its Anglo-Asian theme owed something to his *My Beautiful Laundrette.*

The same mood applied in a set of "plays" Bennett and Frears did for London Weekend: *A Day Out* (1972), *Sunset Across the Bay* (1975), *Me! I'm Afraid of Virginia Woolf* (1978), *One Fine Day* (1979), *Afternoon Off* (1979). To take just one of those, *Sunset Across the Bay* is about a lower-middle-class married couple who in retirement move from the city of Leeds to the seaside resort of Morecambe. This is not the material of a big movie, and the players, Gabrielle Day and Harry Markham, may be unknown to you. They were faces from the crowd, not beauties or touched by glamour. But in the gentle view of sadness sinking with the sun they were so eloquent. *Sunset Across the Bay* is one of the best things Frears has ever done.

To which, he might respond, Well, that was Alan and the actors and the low-budget grace of working in television at that time, plus the subtle social value in looking at the kind of lives being led by most of the audience. Later, Bennett acquired a crust of self-pity and irony hardening in a protective air that came from having become a national treasure and a best-seller. But he was a dry, rather chilly, gentle man who believed in common kindness being chased off the stage by official welfare and then social media. They were both left-wing, watching socialism being compromised by Britain. But Bennett was never better or braver than when writing for television, and Frears was a faithful companion and enabler.

Frears might answer how in Hollywood there were directors as good as Howard Hawks, Frank Capra, Mitchell Leisen, and Michael Curtiz who were also "versatile," bending themselves to different genres, players, and dreams. I don't think that's quite true of Hawks and Capra. Their personalities shine through over years and many films, for good and ill. But it's fair comment on Leisen and Curtiz, and many others, and it stands for the ideal that in Hollywood in its golden age a trusty crew and a good script made one passable entertainment and started on another Monday morning. It was an unromantic way of making dreams. There's some humbug or wishful thinking in that attitude, but there is substance too, and Curtiz is its insouciant model.

Frears has always tried to follow good writing. For decades

now, his oeuvre has been a sequence of these fruitful relationships. Bennett is its model figure—he also scripted the movie *Prick Up Your Ears*—but the line is clear: Neville Smith, who wrote *Gumshoe* from his own novel; Hanif Kureishi, who did *My Beautiful Laundrette* and *Sammy and Rosie Get Laid;* Christopher Hampton—*Dangerous Liaisons, Mary Reilly,* and *Chéri;* Nick Hornby—*High Fidelity, State of the Union;* and Peter Morgan with *The Deal* and *The Queen.*

It's not that those films are uniformly good, or that there haven't been other writers who did single films with Frears. Nor am I suggesting that in pre-production or rehearsal Frears hadn't himself nudged the shape of a story or the fluency of dialogue in one direction or another. But he's never taken credit as a writer—and that self-effacement is not universal in moviemaking. I suspect he'd say that anyone on set can come up with a good line, and isn't everyone trying to make the product better?

On the other hand, there are directors of high achievement who would not think of taking on a film project without generating its idea themselves, before writing the actual screenplay. How can you direct or create, they might ask, without that origination? The list of filmmakers who work that way includes Ingmar Bergman, Jean-Luc Godard, Paul Thomas Anderson, Michael Haneke, Satyajit Ray, the team of Michael Powell and Emeric Pressburger, Orson Welles (with an asterisk), Terrence Malick, and Andrei Tarkovsky. And those are directors for whom it is proper to speak of vision, thematic preoccupation, and artistic integrity.

More or less. We need plenty of asterisks, along with the realization that while Michelangelo Antonioni films list several writers most of the time, it was clear that only Antonioni could have made the films, or understood what they were doing. Where you put the camera, and how long you let it run; whether you use the sound of the wind or compose music for your soundtrack; and whether you cast x or y—those choices amount to authorship and can preside serenely over different people contributing to your script. *Pretty Woman* was chaos in the making, but it looks radiant (and daft) forever because of Julia Roberts—she was its auteuse. She has the same central force in *Mary Reilly*.

Not that Frears would ever permit himself the stylishness (or the vanity) of an Antonioni, or a mise-en-scène so haunted by its own enigma. He shoots simply, for efficiency, but because he prefers a medium minus such personal atmospherics. That's where he's most like Hawks.

Such choices run through this book, and the nature of movie, but in the case of Frears they lead to significant realizations. It's not easy to look at his work and identify a vision or a preoccupation—beyond wanting to make entertaining pictures. Fair enough: he is a model of wry common sense, good nature, and doing his best by people, and that kindness exists in most of his work. Yet it is not as profound as a similar openness to life that one finds in Alan Bennett, who may be the biggest influence on what Frears has done. Bennett knows life can be harder, or meaner, than Frears admits.

But Frears worked through the 1970s on television, a time when comparable movie directors arrived and flowered. That is the decade in which Losey did *The Go-Between*, Kubrick delivered *A Clockwork Orange*, John Schlesinger made *Midnight Cowboy*, Nicolas Roeg gave us *Don't Look Now*, Ridley Scott debuted with *The Duellists* and *Alien* and—in England—the Polish director Jerzy Skolimowski made *Deep End,* a breathtaking erotic dream film with a poetic mystery that Frears seems to mistrust. So at the age of forty, he was rather behind in his career, and easily written off as cautious. He could be regarded as Bennett's house director.

Not that Frears is content to be as provincial and northern as much of Bennett's work. *My Beautiful Laundrette* was a departure for Frears, coming after the Bennett years. It had been designed for Channel 4 with a small TV budget. But the film turned out so well it was decided to give it a theatrical release. It made money and drew attention: Hanif Kureishi's screenplay got an Oscar nomination and Daniel Day-Lewis (in a breakthrough role) won several prizes.

Kureishi was plainly important in a multiracial story, but Frears had no hesitation over the gritty urban setting, or dealing with the English life of Pakistanis, with sexual confusion, political violence, and a film that reached out to younger audiences in a way Bennett seldom seemed to notice. If Bennett was never quite young, Frears has not yet seemed old. Bennett filmed the past wistfully while Frears seemed ready to grasp the awkward nows of English life. That hope has fluctuated. Frears grew up routinely left-wing and well aware of the problems in his world and his London. But he has plunged elsewhere—into the eighteenth century, to Ireland and America. He goes where the wind blows and he is temperamentally less aroused by the idea of a film than by the action itself. It's as if, like an actor, he needed a text to follow and obey. Does this make him less of an individual or even his own man? He has taken on Laclos, Joe Orton, Jim Thompson, and Posy Simmonds with equanimity.

There are Frears films where that reticence is a shortcoming. *The Hit* (1984) had a script by Peter Prince, a novelist and TV writer, one of those interesting one-offs among Frears's writers. It is an original, though the story is redolent of so many film noirs about an outlaw on the run. It's the sort of movieish setup Frears likes. A London gangster (Terence Stamp) gives evidence against his colleagues in court. He has to hide thereafter, and he chooses Spain. He has lived there several years in well-heeled tranquility until the day of retribution. Two hitmen (John Hurt and Tim Roth) come to collect him. They are under orders to take him back to London. That's a contrivance and a failing. It would be enough to execute him in sunny Spain—but the journey back is the convenient structure for a film.

Still, *The Hit* is very entertaining. The dialogue is like razors on a pillow. Frears shoots the action and suspense with unobtrusive accuracy and élan. You feel his sense of American narrative efficiency as a modern mode. Frears likes to make movies because of working with natural actors. The casting is authorship. Stamp is insolent, cheeky, fatalistic. Hurt is icy, lethal, and misanthropic. Roth is a kid thug trying to learn. The film exists in the bitter interplay of this triangle. And Laura del Sol supplies the sex—too obviously erotic—as the Spanish girl they pick up on the way. Effective as it is, *The Hit* is formulaic.

That problem spreads as one begins to wonder how the plot is going to be completed. It feels like an exercise. And as the story winds down, its several deaths are a tidying up. The Stamp character quotes John Donne; Hurt's villain finds some sympathy for the girl. But the fatalism never runs the risk of poetry or philosophy.

Compare *The Hit* with John Boorman's *Point Blank* (1967). Boorman is eight years older than Frears, but they are alike in background and the need to find film work in a freelance life. Boorman's output has been inconsistent. But I think *Point Blank* is more resonant than anything Frears has attempted. It isn't just a noir plot; it's a story of a man against fate, time, and his own confusions. Every time I see *Point Blank* it feels new, whereas *The Hit* goes stale because I know what's going to happen and there's no mystery in that matter-of-fact ending. *Point Blank* thrives on things left unclear—like whether the Lee Marvin character is alive or dead. But I feel that Frears would flinch at that mythic level to a "straightforward" story. He does not like to do the fantasies or the dread felt by his characters. Is there something too fancy or self-indulgent in going that far?

Boorman didn't write *Point Blank,* but it belongs to him, like his voice or an unhealed wound, whereas Frears's film is a stylish jacket he has put on for a party. I think Boorman needed to make *Point Blank;* he committed to its riskiness personally, while *The Hit* was a tidy job and a diversion. What it comes down to is a sense of possession or self-expression in the two films. It may be that Frears is too drawn to common-sense realism to be an uninhibited visionary. Equally, it could be that cinema is better off if directors keep their feet on the ground, or as if Frears had decided that he is English, not French or American.

That is important for any non-American film director. Hollywood hardly exists now, but for decades the challenge of making it in America was inescapable. The opportunity weighed on Chaplin, Hitchcock, Boorman, and Schlesinger. As it did on Cary Grant, Olivier, and Deborah Kerr. David Lean didn't go Hollywood, but he got in the habit of depending on American money. That is a kind of imperialism in the picture business. So Frears had some American money for *Dangerous Liaisons* and *Mary Reilly,* and he went to Los Angeles for *The Grifters* and *Hero.* A few years later he did a Western, *The Hi-Lo Country,* shot in New Mexico.

Hero was the experience that put him off Hollywood. The ingenious film was written by David Peoples (they became good friends) and it could have been a sparkling comedy. But Dustin Hoffman ended up as the lead and he and his director did not get along. Hoffman wanted time, improvisation, and his own central place in the venture. In Britain, and by instinct, Frears had grown comfortable with actors who had less ego or more urge to help. To look at *The Hit, My Beautiful Laundrette,* or the interplay of Gary Oldman and Alfred Molina in *Prick Up Your Ears* (the Joe Orton story) is to get a feeling of Frears as a coach loved by his players in team spirit. Hoffman stuck a thumb in that eye and left it sore.

That reaction was the sadder because *The Grifters,* made just before *Hero,* is nearly as good as *Point Blank.* It came from a Jim Thompson pulp novella about three people in the con rackets: a mother (still young), her son, and the son's girlfriend. Frears was smart to ask Donald Westlake to do his script, an inspired choice and a further measure of how far he felt unable to write himself. The two became close. Westlake drove Frears to find locations and Frears asked him to be on set during the shooting. Better yet, the casting was magical. Anjelica Huston is the mother. John Cusack is the son she must have had in her late teens. And a daring Annette Bening is the mistress.

The Grifters explores emotional fraud or exploitation in as chilling a way as Frears has allowed himself. Quite clearly, the mother flirts with her own son to survive in the film's climax.

It is a shocking, violent moment where the players are fault-less: Bening has not shown such innate, ingratiating dishonesty since. Cusack was in his element as a guy flawed but clinging to immaturity. Huston was austere, forbidding, and like a lonely witch.

The film had four Oscar nominations—for Frears, Westlake, Huston, and Bening—but won nothing. It did reasonably well at the box office but it may have felt too raw for the largest audiences. As time goes by, it looks better than ever, the Frears film with inescapable emotional nakedness. He was nearly fifty, and at his peak. It's not that he subsided afterwards, but back in Britain he did smaller and less ambitious pictures: *The Van, High Fidelity, Liam, Dirty Pretty Things, Mrs. Henderson Presents, The Snapper.*

I'm not sure that was a slide, because Frears was never dull. But any possible decline was arrested by teaming up with Peter Morgan and the actor Michael Sheen, and by seeing that movies might be made out of current events. In 2003, initially for Granada Television from Morgan's script, he made *The Deal,* about the arrangement struck between Tony Blair and Gordon Brown, leaders of the Labour Party, on the order in which they would be prime minister. Michael Sheen was cast as Blair, and he was so fiendishly good one can imagine the real Blair checking in the mirror that he was still there.

The Deal was a provocative venture and Granada were scared it might interfere in the country's actual political process. They dropped out, to be replaced by Channel 4. Then the film played the week before the Labour Party conference. The running controversy over it broke down some last fences between the news and entertainment.

That was the start of *The Queen,* Frears's best-known film, and the most commercially successful. Morgan was the obvious writer with the nerve for putting the Buckingham Palace show up on the screen. And the death of Princess Diana was the fulcrum for its story, for her life and death had been the modern crisis for the British monarchy. They cast Sheen as Blair again, with Helen McCrory as his wife. Sylvia Sims was the Queen Mother, and James Cromwell played Philip. All acute and tidy. Then there was Helen Mirren as Elizabeth. She got the only acting Oscar won in a Frears picture. Her portrait of a lost or deserted leader left on-screen majesty floundering until Claire Foy came along in *The Crown,* another Peter Morgan enterprise that owed a lot to Frears's example.

The Queen grossed over $120 million in theatres, on a cost of $15 million, but at its heart it stayed a television movie, taking advantage of the increasing appetite for celebrity melodrama. I don't think it's actually very good, and Frears the anti-monarchist never recognized how he had helped make that decrepit institution sympathetic. The director was sixty-five by then. Knighthood was whispered about—but would that queen deliver it, or would Frears accept? Was he ready to retire as director emeritus, a renowned teacher at the National Film School and a generous help to younger filmmakers?

No retirement. That eye and ear for TV history seized on *A Very English Scandal,* about the convoluted Jeremy Thorpe case from the 1960s and 1970s. Thorpe's homosexuality had led to an affair with the humble Norman Scott who had then preyed upon the Liberal Party leader to a point where Thorpe thought of "removing" him. This was hard to credit but as touching as it was absurd and very understanding of emotional subterfuge and buried lives in Britain. Russell Davies wrote the script, Hugh Grant was the buoyantly bogus Thorpe, and Ben Whishaw won prizes as his feeble, victim lover. The film kept its wry distance, but it was something new and searching for Frears.

Scott was plaintive about the finished show. He felt he had been patronized and turned into a comic "character" whereas in life he had been as pained as any ex-lover whom people were trying to kill. Which brings me to pain, not the commonest topic in the work of Frears. He sometimes treats it as a bit of a lark, or something that happens to other people and gets exaggerated. Do intense, warped feelings embarrass him?

Well, I can hear him say, People don't go to the movies to be upset, do they? They don't want excessiveness or self-pity. They go to compensate for the pain or distress they feel in their own lives. This is an old Hollywood axiom, and a professional policy, full of good sense. But pain counts. Though muffled, it's there in *Sunset Across the Bay,* if in long shot. It's emphatic in the conclusion of *The Grifters.* Above all, it's there in *Walter,* which may take versatility too far or reveal the director's discomfort.

This was a film chosen to showcase the opening night of Channel 4 in 1982. As such, the nation staggered in disbelief that a new channel should be so severe. Walter is mentally impaired. He cannot handle normal life, especially when his parents die. He is placed inside a mental hospital, and he is abused there. He sees another patient murdered in the hellish place and there is not a glimmer of positive relief. It's nothing Howard Hawks would have touched.

David Cook did the script from his own book and Ian McKellen played Walter. I saw it on that opening night

(November 2) and I have not had the heart to go back to it. For while it deals with pain, it is crushing. It's not just that it lacks a happy ending; it does not get at a raw human vitality in Walter that could allow a glimpse of redemption. It could not have been better done. But it is so downcast one asks why was it done at all, instead of a Frederick Wiseman–like documentary about sadness in such an institution? There was a sequel in 1983, *Walter and June,* by Cook, Frears, and McKellen again, with Sarah Miles as a fellow patient he falls in love with. Can you guess how that ends?

I think Frears likes people and adores women, and they respond. Sometimes there is a jubilant eroticism in his work: like a nude Annette Bening striding forward in *The Grifters.* But those moments are not common, and Frears can be hesitant with sex. *Chéri,* with Michelle Pfeiffer, did not work— against all likelihood. *Dangerous Liaisons* is his film about sex, and it's sardonic and true to Christopher Hampton's shaping of the Laclos novel. But I think Alan Rickman, Lindsay Duncan, and Juliet Stevenson were more vibrant and vulnerable on stage than John Malkovich, Glenn Close, and Michelle Pfeiffer on film. It may be heresy, but I believe Miloš Forman's *Valmont,* made a year later and suffering commercially for it, is a more poignant film (with Bening as Mme. de Merteuil).

Which brings me to *Mary Reilly* and that conversation in Berlin. This is the Jekyll and Hyde story (from a novel by Valerie Martin) done through the eyes and nerve ends of an Irish maid in the doctor's house. Malkovich played the split personality, Julia Roberts was Mary, and there were vivid supporting performances from Glenn Close, Michael Gambon, and even Michael Sheen, who is another servant in the house.

The film was a disaster. Having cost $47 million (it was

Frears's most expensive film) it earned just $12.3 million world-
wide. It had many bad reviews. Roberts and Frears were both
nominated for Razzies, the mark of ignominy. Frears didn't like
the film. So you expect me to say I'm mistaken in liking it?

My feeling is stronger than "liking." For me, it's a movie
about a fearful spirit compelled to watch a kind of horror that
inspires dread and allure. It's a metaphor for any one of us
watching a frightening movie, or a compelling myth. Mary is
timid and hunched emotionally. She is a virgin who has been
beaten as a child. But she is filled with crippled desire and Roberts is daring, and lyrically afraid, in showing eroticism tugging
at her cramped face. So it's a story about a dutiful serving girl
led to confront her own forbidden nature.

Frears did not quite say why the film disappointed him, and
I felt that he had issues with the production as a whole. Or
did its revelations disturb him? It was an expensive film, with
American producers, even if it was shot in London with a British crew. Tim Burton had been the first choice as director and
he dropped out. TriStar, the funding, had talked of Daniel
Day-Lewis and Uma Thurman as the leads. There were stories
that Roberts and Malkovich had been at odds during the filming. And I suspect Frears is troubled by that kind of dissension.
Perhaps he gave up on the film emotionally before it was over
and foresaw its failure.

Commercially and professionally he was correct. But my
feeling may be borne out in time. There's something else of
interest. Despite Helen Mirren in *The Queen,* Judi Dench in
Philomena, and Meryl Streep as *Florence Foster Jenkins,* I'm not
sure Frears is at ease exploring female sexuality or ambition on
screen. Nor does he really trust characters who break out in

will, desire, or madness. He likes them to stay as reasonable as he is. He hardly does dream sequences or expressions of some inward state of being (except for that stag in *The Queen*).

Why protest? The range of his career and its appetite for work are so admirable. For me, *Sunset Across the Bay, My Beautiful Laundrette, Dangerous Liaisons, The Grifters, Mary Reilly,* and *A Very English Scandal* are outstanding. Has he made duds along the way? Of course, except that even the inexplicable *The Program* (about cyclist fraud Lance Armstrong) feels just a folly. Why do it? But then why does Frears pick his subjects? Or does he let them pick him? Is he English enough to be reluctant about going naked when other directors are exultantly born without clothes? Frears has the competence, the wit, and the inventiveness, plus the good nature and the amused impersonality one would hope to find in a head of production at the BBC, or even a prime minister.

Of course, he would duck either job, and say they were undoable. In the same way, he has never seemed persuaded that a movie—much less one of his—could change the world. But there are contemporaries who are bursting for that limelight. Like Scorsese and Tarantino, who have never given a hint that their films are about anything other than their own obsessiveness.

11

THE AMERICAN AUTEUR

In the ten years that followed *Bonnie and Clyde,* it was not just possible—it became necessary—to believe in American movie directors. They were heroes in the culture, storytellers and prophets. The medium and its chance of speaking for us all had raised movies to a rare opportunity and responsibility. America was in an age of war, assassinations, racial ferment, and sexual adventure. It was having a bad time, but a great time, on the same hectic screen.

You could feel the dream and dread, year by year. In New York, in 1976, *Taxi Driver*—by Martin Scorsese, Paul Schrader, and Robert De Niro—seemed like "it," the desperate, ecstatic expression of being on the edge. Not that we were all rogue cabbies with lost lives, shaved heads, ample guns, and an urge to be someone. We lacked Travis Bickle's extremism, but we were being driven, revealed, and directed by the film. We felt our secrets when we saw it. *Taxi Driver* was glory-bound, as well as an unhindered outpouring of destruction.

So many pictures managed to understand and extend the storm in our heads. You did not have to like every film. Their claims on our inner life could be exhausting, but you felt locked in love with the medium. Movie seemed central, and no longer the expression of a cynical business system manipulating us, the public. *Taxi Driver* was a wicked bicentennial tribute from a tripartite heart with Marty's love of fear and outrage, Schrader's scathing liturgical poetry, and De Niro's saintly Aspergian terror. For a few years De Niro directed films just by being in them and staring back at us—"Are you talking to me?" he asked. Yes, that improv line got it all: the impacted exchange between the screen and us.

But add a fourth heart, for here was the last score by Bernard Herrmann, throbbing with the steam that was bursting from beneath the streets. The film historian in Marty—and in us—knew that Herrmann had given wings to *Citizen Kane* and *Vertigo,* which soon would be numbers one and two in the Best Films Ever Made. There was a great tradition, for a moment.

The guys who made the films were younger than the veteran generation of the old Hollywood. They thought they might be artists, exemplars of ambition, paragons of wit and impulse on late night talk shows, mysterious and insolent, accompanied by limousine service, inventive lawyers, and astonishingly beautiful women who said hardly a word. The guys thought of being Michael Corleone *and* Warren Beatty. They were going to make the Great American Movie—until they realized they had done that already, almost before they had begun. They were going to take command of a new movie business, until they realized how their brief glory had brought that business back, like a Michael Myers who refused to stay dead in *Halloween* (1978).

There were ironies from the start if you cared to see them. They were like the Rolling Stones lamenting their failure to find "Satisfaction" (1965) when their songs made them resplendent, infamous, very rich, and wasted pioneers in just how satisfied a boy could be. Mick Jagger was as big an inspiration and model for actors as Marlon Brando, and Mick doing his snaky wild thing was a model of self-love married to self-pity. Just so long as no one asked him to act, to pretend to be someone else. Writhing across the stage in indignant mock orgasm was his jazz.

In the same sardonic spirit, it was a treat to observe what had happened with *Easy Rider* (1969), the archetypal young arrival in which Peter Fonda and Dennis Hopper had said, Look, anyone can do this, and been proved right to the extent that a whim and about $400,000 had turned into $60 million, and persuaded the "business" that these kids might be a new financial plan. Just so long as no one bothered to notice (or say) that *Easy Rider* was godawful crap and pretension. Hopper would prove to be a world-famous human mishap, a legend without credentials and a phenomenal actor or a roaring presence. Always aggrieved at not being James Dean, he would get to be Frank Booth in David Lynch's *Blue Velvet,* a hipster monster more alarming and eloquent than Michael Myers.

Anyone could do it—even a movie nerd who had grown up in the dark. Peter Bogdanovich was an American Godard (for a few years). Born in 1939, he had studied acting with Stella Adler (and he has always been a reliable supporting player). He loved old movies and saw so many of them that in his head he began to be in them. With his wife, Polly Platt, he gave up the East Coast, where he was curating classic movie seasons (he did Howard Hawks at the Museum of Modern Art in New York) and writing film books, to try his luck in Hollywood. Roger Corman let him throw together a remarkable debut film, *Targets* (1968), that was as wary of great movies as it doted on them. With that start, he delivered three beauties in a row that were exactly what a restless film critic might have made: *The Last Picture Show* (1971), *What's Up, Doc?* (1972), and *Paper Moon* (1973). The last of those was a tribute to John Ford and Jean Renoir; *Doc?* was a screwball comedy in thrall to Hawks and Preston Sturges; while *The Last Picture Show* was from a Larry McMurtry novel and nothing less than an account of young people trying to grow up after a cinema closed in desolate places in sad parts of Texas. (That last show was *Red River.*)

It seemed Bogdanovich could do no wrong and he should have heeded that as a story setup. But he was not quite living in the modern world. He was a shy young man, lacking confidence, but putting on airs of authority. He dropped Polly Platt for his young discovery, Cybill Shepherd, and he thought she could be Carole Lombard. He subbed for Johnny Carson on *The Tonight Show.* He came to be regarded as insufferable, which was as much the envy of onlookers as a fair commentary on Bogdanovich himself. He began a book-length interview with Orson Welles, a man and a model to whom he aspired with intense romantic allegiance. And by the late 1970s, he was over. He would do impersonations of famous movie people, until the world hardly knew who his subjects had been. He was a decent, kind, talented man (he could have been Lubitsch in the 1930s), and yet he was mocked as someone who had swallowed his own publicity. So he had three gems in three years. He had made it look as easy as Hawks had done. But Hawks went on for thirty years. Lifetimes were so much shorter now, and American success was coming to understand itself as a precarious place.

Robert Altman was older and from a different world. Born in Kansas City in 1925, he had flown bombing missions in the real war and then he had drifted into industrial filmmaking in the Midwest. He codirected a maudlin tribute to James Dean in 1957 and he worked in television, but he was thirty-five by the time he made *M.A.S.H.* (1970), with a lacerating humor and utter ease in having the Korean War serve as a metaphor for the chaos of Vietnam. Altman had arrived, and in the next five years he delivered himself as a mordant deconstructor of old Hollywood attitudes. *McCabe & Mrs. Miller* said the old West had been humbug, but he brought it back to life in the form of Warren Beatty's rambling, inept but oddly likeable failed businessman.

His version of *The Long Goodbye* (1972) was a charming form of film commentary (not far from Bogdanovich, but quirkier and more surreal) in which the legend of Philip Marlowe had been stolen away and given to a stoned, failed actor (that was Elliott Gould's casual charisma) so that this sweet-and-sour goodbye was farewell to Bogart's epic champion from Hawks and 1946. Altman's film is silky and alluring, picking up the light, like a dress dropped on the floor. But the public did not pick it up. And by the time he made *Nashville,* the satirist felt inflated by a weird bicentennial impulse and by the praise of Pauline Kael hissed in his ear. In the early 1970s, in love with wide-screen, restless camera movements, and multitrack sound (as if the show was real), Altman had done definitive work. He sank, though he would come back with films as good as *The Player* and *Short Cuts.* But there was that moment when a silliness like *The Long Goodbye* could feel as sharp as a few songs by Cole Porter or Harold Arlen from thirty years earlier. Songs mattered in the heyday of rock. Gould and Beatty had half sung their rambling monologues. And the repetition of different versions of the song "The Long Goodbye" was as important as the aching low-light deep focus from Vilmos Zsigmond, the cinematographer. Some complained they couldn't hear what was being said in those Altman films, and there was a similar unease over how or where to look.

It was said of another cameraman, Gordon Willis, that he lit color films so dark they were nearly invisible. Willis was a directing agent, in his way, a visionary who shaped his movies, and Willis would shoot *Klute* (a sinister, moody New York that made the word "noir" seem quaint and a throwback). Then he did both parts of *The Godfather, The Parallax View,* and *All the President's Men.* This was a new, dangerous way of seeing in which the photographic texture was music for the melancholy. Willis worked without Academy respect: he was a rebel, not ingratiating, and that brought a mordant intensity to his projects. He only got an honorary Oscar, years later, but Alan Pakula and Francis Coppola could not have been themselves without him.

Not that Coppola was ever other than himself, but even the dominant director of those early 1970s might be insecure or unsure how to proceed. It was inevitable in the vast success of the two *Godfather* films that Coppola would be hailed as a hero and an auteur, a Corleone. Sure, there was an affinity between the director and his emerging character, Michael, the good boy from Dartmouth who became the fount of authority and was left at the end, like a bleak president surveying lies and punishment—and *The Godfather* belongs to the Nixonian moment, without a resignation. But in his upbringing, Francis was closer to the weakling brother Fredo (John Cazale) than to Michael or Sonny (James Caan). He had been the outsider looking in, and so many directors fit that character type no matter the mastery they may like to act out in public. Directors have to give orders. Only Altman had had military experience. Film is so often a matter of innocence looking at glory, sexual triumph, and violent prowess. There's very little sex in *The Godfather*, but that leaves more room for the adoration of power, control, and directing the world. So Michael orders executions and Coppola carries them out. *The Godfather* celebrates a kid who gets to run a black mass. That influence lingers in Hollywood and in our politics. It is not accident that Donald Trump can sound like a gangster. He grew up on such movies. They make us an offer we can't refuse. *The Godfather* is the admission—and secret approval of—the pact of corrupt power that directs America. So you can't attain power now without being trained for screening.

With *The Conversation* splitting the two parts of *The Godfather*, Francis Coppola had had a richer three years than Bogdanovich. He became a cheerful exponent of his own power, especially in San Francisco, which was his city, and the gathering place of a rare band of filmmakers, American and international. He financed the restoration of Abel Gance's *Napoléon*. He was a screenwriter (he had won an Oscar for *Patton*, another tribute to command) but I'm not sure he ever had the need or the character to dig deeper into himself.

Apocalypse Now was too obviously a meeting of the Big Director and a Big Subject. It is riveting much of the time, but with Brando at the end it stumbled into a creative quagmire in which the director or the auteur could not quite grasp what he was doing. It was telling that in time Coppola reconstructed a new version of his film, *Apocalypse Now Redux* (it opened up forty minutes of closed rooms and new characters), a way of saying this film business is about great artists who cannot always make up their minds. After so many viewings of *The Godfather,* I do not feel clear about Francis's identity. It is still Mario Puzo's concept as carried out by Coppola. It was an assignment more than a compulsive original (*The Conversation* is closer to the man). It's as if he still longs to be a director more than the helpless visionary of human destinies—like Hitchcock or Buñuel.

Francis had a collapse during *Apocalypse Now.* The project was out of control, and he was distracted enough to say its ordeal was the equivalent of Vietnam. This is painfully and tenderly recounted in the book *Notes,* by his wife, Eleanor. A financial slump followed and then films that do not feel made by the same man. In history, it may appear that Coppola lost interest or passion in his films, but he became a modest don in food and drink. His house in Rutherford, in the Napa Valley, became a winery so the name Coppola was on every smart table. In the same way, *The Godfather* still plays in all our households, for its fascination with male power going austerely insane is too American for us to revoke it.

I realize a pattern is emerging, that of sudden personal expression and fulfillment, to be followed by years of relative failure or diminished energy. It is notably different from the persistence of Hitchcock, Hawks, or Buñuel, but I think it bears out the new public reputation of movie directors in the late 1960s and the lessons of the auteur theory. It is very hard to stay famous in our fickle America, or to concentrate on your work in the way a Picasso, a Matisse, or a Lucian Freud might just keep painting day after day, never mind the fame or the auction prices. Orson Welles inaugurated so much in film history, not least the principle that a kid makes his great movie *first*—the excitement of doing it is like getting laid for the first few times.

There are other notable firsts. In 1973, a thirty-year-old named Terrence Malick raised about $300,000 from a few richer friends, including Max Palevsky and producer Edward Pressman, and made *Badlands,* a sumptuous debut and an exquisite combination of the open-road Western and a wanton desperado itching for fame or the murder of insignificance. It had Martin Sheen and Sissy Spacek as babes in the wood, dancing in their car headlights, doing a few offhand killings and . . . getting attention. Just like *Bonnie and Clyde, Badlands* is a parable about the unknown American finding self-expression across the horizon of modern legend—of having his story told. That relentless urge to say, It's me and I matter, was a pressure in so much directing. Audiences went to movies to find a fantasy self—but so did directors.

Was Malick ever as good again? His next film, *Days of Heaven,* was ravishingly beautiful and deadpan lyrical in its flat narrative by the Linda Manz character (another immature but penetrating girl). But I felt the beauty was smothering story; the film was so studied and lacking the immediacy of *Badlands.* It felt like the early twentieth century. That was its declared subject period, but its self-respect was overwhelming. It also felt like spreads from the magazine *World of Interiors,* admiring and pricing the past.

Malick stopped directing. He had always resisted being a public figure, declining interviews or introductions to his own work. That was self-effacing, or unimpressed by show business. He was of Lebanese and Assyrian descent, the son of a geologist. He was a scholar, fascinated by natural sciences; he taught philosophy at M.I.T. and published a translation of Heidegger. That may infer a lofty creative attitude (not exactly Hawksian), and it can be hard for film directors to stay that detached or withdrawn. The financial pressures usually require a personal push—going on the road promoting their work. Ingmar Bergman liked to be remote, or out of reach, as did Stanley Kubrick. Still, Malick is as close as American film has come to the retreat or the nonpresence of a Salinger or a Pynchon.

Malick did mount a stage production, derived from Mizoguchi's great film *Sansho the Bailiff,* an anguished human story but seen from an emotional distance, as if observing wildlife. Then he came back after twenty years away, and made one more outstanding film, *The Thin Red Line,* maybe the first American war film in which the human beings seemed like noisy plants fading into the jungle of botany and time. There are also remarkable things in *The Tree of Life,* but I think by then Malick had become a source of disappointment and dismay to his first admirers. He was making "Terrence Malick" films now, awesome sometimes in their sense of nonhuman worlds but less attentive to story. The collision of the two young people in *Badlands* remains alive and arresting, but it feels like a forgotten direction for the director. He could say that is just my opinion. But are we at a point where a filmmaker can start to forget audience? That's not a casual question. We may yet have an era of films that concentrate on atmosphere and passing time. In an age of drastic climate change, are those the pressing verities?

In that mood, I put off seeing *A Hidden Life* (2019), a three-hour contemplation of a humble Austrian farmer who enabled his own execution, in 1943, because he would not swear loyalty to Hitler. I could tell from the trailer that it was beautiful, and I was wary of that in Malick by then. How stupid. *A Hidden Life* is an oratorio on farmland and urban prison, and on fragmented wide-angle close-ups that split time. And it does family life as if breathing in dung and blossom—no one feels young children better (a topic our directors tend to neglect). It is ravishing in its ominous simplicity and Malick's great work. It was also the fullest warning about this country's damned leader.

Isn't it enough to make a film as absorbing as *A Hidden Life,* especially when it is identifiable as his? Didn't Hawks make his essential film over and over again, and wasn't Hawks in a dream? But I always feel his thrill at the fun in doing it as if for the first time. Is film an explosion, or can it be a fire that burns as long as contemplation? Malick has always filmed fire as if it is the holy ghost.

I didn't mean to write this much about Malick. It surprises me how much he—and the implications of his rare career—stay in my head. Perhaps some of his pictures are hopelessly abstract, or nonconcrete now, yet I find myself drawn to that mood. So sometimes I'm stupid. I feel I prefer directors who don't quite own up to that blunt job. I think David Lynch, say, is more interesting than Ron Howard, Ridley Scott, or Steven Soderbergh, all remarkable for their versatility. A career that functions like exact machinery can seem the most empty and defeating, and that extends to our famous achievers, Steven

Spielberg and George Lucas, guys who seemed to shut down on the art they kept talking about.

They are easily the most successful figures of their time, and Spielberg has not lost his appetite for making films for himself, even if George Lucas gave up the drive or the need to be an author—as opposed to a producer presiding over an empire. There are few Spielberg films that I find boring or a waste of time, though I don't desire to see some of them again—*The Color Purple, Jurassic Park, E.T., Bridge of Spies, The Post,* and even the exemplary *Lincoln*—you see what a curmudgeon I am, or how unimpressed by uplift.

Not that Spielberg really tolerates indifference or failure: if you don't like *Jurassic Park* for 1993, here is *Schindler's List* (they are both chase films). Not just because of its subject matter, the latter is a commanding picture. It is so well acted. The re-creation of Cracow and Auschwitz is so haunting; Liam Neeson's Schindler is one of the most ambivalent characters in American, or Jewish film. There is even a perilous approach lurking there in which Schindler might be unlikeable and the whole fabrication of salvation could be seen as a trick for turning the Holocaust into a showbiz triumph. Which I think it is, as cunning and calculated as the little girl's red coat, a nudge of italic in that desolate black-and-white. But then you have to remember that Spielberg made *Jurassic Park* and *Schindler's List* at the same time. Is that startling conjunction really human?

Or does Spielberg need to be seen as a producer, or even a movie studio? That's not far-fetched: he has sustained the industry in so many ways, from *Jaws* to *Saving Private Ryan,* which are gripping processes, long after their suspense has relaxed. As if "gripping entertainment" was the acme level of the human imagination. It need not be, even if cinema made that claim for us. Spielberg has also done films that refuse to settle into the ruts of box-office rapture, but leave us wondering and uncertain how to feel: I think *Empire of the Sun* (his masterwork), *Catch Me If You Can,* and *The Terminal* are indelible films. I see them as often as I can, and I love them just because as productions, or as attempts to take the showbiz citadel, they are irrational, or blithely misguided. It is in being so rigorously sensible and accomplished that Spielberg can seem limited—and antique.

George Lucas had been a shy hanger-on at first in that romantic shift among young filmmakers who might save or renew the soul of the business by moving from Los Angeles to San Francisco or northern California. George was from the inland town of Modesto (born there in 1944), a humdrum place on the way to Yosemite. But he had been an outstanding film student at the University of Southern California (while Coppola was at U.C.L.A.). George had depicted a gloomy dystopian future in his first film, *THX 1138* (1971), a personal statement movie, pretentious and foreboding and ultra-European. Two years later he latched on to his real experience and did *American Graffiti*—let's say the best film he would ever make and the only one that tapped into his ordinary life.

Francis had had George as an acolyte and someone he encouraged. Coppola had been producer on *Graffiti* and a godfather to its life at Universal where it went from being disdained to earning $140 million on a budget of $777,000. And then George got it into his head to make this space adventure, with young actors and adolescent special effects. They called it *Star Wars* and George had the wit and the nerve (and even the offhand luck) to negotiate the merchandising rights from Twentieth Century Fox when that grand old studio had hardly thought what merchandising rights might mean.

George directed that first film himself, in a normal, industrial way—and industrial was the word that sank in. His special effects company (an engine that drove computer-generated imagery) would be called Industrial Light and Magic. As you think about it, that interaction of industry and magic (in the orgasm of light) is very American and very Hollywood. As it turned out, the northern Californian quest for salvation and creative wholesomeness ushered in a new force in the picture business that was founded in nature being supplanted by effects, mythmaking in technology, and a young roller-coaster audience who did not want to be seen growing up. Was there no future in that in America? That may be pompous snobbery. Whatever, the business came back, and soon enough it was revealed as a vehicle for advertising. The merchandise was always the force.

For years, Lucas did not direct another film, not until 1999, when he got back to the pre-story to *Star Wars,* episodes 1, 2, and 3 in the serial.

In 2012, Lucasfilm was sold to Disney for $4.1 billion. George had done so much and was as tired as any tycoon who stops short at the point of running a corporation, instead of the whole country. Lucas did not have that kind of personality or ambition. But he had made a world and reached an offer he could not refuse. If you loved *Star Wars* in 1977 and the next few episodes, and then the exuberance of *Raiders of the Lost Ark,* which George produced and Spielberg directed, then you might be wistful. But your media and your imagination and those of your children had been shaped and directed by George Lucas. So it was entirely appropriate that he had folded himself into the gentle yet very firm embrace of childishness, the Disney idea.

The characters in *Star Wars* and Indiana Jones faced so many dazzling adventures and perils, but those films were as safe as houses, or the bank. They did not want to get into that greater danger of the relationship we had had with a Travis Bickle.

To the extent that this book is a history of directing movies, with case studies, I have omitted so many people. Not least people from other countries who came to America on the notion that movies are American, and that you have to try your art or your business in Los Angeles to be sure who you are. That is no longer true. The semi-religious principle that movie was American, and that the United States was a continuous motion picture, has collapsed. But LA had become a lush, numb set, a mood to inhabit. That absurd kingdom lasted seventy years without much dismay, while the megalopolis acquired less and less faith in movies. New kids looked at the HOLLYWOOD sign and wondered what the label thought it meant.

But sometimes the visitors, the refugees, caught lightning in a bottle. In 1974, it took a Pole so often on the run to make an essential American film: *Chinatown,* by Roman Polanski, with a script by Robert Towne (the writer of that moment), and with cocksure Jack Nicholson fit to be undermined as the private eye wiped out by malign authority.

Is it hard to talk about Roman Polanski now? Is he somehow not quite proper? No doubt about it, and no question as to how many film directors, through sheer creative participation, began to be like characters in their films. So in *Chinatown*, it's Polanski who goes up to his great star and seems to slit his nose—It's me, Roman, I'm doing this! Don't you forget it, Jack!

Before *Chinatown*, he had done *Repulsion, Cul de Sac,* and *Rosemary's Baby.* How could anyone think this auteur was calm or comfortable when unease was his air? Did he behave badly or in a gamble? Always. Has the whole matter of his "case" become grotesque and beyond repair? Is anyone really fulfilled or satisfied that this crafty, disconcerting genius, this ruffler of feathers, can't come back to his America, the one he helped define? Don't fret too much—it's Chinatown. He has been on the run all his life.

There was never any question but that Jake Gittes in *Chinatown* was going to be Jack Nicholson, if only because he was friends with Towne and the film's producer, Robert Evans (his own work of art). Nicholson was even more an auteur, or a generating presence on the screen, than Robert De Niro. He was a surprising support in *Easy Rider,* and there is much more, including two films for Bob Rafelson—*Five Easy Pieces* and *The King of Marvin Gardens*—when Rafelson was unruly, impetuous, and sensitive if you waited. But in his great 1970s, Jack also did *Carnal Knowledge, The Last Detail, The Passenger* (for Antonioni), *One Flew Over the Cuckoo's Nest* (for Miloš Forman), *The Missouri Breaks* (with Brando and Arthur Penn), and then *The Shining.* For me, that is the majestic film from Stanley Kubrick, the one in which he finds a character, Jack Torrance, whom he can love as an antidote to his perpetual misanthropy. And up in the Overlook Hotel (in Colorado or Ultima Thule), as a manifestation of Kubrick settling away from America, in a country mansion outside St. Albans, *The Shining* is a model of the single-minded director who is worming his way into his own story and being caretaker in its haunted house. There is no better short description of what a director is, and no other film that so demonstrates the incoming tide of Jack.

There are other directors who were curiously waylaid or cut short. Michael Cimino (born in New York in 1939) made *Thunderbolt and Lightfoot* (a Clint Eastwood film, so get out of his way) as a warm-up. Then, all of a sudden, he was in charge of a film born in confusion, against all odds, by turns profuse and wandering and then lethal and exact. But *The Deer Hunter* won best picture and best director, no matter if the Vietnam politics offended or if it had let a Russian wedding scene in a Pennsylvania steel town triple in length because it was so full of good stuff. And if it had mishandled the Russian roulette scene (contrary to the facts of Vietnam), it had still had time and insight to see that Meryl Streep was going to be a great actress (or was it merely *the* Great Actress?).

He went on to do what would be *Heaven's Gate,* a project on which his arrogance and his visionary insistence overwhelmed budget, sense, and the ancient edifice of United Artists. This led to one of the best books about directing, *Final Cut* by Steven Bach, who had been a studio executive suffering under the aloof "genius" of Cimino. In theory and at the box office the film was a debacle. It brought down that studio. But life is more complicated—the full *Heaven's Gate* (219 minutes and $44 million, or four times the starting budget) is a masterpiece. Try to see it on a big wide screen as a movie—or is that paradise as remote now and unrecoverable as the Wyoming of the 1890s? Cimino was never as interesting or ambitious again. He went off to France; he made bad films; he wrote a novel; and he followed his instincts.

All through the rise and fall of Cimino, a totally beloved American director kept making tidy, financially responsible films, one every year, that generally delighted the public, from *Annie Hall* through *Radio Days* to *The Purple Rose of Cairo,* and beyond. Woody Allen was a treasure—everyone said it— and we hardly bothered to notice his preoccupation with guilt, duplicity, and regret. That intelligence is too late now. Woody has been made an outcast, a chronic director (at eighty-four) whose films cannot be released in his homeland. It's another kind of Chinatown, and we only have to live long enough to see how belated amnesia (in us and the U.S.) will one day resurrect him as an American master (with an asterisk).

Is there an American director now, more young than old, an uncompromising auteur, in whom I see great quality? I would answer Paul Thomas Anderson. I can't say I love all his films: for me something takes *The Master* off track, and *Inherent Vice* makes me realize that I don't inhale. But to think that some- one who was born in 1970, the year of *Five Easy Pieces,* who was six when *Taxi Driver* opened, has already made *Boogie Nights, Magnolia, There Will Be Blood,* and *Phantom Thread* is a source of wonder. Just to take the last of those four, it's worth saying that *Phantom Thread* is a tender, comic dismantling of a director figure by a young woman who was waiting table and just took his greedy order for breakfast—the study of directo- rial breakfasts is a topic I am defaulting on. That film is a love story in which the woman rebukes and chastises a great man, without disputing his worth. That sort of story is seldom told in our movies—and that makes a serious vulnerability in the cult of male directing.

There is a Scorsese film I love above all his later work because of a similar narrative insurrection. In *Casino,* the wife Ginger (Sharon Stone) betrays and trashes her De Niro just because he is a control freak and she is out of control. I think it's as good as *Taxi Driver* and a way into the terribly neglected *New York, New York.*

Of course, *Casino* is another gangster film (*Goodfellas* goes West) in which Joe Pesci unleashes his entrancing Rumpelstiltskin, and Las Vegas is treated as our poisoned Church. Still, I felt some irony over the essentially besotted, seventy-five-year-old Scorsese being allowed to make *The Irishman,* as if the unfeeling system had never let him make a gangster picture before. Netflix paid for it and made their tough bargain: the film would get three weeks in theatres before it found its home, streaming in our domestic cinemas. Yet could it be as interesting as its rivals in that arena, from *The Sopranos* and *Breaking Bad* to *Babylon Berlin* and *Ozark*?

In that contest Scorsese might have to stand up against unlikely rivals, like Michelle MacLaren (born in 1965) who had done eleven episodes of *Breaking Bad,* three of *The Walking Dead,* four of *Game of Thrones,* a *Westworld,* and the pilot for *The Deuce,* and done them with absolute efficiency and directness, anonymous but right for each show. That's how directing worked in the new world of long form on the small screen. It was as if she was the natural child (granddaughter it would be) of Michael Curtiz, who had won the directing Oscar for a thing called *Casablanca* in 1943 and directed it as if he was driving a dodgem car on a crowded rink, expertly and impersonally, and as if the whole venture was what one of its screenwriters would call "slick shit." From 1940 to 1945, all at Warners, Curtiz had directed ten pictures as habitually as eating fresh bagels for breakfast.

Plus Michelle MacLaren had another credential: she was a woman.

12

A FEMALE GAZE

In January 2020, when the Oscar nominations were announced, there was disquiet at Greta Gerwig not being nominated for directing *Little Women*. Maybe there were larger reasons for unease: Did the picture have to be called *"Little" Women*? Was Céline Sciamma a more deserving case for *Portrait of a Lady on Fire*—or Terrence Malick for *A Hidden Life*? After all, the field of neglected and denied talent observes no gender lines. Never assume that "talent will come through": that is another of the American pipe-dreams in which effort + character = success, or Success. Oscar has been dumb and misguided so often in its past: there were no nominations for *The Shop Around the Corner, His Girl Friday, Notorious, The Night of the Hunter, The Long Goodbye....* The worst thing about Oscar has always been its blind eye (the face has no features on the famous statuette).

In Britain in the 1950s, women didn't play soccer, they weren't prime minister, and they didn't direct movies. Yet they were a center of attention—whether they liked it or not. Even as a child when I saw someone like Yvonne De Carlo or Rhonda Fleming on display in a film, I knew that men were framing the odalisque. There was a scheme of ownership and consent in the air that was furtive but deranged. By 1963, there was this photograph of an apparently naked young woman sitting in an artful Scandinavian chair, gazing at the camera, insolent or numb, a sacrifice on the plate of public voyeurism: Look at that naughty girl—eat her up. Her name was Christine Keeler and she had done what men so much wanted that they had to scold her for it.

In 1958 there was a film with Jeanne Moreau on the night streets of Paris, luminous in the new Tri-X black-and-white. She was all alone, walking, waiting for her man. Nothing else was happening except for Miles Davis on the soundtrack: he had improvised as he watched the footage. I guessed a man had made this scene (it was Louis Malle's *Elevator to the Gallows*), but it dawned on me that Moreau's bitter sensibility might control or author a film, just by being in it while nothing else happened. Even if Louis and Miles had both slept with her.

Moreau had authority. But just because men are so disposed to watch, we can argue that the history of film has been that of men surveying and "directing" women. It's there in D. W. Griffith beholding Lillian Gish, Kenji Mizoguchi asking for regret in Kinuyo Tanaka, Preston Sturges painting Barbara Stanwyck with ironic aplomb in *The Lady Eve,* and Hitchcock and Hawks hiring so many women to be looked at, from Suzanne Pleshette to Dorothy Malone. It's there in the impassioned standoff between Godard and Anna Karina in *Pierrot le Fou.*

Can women only be in charge when they allow themselves to

be seen? Is Stanwyck actually directing or conjuring *The Lady Eve*? She really is the object of its camera, with two dame roles to make life richer. Did she ever think to direct herself, or did she honor the orthodoxy that that was not what women did? I realize Preston Sturges is a hallowed name in auteur schemes. Andrew Sarris put him in category 2, "The Far Side of Paradise," and loved "the frantic congestion of his comedies." That is well said, but face some facts: the great Sturges may have seemed blessed for a time; still, his glow lasted only a few years, at Paramount. When he got bigger and more revered, he fell apart. He lasted five or six years while Stanwyck prevailed for four decades, tolerating the routine films she found herself in and waiting for the caviar.

In the history of the Academy (the one with its male statuettes), a woman has been nominated for best director five times: Lina Wertmüller for *Seven Beauties* (1976); Jane Campion for *The Piano* (1993); Sofia Coppola for *Lost in Translation* (2003); Kathryn Bigelow for *The Hurt Locker* (2009); Greta Gerwig for *Lady Bird* (2017).

Can you hear the patronizing murmurs—Well done, ladies—in the smoking room of the male club? Is there even a snide joke that the one winner in the five, Kathryn Bigelow, took home an Oscar because she had made the sort of movie a guy would make? Like it or not, *The Hurt Locker* is obsessed with men in armor in the desert having to do frightening things. Its central character, Sergeant First Class William James (Jeremy Renner), is a flat-out toughie, a wild one, on the brink of self-destruction. War and danger are his drugs. The film is very well made, taut, desperate, and convincing, even if it is its own dead end. Its story restricts narrative depth because James is merely implacable, and the film never challenges that male response to being lost and in great danger. *The Hurt Locker* is not just *about* its predicament; it *is* that predicament, without resonance or metaphor, as if to say, This is what mad men must do. And in the male club that could prompt honest awe and stupid admiration—how can a girl know about such things?

How did Ingmar Bergman know so much about women for *Persona* that he was not questioned? Was it by watching them, by wanting them, by taking advantage of them—or in the high fancy of art? You don't have to have been or lived a film to make it. Flaubert could say he was Madame Bovary, but he was not; instead he was an imagination staring into the window of that character, and her possibility. The cinema has always been fixed on pretending: the overwhelming screen reality does not touch or hurt us—we are safe; that is our terrible liability and the imaginative pressure in the medium.

Steven Spielberg did not take part in D-day landings, and Kathryn Bigelow never served in Iraq. They can say they talked to soldiers and studied weaponry—they did their research— but the power of their films, and the illusion that we are beholding the real, fearsome thing, is because of their imagination, their cinematic talent, and their elemental need to tell all obstacles in the process of gathering together a movie, *"Fuck you, I am going to do this!"* The effort in doing that has to be fierce—and men have tended to say that ferocity is *their* thing.

That also entails the chutzpah, the bullying, the lying, and the lack of sleep to get the budget that will pay for the weapons, the uniforms, the explosions, and the sound of it all. That means getting other people's money (OPM); that fundamental resource is as important as CGI: *Saving Private Ryan* soaked up $70 million, while *The Hurt Locker* needed $15 million—well, I'm sure it needed more, but that's what it got.

I am talking about a determination, and a refusal to take prisoners, that is close to Sergeant First Class William James's extremis. That's a reason why so many films are about obsession—it's the ordeal in which they are made. And somehow we still think that obsession is a male condition.

Did Kathryn Bigelow "serve"? Yes, in art school and film school and in the relentless battleground of getting something made. Her campaign medals would include being married to James Cameron, who surely taught her plenty. She is not remotely a guy, but in the best sense she was imaginatively horny about being one.

She won a landmark victory such as her Sergeant James would comprehend in being the winner in that five. Not that there was any need for her to feel in competition—beyond the plain fact that American filmmaking is a battle, very well described by Samuel Fuller at the party in *Pierrot le Fou.* That tension dominates Hollywood, and it can be seen as the muscle tone ready for athletic contest, or early onset rigor mortis. In a previous film, *Blue Steel* (1989), Bigelow had cast the highly buffed Jamie Lee Curtis as a cop in an affair with the psychopath she was tracking. Curtis was an emblem of bravery after *Halloween,* and she dominated the screen like a honed athlete.

But Bigelow's Oscar was also part of the panic that has overtaken the Academy, and which it thoroughly deserves. It needs to include women. Alas, the Academy has become an institution, hardly able to remember that it was originally not just a male club but a maneuver to forestall unionization in the picture business, to divert unease over Hollywood scandals, and to celebrate self-congratulation. Women played no great part in setting up the Academy, but legend has it that when Cedric Gibbons sketched the figure of the statuette, Margaret Herrick, later the Academy librarian, said it looked like her uncle Oscar.

In 2009, when *The Hurt Locker* won best picture and best director, the Academy of Motion Picture Arts and Sciences had a membership of around five thousand and it was predominantly male, white, and becoming elderly. In the ten years since, the Academy has determined to become more open to women, to people of color, and to just about any minority interest that can muster a voice. The membership has doubled and women are now up to about a third of the total. That change is understandable, if sometimes hurried, but it has not begun to address the deep-seated ways in which movies were the enactment and the promotion of a male gaze. There are more films being made by women and getting seen. But the monuments to male righteousness, self-pity, and "wisdom" are still being made, though sometimes they seem stranded now—would its flawed, brutal but inescapable male camaraderie make *The Irishman* a film for 2019, or 1949?

The Academy faces many dilemmas: not just whether the time is ripe for some gender modification of Oscar—should he/it keep the sword and a shy manly profile, or is it time for Olive or Opal or Orianna to have a tactful indication of breasts and hips (things Hollywood used to do with enthusiasm)? Or do they go straight to a trans figure? More significant than that matter of design, how does the Academy sustain the faith of "professionals" voting for quality when it has always been plain that the clinching prizes of cinema are counted at the box office. Thus, in 2009, *The Hurt Locker* grossed only $49 million (much of that after its awards), while one of its rivals, *Avatar,* made by Cameron, brought in $2.79 billion at the box office. So it's an affectation for Hollywood to pretend it is making art when it knows that it is swayed by the numbers. You can bring in more women, more people of color; you can nominate more foreign language films; you can open the doors to left-handed people, to those on the spectrum (that range is growing); you could even nominate a category of losers or bad pictures—even if that has been flourishing since 1927.

The history of women making films is more complex than you might think. Alice Guy-Blache (she was born a Guy; Herbert Blache, another director, was her husband), began as a secretary, but she rose on talent, ambition, and good luck and she ended up producing, directing, and controlling hundreds of films. These are still very little known and it is sentimentality to believe there is an audience ready to retrieve such bodies of work. Well, yes, the club will admit, but this lady was French and things are different there—yet most of her work, in the first decade of the twentieth century, was done in New Jersey.

Only a little after Alice Guy's heyday, there was a Canadian girl, Gladys Smith, who had unrivaled authority in Hollywood. As Mary Pickford (1892–1979), she was not simply one of the most comprehensive star personalities but also a commanding business person—she was the fierce brain in the United Artists experiment, and she was a founder of the Academy. She produced most of her movies, which was not just a polite credit but affirmation of her power and her vision. She was not credited as a director, but that was in a working system that did not bother to remark on direction as a rival to Mary's identity.

But if you only believe in credits, then there was Lois Weber (1879–1939), actress, producer, and director of 141 films. Her career was managed with no more opposition than any man would have faced, and is breathtaking as a possibility that might exist now. Directors don't work as much as they did then: in the decade since her awards, Kathryn Bigelow has made two films—*Zero Dark Thirty* and *Detroit*. Hawks did five in five years—he was a Woody Allen. Work was as steady as the audience.

Women were behind the scenes. I doubt we would know Rudolph Valentino but for the decision by screenwriter June Mathis (1887–1927) to notice him, then discover him for *Four Horsemen of the Apocalypse,* and to guide his rather empty-headed beauty toward an astonishing stardom cut short by early death. Mathis never directed anything, but she was recognized for her power and insight. You can argue that she was known for perfecting a rather foolish fantasy for women (but a pioneering escape for gay men, too), while Mary Pickford was utterly calculating in presenting a childlike sweetheart archetype that made all sexes and ages comfortable.

Pickford is not fashionable now in feminist remapping of cinema. In his immense—over fourteen hours—and earnest documentary *Women Make Film: A New Road Movie Through Cinema* (2019), Mark Cousins does not say much about Mary, but he is attentive to the claims of Dorothy Arzner and Ida Lupino. They are the only women who directed American films in the first decades of sound. I stress that because if the chances for women diminished in that time it may have been because sound gave movie fuller life as an imitation of reality, a fantasy illusion in which sex or intimacy was more pressing than it had been in silence. There was an aura of male privilege in the look and the hush of films (human silence only became precious after the invention of sound).

It's a measure of that empire that women never got to photograph films. To this day, four percent of American cinematographers are women in a country that has known Dorothea Lange, Lee Miller, Helen Levitt, Diane Arbus, and Sally Mann among so many others. In 2018, Rachel Morrison was the first female camera person nominated for an Oscar, for *Mudbound.* It is as if looking had a magic that women were not fit to share. If that sounds ridiculous, you are learning more about the occult nature of Hollywood, and the imprisonment involved in its putting women on display for us.

Arzner made some entertaining films but she was never in the top rank of directors, and it's hard to say whether that was because of her or because obstacles were steadily put in her way. David Selznick knew he was making a woman's picture in *Gone With the Wind,* as well as a portrait of Scarlett O'Hara. He said he believed in women and loved them (as he chased them). He had trouble with his male directors on his big picture and went through a handful, assured in the belief that the movie—if it got done—would be about Margaret Mitchell's vision and Vivien Leigh. But he did not think to ask a woman director to come to his aid. *There are none,* he would have cried.

There was one woman available, and she was in Los Angeles in December 1938 as shooting on *Wind* began. She was shown around town as a celebrity by Louis B. Mayer and Walt Disney and her films were highly praised. You may flinch from this, but I believe she had already made the most striking film then directed by a woman. Moreover, it had the élan of male prowess that was so treasured in Hollywood pictures. You can hear it in the title, which could have been an epic American adventure— *Triumph of the Will* (is that the subtitle for *Rambo, Part VIII?*). The director's name was Leni Riefenstahl, one of the great dynamic sequence-makers in the history of film, an eye avid for glory, and a woman who had handled the apparatus of Nazi control and interference to make the film the way she wanted.

You know not to like *Triumph of the Will,* though perhaps you have not seen it. So, in its malign obscurity it becomes hateful. It is natural to be intimidated by any achievement overshadowed by the word "Nazi." But there are autobahns and automobiles, public buildings and even movies—like *M* and *The Testament of Dr. Mabuse,* on the cusp of disaster—which you may still admire, and which smack of the authoritarian control that turned so ugly. I don't think Riefenstahl was a war criminal; nor do I believe she slept with Hitler or Goebbels— these are shards of gossip that cling to her. She preferred studs.

Yet I suspect she was not pleasant to know in her single-mindedness about film and other things. I think emotionally she was a fascist, yet I sometimes feel the same lust for command and unkind order in Bergman, in Kubrick, in Scorsese, even in Chaplin. To talk about Riefenstahl is to describe attributes that would fit many American directors who strove to enact "directed by" for the public and themselves when not being in control seemed such a source of fear. "Directed by" tells us to trust bold auteurs in our lonesome dark.

An engine of accomplishment or executed plan exists as potential in all cinema, and the rousing affirmative of *Triumph of the Will* is not so far from the martial positivism of *Sergeant York, Casablanca,* and *Sands of Iwo Jima.* It's there in the way John Ford looks at the cavalry. Something similar (yet more implacable) exists in our modern epics in which computer-generated imagery has taken over from actuality so that our heroic titans, digital superoids, can defeat every phantom enemy time can fabricate. Isn't there fascism in the kill counts of the ancestors of such films, the video games?

Suppose fascistic instincts lie close to the motor of movies.

Leni Riefenstahl was born in Berlin in 1902. She had wanted to be a dancer and by the age of twenty she was a handsome Aryan, exultant about the human body. But an injury ruled out a dancing career, so she thought she should act. In the 1920s, she cultivated the role of a mountain girl, not Heidi but a spirit of altitude and extremism, sometimes close to naked in the light, and an object of infatuation for Arnold Fanck (born 1889), who directed her in *The Holy Mountain* and *The White Hell of Pitz Palu.* By 1932, Leni produced, directed, and starred in *The Blue Light,* about a mountain woman regarded as a witch by villagers because she can climb higher than men. It is an ecstatic, daft parable, and an unalloyed glorification of the feminine. It launched a career that led her into a one-hour documentary about a Nazi rally, *Der Sieg des Glaubens* (The Victory of Faith). It is not very good, but Hitler and Goebbels liked it enough to urge Leni into something more ambitious. After all, it was no great stretch to make Leni at thirty seem like an outlaw angel. But could she turn Adolf into a Führer?

It happened. We are high in the sky in an aircraft. We see or feel the flutter of its propellers and hear the stirring of grandiose music. We are amid white clouds like churches and harbingers of history. We are getting the works from a childlike visionary, looking down on life. As music swells, the mist of clouds disperses and we can see the dark, Gothic shapes of a medieval city: it is Nuremberg, where the great rally will occur. We see the shadow of the aircraft moving across the city: today, you feel that must be CGI, but in 1934 they had to get the real thing! There are phalanxes of uniformed troops marching in the streets. We have not seen the Führer yet; it is as if he is the monster or the divine one. Why not both?

You have to see this for yourself, and trust that you are mature enough not to be swayed by it while understanding that the pulse in the film is getting to you. For all you know of history, eighty-five years later, this encouragement worked.

The plane lands, to roars of approval and bliss. We see Hitler, that sheepish mess of a man, and Goebbels more sinister in a belted white raincoat. Then there is a motorcade from the airport to the heart of the old city. Somehow—isn't this magic as befits an inspiring figure?—we are behind Hitler, standing in his car, but in the right place for us to see the rather limp upright of his hand saluting salutes and to see how sunlight fills his palm like gold or milk. But then we have a fuller view of the motorcade and there is no camera behind Adolf. How did they do this? Was the moment rerun for a different camera position? Is this actuality or legend?

Then the car halts: a mother with a child has come forward to greet the Führer—just a stray moment? spontaneous?—but after he has blessed them, she steps back away from the car, and into the sunlight of myth. This seems like newsreel, but it has the directed intent of a fiction film. And Leni Riefenstahl did it. There are so many movies in which a male director makes love to a beautiful woman, but here, in 1935, is a picture where a female gaze says she wants that man—that one, the jerk with an inept moustache—and the film tells us she must be obeyed.

Of course, there were things in history after 1935, horrors we can't get out of our heads. And it's not that those things weren't fed by *Triumph of the Will,* like blood nourishing an organism.

It's not that Leni wasn't fascistic. But she had thrown out any hint of being ladylike or genteel. She was as fierce as Sergeant James in *The Hurt Locker*. This is not just the screen dynamic of *Triumph*, it's the way she cajoled and dictated to the Nazi Party how to do a rally fit for her film. It was one thing to handle a Mayer, a Thalberg, Jack Warner, or Harry Cohn, but Riefenstahl faced down the stupidity and the male supremacy of authentic thugs. She had made a film like a man; it thrusts forward in its tracking shots, and it films the linked arms and the leather belts of a line of storm troopers as if they were Astaire going across a smooth floor. (*Top Hat* was 1935, too, and surely no one but Fred directed that film.)

I hope that comparison is upsetting, because for just a few years, with *Olympia* following the Nuremberg picture, Riefenstahl swept the house clean of so much attitudinizing and ushered in a strange new superwoman with a willfulness that could handle Goebbels and might have trashed Harvey Weinstein. The central *Will* was hers. Remember, I have warned you, to be a film director is to discard some degrees of common humility and decency. That discipline assists anyone going for the job. And it leads me to a disconcerting aspect of this chapter and of the medium, too.

I had a list running in my head of the female directors who deserved consideration. Naturally, Ida Lupino has to be there for her run of pictures in the 1950s that manage to be feminist while serving themselves up with B-movie panache: *Outrage, The Hitch-Hiker, The Bigamist*. But is Lupino more a historic breakthrough than a profound talent—like Jolson in *The Jazz Singer*? Am I being sentimental in thinking that the Ida who was so unexpectedly piercing as an actress in, say, *They Drive by Night* and *The Hard Way,* had more depth than she was allowed to show in "her" films?

But I can imagine male directors who might have been more revelatory if they had been granted time, a better cast, more budget, and less pressure. Is it possible that Nicholas Ray could have made Willa Cather's *The Professor's House* (a dream I am inventing) if Hollywood of the 1950s had understood that he was *Nicholas Ray*? Or was he most himself as a Prometheus forever torn apart by unfair pressures?

My fond list would include Lisa Cholodenko, Clio Barnard, Barbara Loden, Larissa Shepitko, Claire Denis, Patty Jenkins, Sarah Polley, Jennifer Kent, Andrea Arnold, Chloé Zhao, Ava DuVernay, Debra Granik . . . and Ana Lily Amirpour.

That last name may be the least known. Amirpour was born in Margate, England, in 1976, though she is of Iranian and American descent. She was educated at San Francisco State University and U.C.L.A. and she became one of the many people trying to make personal films that could still find a public. She raised about $50,000 to do *A Girl Walks Home Alone at Night* (2014), a black-and-white vampire dream shot in a desert town near Bakersfield, California, and a feminist landmark, cruel, comic, and lovely, with a serene performance from Sheila Vand. It cries out with inspiration and daring, but Amirpour has had great difficulty in following up after a film that hardly recovered its costs. She may have had no triumph greater than raising that $50,000.

That story makes it more impressive that Jane Campion has sustained a career as one of the best directors in the world. She is female; she has married; she has had children—one died at twelve days. I hate the predicament of saying things like, "The best woman director we have," or "The greatest black filmmaker in the world," or the most intelligent Jew, the finest Aquarius, or the most lucid left-hander. (Of course, left-handedness is plainly facetious, or so you might think, until you appreciate how steadily Hitchcock favored left-handed players—Kim Novak, Eva Marie Saint, Cary Grant, Anthony Perkins—as if that slight departure from visible routine permitted an extra glimpse of pain or neurosis.)

I have no idea whether Jane Campion is left-handed, or whether she can pretend to be if she senses an opportunity. She was born in New Zealand in 1954. Though her family was active in theatre, she read anthropology at university and then went to the Chelsea Art School in London. That preceded studying at the Australian Film, Television and Radio School in 1981. Soon after that she started making short films that won attention at film festivals. But her feature debut, *Sweetie,* waited until 1989. It was in 1993 that *The Piano* won the Palme d'Or at Cannes. Why not? It is one of the most intricate studies of emotional liberty and societal restrictions ever made. It has an awesome level of real, wild life in New Zealand before "modern civilization," but it is also worthy of Buñuel in its unforced depiction of pathological states. It also won performances from Holly Hunter, Harvey Keitel, Sam Neill, and Anna Paquin that seemed as good as the acting in Bergman. *The Piano* was nominated for best picture, but that safe prize went to *Driving Miss Daisy.* I don't attribute that to prejudice against women so much as a general fear of dangerous windows into our inwardness.

I felt nothing but excitement when I heard that Campion would next make a film of Henry James's *The Portrait of a Lady,* with Nicole Kidman as Isabel Archer. For me, the film that emerged is a thoughtful travesty, wrong-headed and pretentious, yet clearly the work of a major director who may have been led astray by thoughts that she should be a woman if not a lady. But our respect for great auteurs should trust them to produce poor films every now and then. So I'll try to make amends by proposing that Campion's most mistreated picture, *In the Cut,* may be her best. Taken from a novel by Susanna Moore, and developed and produced by Kidman, this is nothing less than a film about a woman who feels she has as much right to sex as a man—without being a porn star, or a Russian empress.

Instead, Meg Ryan plays Franny, a high-school literature teacher, on her own in New York City, but eyeing men who look at her. She takes note of new words she comes across— like "disarticulation," which is what has happened to a female corpse found in her garden. She hears this from an investigating detective, Giovanni Malloy (Mark Ruffalo). They have good sex without trusting each other—is that why it is good? *In the Cut* (2003) is claustrophobic with its sensual close-ups, and we realize Franny is as reckless and out on a limb as her subway poets. There is a feeling of New York heat that is not just weather. The film is casually candid sexually, and Giovanni is as naked and as abandoned or fulfilled—which is it in movies?—as Franny. An aura of menace hangs over the film, like the smell of sex, and we wonder at how women are less hidden over pleasure than men who are still insistent on their control. That is what drives murder in so many films.

Something about *In the Cut* was deemed shocking or unwholesome, and I wonder if male expectations felt suddenly vulnerable or exposed. Meg Ryan gave herself to the picture with such courage, and it ended her romcom career. Still, it is one of the best films about sexuality from a time when that subject matter was not hedged around by the defense works of correctness or disapproval.

It may be that reactions to *In the Cut* fueled the extraordinary *Top of the Lake,* made as a 2013 TV series (codirected with Garth Davies), set in desolate parts of New Zealand's South Island. It is another murder story, about the disappearance of children. And murder, let it be said, is an action in life that is much more common in men than in women—but far, far less prevalent in ordinary life than our movies would suggest. Elisabeth Moss played a police detective (the part seemed to give her career more daring) and Peter Mullan is a crooked father figure on the horizon. It may be Campion's most personal work (better than the sequel, in 2017), as beautiful as it is frightening.

It's not just that it seemed to benefit from a woman's point of view, but also that we were closer to a human understanding and disillusion where distinctions between genders were artificial. Moreover, *Top of the Lake* was part of the trend in which the best and most demanding entertainments were appearing not in movie theatres but on what we once called television screens. The image was smaller, but it did not seem constrained. It could be a way into smothered inwardness that had been promising since we saw Lillian Gish in *The Wind* (1928). Gish was the driving force on that extreme subject—it was meant to be about a woman going mad after she had accidentally killed a sexual aggressor. She persuaded Thalberg to do it; she hired Victor Sjöström as the director. But then, in the crisis, MGM wanted a happy ending instead of madness, and Gish had to abide by the trite resolution. The picture business titillated us with sexual suggestion, but it was terrified by the real thing. Bit by bit, screen fantasy enshrouds our awkward truths.

There is another recent film, Kitty Green's *The Assistant* (2019), in which a young woman (played by Julia Garner) starts to work at an unnamed film company in New York. She is working for He Who Must Be Obeyed, a monster who makes films in the old male way that includes the indifferent, impersonal exploitation of women trying to get on in the business, and the show. And we know—I think we have always known—that that has happened as a matter of course. I do not know the biographical details, but I would not be surprised if an Ida Lupino had had to barter herself along the way, first to be an actress in pictures, and then to get the chance to direct. As far as I know, she never complained, because complaint was not in the Hollywood climate then, or in the general way of life where females were raised in pretty obedience. It was taken for granted that the picture business, and its art, was the manifestation of male opportunism. That was not just screwing actresses on the couch; it was shaping stories in how to digest romance; it was the principle that women should be "beautiful" and shut up.

Women went to the movies (a little more than men). Women were certainly *in* the movies, on our screens, in a kind of hushed, voyeuristic mood of autopsy. But the enterprise was a male venture (or adventure) in which everything was directed by male ambition and men's sense of how the world worked. Sometimes you could think that cinema only existed because of the male gaze that longed to see, to a point of deciding that is how the world should be. . . . Try imagining Genesis written by Eve. Do it as if she is Marilyn Monroe, or Elaine May (because God came to Elaine and said he thought he needed a rewrite with some humor).

Think of *The Godfather* as Kay's stream of consciousness—she is Michael's wife, played by Diane Keaton. In its first two parts this is a landmark film, made with meticulous craft and refinement so that its slaughter and its unchallenged male gloom reign. It is a film for and about guys. In truth, this culture is hideous (and one we loathe in public): it is the establishment of gangsterese as a vital American tradition, a "bad thing" maybe, but one that guys aspire to. Any mature creative approach to its ritual might decide that its thrall and its empire need to be challenged. In some speculative remake of the film—it is a power in movies that this urge is a natural response—I have proposed a narrative turn in which Kay opposes Michael. She becomes a witness against him. She believes the Corleone thing must end (rather as she might oppose slavery). It may be in that process that she could be destroyed, or made an outcast. That is what the story needs, for all our sakes. God knows, the "story" of *The Godfather* is so immaculate its horror becomes like a religious passion. But we have a right to talk about the content of our movies, and to decline to be taken in and fobbed off by how well the bad stuff has been done.

So female directors are becoming more powerful in the modest way of getting a chance. But that has not yet altered the power of the weather system. At the Telluride Film Festival, in 2019, when it premiered, *The Assistant* faced some resistance from movie people, good friends. Yes, they said, the film was well done, but they wanted more, including the revelation of monstrousness in this company being spelled out *and van-*

quished. Perhaps they foresaw a Weinstein figure emerging from the shadowy, withdrawn way he was framed out of sight. They wanted this woman to pull the rotten castle down? These were guys, and movie men are raised to get wins.

In a way, that's the punitive energy that I am proposing for Kay in a new version of *The Godfather.* I want her to be like the sheriff in *High Noon,* like juror No. 8 (Henry Fonda) in *12 Angry Men,* or like Chaplin at the close of his films. Not defeated. Not beaten down.

But I'm not sure that that persistence and willed glory in women is really consistent with the atmosphere of the movies. In the age of *Cleopatra* and *The Great Escape,* in *The Fire Next Time* (1963), James Baldwin observed the valiant attempt by blacks to gain access to white society. But consider, Baldwin asked: why should black people betray themselves by seeking admission into a white culture that had behaved so badly and for so long? That hesitation applies to what I'll call cinema. Should women directors make male films—like *Triumph of the Will* and *The Hurt Locker*—or can they insist that we are better than this dark, narrow enterprise movie has lived in?

In 2019–20 the country was being led and misled by a monument of infantile male supremacy. It wasn't just that Trump was a bad man, he was the epitome of so many false and damaging constructs in how we live. It is not just that he needed to be replaced by a good guy. That win/lose test is trivial compared with the startling ways in which Trump expressed and identified so many rotten American desires—and its mania for desire fulfilled leading to "greatness." Instead, we need a weather in which guys can be forlorn, quiet failures and unable to seize a narrative and direct it. But is that un-American?

As I came close to finishing this book, I was talking with my editor about a title and a subtitle. We both liked *Directed By.* It made clear the area of concentration. It promised the study of some exceptional directors seen in the line of history. It was open to many different levels in which films were made and shaped and sold. But the subtitle gave us trouble: "Who Runs the Movies" was one idea, but we flinched at its assumption of power or authority, for we knew that the reality of film production had to accommodate not just degrees of collaboration that were often hard to track but also an inherent directional thrust in the medium itself: Sit in the Dark and see the Light—it is a model of authoritarianism. So many cultural assumptions flow from that instruction. And it has damaged all of us. For we are talking about how we have learned to think and feel. And cinema has started with two far-reaching lies: that we are in the dark, and that the light will save us.

These are mythic principles that Leni Riefenstahl would have endorsed.

It may yet prove the vitality of the female gaze is to teach us there are better things to look at than a movie screen. It was a secret motive in *Triumph of the Will* to urge Germans: don't waste time on the awkward realities of a nation, look at glory instead. The female gaze needs to see through so much bogusness.

13

___

ALONE: THE NATURE OF A MINORITY

I showed the previous chapter to a friend, and she suggested that I had overlooked Sofia Coppola, Joanna Hogg, Kelly Reichardt, "possibly even Sally Potter might get at least a name check. . . ." The list could extend, but I have this problem: I don't like all these directors' films. In the same way, I am not a fan of Michael Bay, Tony Richardson, Lars von Trier, Clint Eastwood. . . . I'm going to admit it: I would rather read Geoff Dyer's book *Zona* than watch its subject, Andrei Tarkovsky's *Stalker.* I know, this is disgraceful, but it's important to keep a pantheon of directors you *don't* like. Yet I sometimes wonder if correctness could one day request that all directors are worthy, because what they do is difficult. I dread that claim.

So many points come out of that comment, not least the pathos of being "minor" in a profession bursting with a lust for attention and significance. Movies are announced in advance. They bristle with purpose before a foot of film has been shot. Grids or gospels appear—the screenplay, the contracts, the schedule, the budget—that may crush creative spontaneity and set up anxiety in the minds of the filmmakers. It is so hard to have the feeling of possibility that can hover over a blank page, a keyboard as a song germinates, or a first pencil arc on drawing paper. The directors may be so determined to be in charge of the enterprise, so fierce and *obsessed,* that they cannot allow themselves to let it live and grow in their minds.

It has never been the plan in this book to name-check every possible director. Even if such a project had been undertaken, there would be omissions. Any biographical dictionary is blind, forgetful, or unaware. I know that I have not found room or proper space for directors and pictures that I adore: just quickly, I think of Michael Powell (*The Red Shoes*), Jerzy Skolimowski (*Deep End*), or even Ernst Lubitsch, a famous master and director of *The Shop Around the Corner,* which may be the film I love most today. So I tell myself I have been strict with the history while hoping that that policy might seem legitimate.

Still, in the last chapter, I did pause over the name Barbara Loden, just because her story is so instructive, and poignant. Loden began as an actor, and she has small, vivid moments in two films by Elia Kazan, *Splendor in the Grass* and *Wild River.* Kazan was the most esteemed American director of the era that began with his *Streetcar Named Desire* on stage (1947). He had graduated to film and he had made *On the Waterfront, East of Eden,* and *Baby Doll.* He is a barefaced omission from this book, and now I am adding a little insult to injury by including him because he had an affair with Loden and married her.

He was moved by her and her difficulty, when I think he favored pliant women, like the sweet Abra (Julie Harris) in

East of Eden, who would allow herself to be shifted from loving Aron (Dick Davalos) to understanding Cal (James Dean). Kazan was a womanizer all his life, but that doesn't mean he didn't sometimes have rare insight into women. I think he knew Loden was never going to be a star actress, just because she resisted the need to be obedient to male designs. Sweetness never softened the resistance in her face.

I suspect that that look had been intensified by watching Elia, "Gadge," a habitual manipulator. Distrust is character-forming. Still, Kazan cared for her enough to give her about $100,000 so that she could make *Wanda* (1970), in which she plays an exhausted, wiped-out woman existing on the edge of dereliction, not just homeless but without any place or hope. She inhabits the most crucial minority state we know, that of isolation. *Wanda* is an essential film, a great film if that is the terminology you rely on, but it has taken forty years or so to gain proper appreciation. It is a film that has no faith in story saving us, in the redemption of character, or the mercy of "entertainment." It adheres helplessly to a persistent state of alienation, aloneness, and the absence of meaning, and Kazan—a radical in some ways—knew enough about the business to judge that it was a film without an immediate future. It is about feeling, not feeling good. Yet today, *Wanda* may be more closely examined than many Kazan films. Indeed, it makes the arranged moral lesson of *On the Waterfront* look archaic and foolish.

But it is a movie about a woman who did not deserve to be in a picture by the standards of 1970. In her way, Barbara Loden was saying, Look, this is the end of old cinema. She never made another film—she was dead at forty-eight, decades before Kazan died, which was a few years after his honorary Oscar for

Lifetime Achievement (a lofty label that usually carries capital letters).

Barbara Loden was trying to be a female director of American films when there was so little space for her gender in a director's chair in Hollywood, and when the spirit of "independent" filmmaking was in its infancy, though Shirley Clarke was at work with *The Connection* (1961) and *Portrait of Jason* (1967), the latter a haunting portrait of two other minority conditions, being black and being gay.

But in mentioning Clarke, I am reminded that I have omitted John Cassavetes (truly a larger force in the attempt after 1960 to make a kind of movie that inhabited the rampant untidiness of American life, its raging at failure), and even Alan Clarke (1935–90), a figure in British television who seems to me one of the outstanding British artists of his time—*Scum, Made in Britain, The Firm, Elephant,* and *Road*. Alan Clarke is not much known today, though Stephen Frears is still in awe of his example. Clarke was part of a lively group of friends and collaborators, yet I'm sure he felt alone. And that is the fundamental minority condition in filmmaking, no matter the money and the lifetime achievement awards the job may have gathered.

There is another loneliness that comes into play: for instance, I have discovered over the years that I like *Wanda, Deep End, Elephant,* John Boorman's *Point Blank,* and Pedro Almodóvar's *Pain and Glory* rather more than many other people who also have respect for those films. In a romantic way, I feel those films go to "the heart of the matter," and that inspires me to write about them. Similarly, vanity and its search for eloquence always motivated me with *Citizen Kane, The Big Sleep,* and *Celine and Julie Go Boating.* Criticism, let alone good writing about a film, comes out of a desire to express (and end) one's solitude.

As a matter of history, I believe that this status affects all film, all art. A part of me resents the need to develop and exist in such categories as feminine cinema or black cinema. Perhaps that is window dressing for my being a white male and for the profound but unwitting lessons I absorbed in childhood that film was the manifestation of a kind of white, male authority. Those codes are being taken apart now, and the urge to make reparations is not just a matter of film history; it concerns our total culture and the instinct that white males have had their shot at running the world, without really pulling it off to humanity's benefit or satisfaction.

There is another minority pressure too easily missed in film history. American film was, and in many respects still is, Jewish. It's not just that the foundational figures in Hollywood were invariably Jewish: William Fox, the Laemmle family, the Schencks, the Mayers and Thalberg, Sam Goldwyn, the Warner brothers, Harry Cohn. Nor is it a matter of so many directors being Jewish—Woody Allen (a treasure once and now excluded without legal process), Stroheim, Sternberg, Curtiz, Lubitsch, Wilder, Wyler, Mankiewicz, Cukor, Ophüls, Kubrick, Jerry Lewis, Spielberg, and even Chaplin, who nursed the romance that in his uncertain parentage he might have been Jewish. It is also the way in which the movies were the persistent celebration of many traits of Jewish storytelling, just as show business was led and peopled by Jewish business operators, their nerve, their energy, their ambition, and their chutzpah. The crazed enthusiasm of film promotion is one of the great Jewish songs about immigrant triumph.

For all the cheerful celebration of Hollywood, we have still done so little to trace and understand this immense display of Jewish idealism (and how it shaped American morality). We should also note how far it helped color anti-Semitism, both in America and the rest of the world. In our sense of film history, there is no film more deserving of rueful attention or autopsy than *The Jazz Singer* (1927). This is not only famously the start of talking pictures, with Al Jolson's character talking to his mother and singing in time with his moving lips. It is also a monstrosity in which Jewish sentimentality tries to ride on grotesque abuse of blackness and the iconography of enslaved black America. Time and again, film history needs to set aside its masterpieces and concentrate on its great moral disasters.

That brings me to the last neighborhood of this book. It was impossible or effectively illegitimate for a black person to direct *The Jazz Singer*. There were no leading black players in our movies because the very sight of blackness was deemed an outrage to decency. We may treasure modest steps forward. Hattie McDaniel was the first black player to win an Oscar, for Mammy in *Gone With the Wind*. Yet David Selznick, the producer of that epic and more its creator or director than anyone else credited for that job, acceded to pressures from Georgia so that Hattie was not invited to the Atlanta premiere of the film—a grand event that included just about anyone Selznick could think of.

At the Oscars night where *Gone With the Wind* swept the board, Hattie and a companion were at the banquet so she could step forward to receive her Oscar and talk about being "a credit to my race." But she was required to sit at a small table in a corner of the room, instead of being at the large Selznick table that included Selznick and his wife, Vivien Leigh and Laurence Olivier, Jock Whitney and Olivia de Havilland, Gable and Lombard. The best table in the room in a community and a culture that prizes the best table as a semi-religious shrine.

That was hideous in 1940, and it is either absurd or soul-destroying now when one realizes how far the best-table culture lingers. The improvement in the state of racism in America since 1940, and the healing of the wounds of loneliness, is so minor as to shame us.

I hate the culture in which there should be chapters for female directors and for black directors. It seems anathema to the Constitution (or its evolution) and to Americanism that quotas of respect need to be enlisted. To perpetuate the term "a black film director" is a way of eclipsing the prospects of "a humanist filmmaker," "an optimistic filmmaker," "a cruel filmmaker," and so on. One of the more crippling burdens on a black director is the instruction that he or she make black films. So I relish the fact that Spike Lee's prodigious, inventive, and unyielding oeuvre includes films with both black and white characters, in hostility and friendship, wrath and humor. He is the director of *Do the Right Thing* (the cast of which includes Danny Aiello and John Turturro), and *The 25th Hour*, with a cast of Edward Norton, Philip Seymour Hoffman, Barry Pepper, Anna Paquin, Brian Cox, and Rosario Dawson.

She plays an exquisite woman named Naturelle; Puerto Rican, she's an emblem of allegiance as her guy goes off to prison. There are bad black cops in *25th Hour* as well as Lee's torment over New York. The film has a diatribe against the clamoring ethnicities of the city—and then a fond embrace of them all. Spike is thoroughly mixed up. The picture vibrates with tension between agitprop lecture and emotional drama, especially in the finale where a dream of escape into the expanses of America settles for prison. None of his films is more moving.

Spike Lee (born in Atlanta in 1957) is one of the most significant and challenging Americans of his time. If you ever met him as he brought his first feature film, *She's Gotta Have It,* to public screens in 1986 then you can see the argument that no minority status is more influential than trying to be a filmmaker and sketching borrowed credit cards together to pay for a picture (it cost $175,000). Lee is indefatigable in his cheerfulness, his stamina, his unstoppable urge to put provocative stuff on our screens, and his general acceptance of getting so few Oscars or nominations. He did get an honorary Oscar in 2015, and then he really won with his screenplay for *BlacKkKlansman.* He is as heroic and signal as D. W. Griffith, John Ford, and Frank Capra. And he lives and works under the weight of having to be black, whereas a Howard Hawks, an Alfred Hitchcock, and a Jean-Luc Godard never had to notice being white.

Still, just as I do not much like the work of Ford or Capra, so I am not bowled over by Spike's films despite believing in him as a public example. Mere liking or opinion need not be important, but it is a habit we should not give up. As it happens, I am personally more impressed and moved by films by Carl Franklin—especially *One False Move* (1992), *Devil in a Blue Dress* (1995), and *One True Thing* (1998).

Perhaps that was his purple patch. Perhaps Franklin has had difficulty in mounting other pictures that might be in that class. Perhaps you missed those films, and hardly know that Franklin in recent years has done a lot of series TV—including *House of Cards, The Newsroom, Homeland, The Affair, Ray Donovan,* and four episodes of *Mindhunter.* You may have seen some of those episodes, without noting the name of the director, or reading the episodes as more than being in line with the tradition and the weather system of their series. Franklin is seventy now, and he may not get the chance to make another great film on a par with *One True Thing*, which is played out by Meryl Streep, Renee Zellweger, and William Hurt (all at or close to their best).

There are others: John Singleton (*Boyz in the Hood*), Charles Burnett (*Killer of Sheep*), Ryan Coogler (*Black Panther*), Jordan Peele (*Get Out*) . . . and John Akomfrah. He was born in Ghana in 1957, just months after that country ceased to be the "Gold Coast." He went to Britain, studied there, and became a founding member of the Black Audio Film Collective. The film of his I know and love is *Vertigo Sea* (2015), an installation of three side-by-side screens that run forty minutes in a panorama of oceans, voyages, whaling, and slavery. You may regard it as a movie, yet I saw it in an art museum as an amalgam of old footage and fresh scenes arranged by the director. So to see it, you need an uncommonly long room. But it is as worthwhile as anything else available.

Film directors are their own minority. They are always alone, trying to find their break, their opening, their moment, never sure that it may not be a dead end or a mistake. They are no longer under contract as directors, sure of a couple of pictures a year. So they take a commercial here or there and a television episode—impersonal assignments compared with *Phantom Thread* or *The Irishman*. They have to maintain their presence.

In that suspense, some life companions may have decided these directors cannot be lived with, because they are crazy, selfish, or too determined to be alone. And by now that obsessive solitude has been deepened because the generous, uplifting togetherness of cinema is less compelling or common. Hawks and Hitchcock excelled and seemed nonchalant because they trusted that "everyone" was awaiting their films. Orson Welles and Jean-Luc Godard guessed that euphoria had to end. The audience—the public—was shifting toward being a mass, just as the term "mass media" had always foreshadowed. Today's intense assertion of minority isms and choices is fighting the tide of uniformity in which individuals do not exactly make or watch films. The stream is the auteur; digital has eclipsed the poetry in things seen; the screen is our conscience, but it does not care if we are there.

14

THE KID FROM THE VIDEO STORE:
QUENTIN TARANTINO

There was always a passion likely to produce a brilliant film-maker who cannot quite refer his pictures to a thing called life. From the very start, Q was making movies about movies. The brilliance was so ecstatic it hardly noticed its dead end.

I had to check this out—it didn't seem possible after I had seen *Once Upon a Time . . . in Hollywood*—but when some members of the Manson gang took over 10050 Cielo Drive, off Benedict Canyon, on August 9, 1969, and when they did what they did there, Quentin Jerome Tarantino was six, more or less the age I was when I saw *Red River,* and rode along with Dunson and Garth, taking that herd of cattle across the Red, all the way to Abilene. Which only puts me in mind of how we have been dreaming, and what we have made of our Abilene, or Cielo Drive.

What sent me back several times—just to check the dates— was my assumption that the spirit behind *Once Upon a Time* had been *there then,* in Los Angeles in 1969, and regarded it with a mixture of rue and nostalgia. What makes Tarantino's fairy tale so good is his air of knowing the place, the narrow roads into the hills of trees, the habit of letting your car snarl and swerve into the blind downhill curves, because *probably* there was no one coming, and then the ketchup of music, dumb television shows, and that assurance that the air of L.A. then had been as much to treasure as any old movie. Somehow, life had turned into a screened phantom.

That was absurd: Tarantino in 2019 had the look and regret of someone in his late fifties, even if his mantrap grin made you afraid that growing up was out of his question. He really is so good, and that bad. So how could he have been six, about the age of the best female in the picture—Julia Butters (actual age ten), playing the child actress Trudi Fraser (in the class of Margaret O'Brien from *Meet Me in St. Louis*)? You see the temptation and the peril in referring every face or sight to movie ancestors?

Quentin had seemed such a brilliant kid at first, a whiz student who never went to college. All you had to do to acclaim him as the best new thing in movies was to overlook the meticulous vileness of *Reservoir Dogs* and its geometric nihilism. It helped that Quentin himself couldn't stop talking, like the clerk in a video store who had seen every film, and could recite the dialogue, especially from the pictures you weren't interested in—the exploitation films, cheap horror jobs, slasher gore, and beautiful violence inflicted on bimbo actresses who screamed more than they talked. What did we expect when a city factory put out stories that made life seem sheepish?

It's a good question: what did the "culture of film comment" expect as its own paint flaked away in the desert light of screens, digital, CGI, and the lost glow of film? The great generation of the late 1960s and 1970s had peaked; they had grown old, institutional, or they had died and drifted into modest disgrace. What could film academe do in 1992 but be awed by the arrival of Tarantino as a kid without what was called education who was dazzling? Hadn't teachers told students to see as many films as possible? And hadn't Quentin done that beyond counting or comparison? So how could they be troubled that a movie brat's prodigious absorption of all the movies ever made could produce pulp so pretty and aromatic you felt you should eat it—as if it was a *royale* (a French cheeseburger)?

Tarantino had been born in Knoxville, Tennessee, in March 1963. His life was a riot of contrary directions. His mother and father broke up very quickly. She married again, and the stepfather took the child to grown-up movies. The actual father was some kind of actor and producer. The boy, an only child, moved back and forth between Los Angeles and Tennessee. The mother fell ill, and grandparents helped look after the kid. There was an absence of family, stability, and education—Quentin dropped out of school at the age of fifteen. Who cared? Wasn't he at the movies and hadn't there always been a feeling in the New Wave ideology that all a kid needed to do was go to the movies, get out of the light and into the dark? How many times had teachers told such promising students to get a broader education, to read Flaubert and Henry James, to look at paintings and listen to music, to walk in the countryside, to get into their own demanding and complex relationships? And some of the kids had stared back like hardened cops who scorned your pathetic story.

What right do I or anyone have to pass comments on the life Tarantino lived? None at all. But I have seen the films and felt a need to speak.

Reservoir Dogs was always a mysterious title. Before I'd seen the film, I understood the curious melancholy of reservoirs in cities—the dark waves lapping quietly, the aroma of fresh decay—and imagined the stray dogs that gathered there, somewhere between disturbed and dangerous. So it was a letdown to hear that the title was actually a joke, picked up from someone in a video store asking for Louis Malle's *Au Revoir les Enfants* but saying "reservoir" instead. That store, Video Archives in Manhattan Beach, had been Tarantino's university, where he clerked for five years.

Then he'd started writing scripts and at first *Reservoir Dogs* was going to be a homemade film—just Quentin and some buddies—until Harvey Keitel heard about it, talked it up, and pulled together $1.5 million and a gang of actors to wear the black suits, the white shirts, and the blood and to forsake real names for colors, like the balls on a pool table. You could think of the whole picture as a frame, a set-up, punching its balls into the pockets. Tidy and lethal. And as arbitrary as any game done for its own sake. There were efforts to place this debut in terms of influences and history. Quentin said he had thought of Kubrick's *The Killing,* which was best set aside in case you began to remember the rich malice and anguish in its Peavy marriage (Elisha Cook Jr. and Marie Windsor), or even the smothered affection the Jay C. Flippen character has for Sterling Hayden. Kubrick was not the warmest fellow in movies, but *The Killing* had been about people not colors. .

I don't sneer at the pool analogy, much less the way many movies can be perceived as closed games. Robert Bresson's *A Man Escaped* is like a tiny test of getting a man out of his hole, but when it works there is a release of spiritual exaltation that makes the Mozart finale seem appropriate. *The Big Sleep* can be regarded as a sardonic grand master engaged in several games of simultaneous chess. But at the end, you appreciate that man, not to mention the several dames he does ping-pong with. It's easy to say the afternoon at the Acme Book Store is a metaphor for sex (everything in Hawks rises to that test), but it is also a revelation of two people, a grown-up offhand opportunism and the consensual culture of literacy. (Dorothy Malone's unnamed clerk does know her books.)

But the entourage without a center in *Reservoir Dogs* discloses nothing about the several guys beyond their interchangeability, their antlike roles in the absurdist task of occupying the screen for ninety-nine minutes, their stand-up facility with talk and their undeviating dedication to formula. The Mexican standoff is their formative diagram. Thus in an elegant and assured piece of gamesmanship, the setup turns hideous. I am talking about the scene in which Mr. Blonde (Michael Madsen) tells a tethered captive that he is going to cut off his ear with a razor—leaving us to work out how we are prisoner too in this cruelty, caught between horror and gloating.

It is possible that any movie can be analyzed down to the elements of an executed plan—script to screen, or story to money. But isn't it in the nature of stories, and our dependence on them, to draw on some human interaction, with comedy or pathos, tragedy or resignation, even with triumph? And isn't there inherent in *Reservoir Dogs* an intimation that our humanism is being erased?

That sounds solemn, but thirty years before the film was made, neither its violence nor its nihilism would have been permitted by the Code often mocked as archaic. Yet maybe there should be skepticism for a culture that revels in the voyeurism of the ear scene, and which is not dismayed at Mr. Blonde shuffle-dancing to the predatory "Stuck in the Middle With You." (See *Au Revoir les Enfants* instead—it's magnificent, unexaggerated, and humane.)

In 1992, I wanted to walk out on the picture at that scene, and to reject its vicious smugness. I still feel that. But *Reservoir Dogs* began the Tarantino cult in a world craving impudent, raw genius. The film debuted to acclaim at the Sundance Film Festival. It was taken on for distribution by Miramax and by Harvey Weinstein, who would be Tarantino's patron for many years. And the film was a box office success.

It's an unusual dilemma—or it was in 1992—for a film critic to feel alarmed by an independent movie made by a young person with such talent. Moreover, the profuse talk among the guys in the opening scene was inspired and nearly delirious. Dialogue can be a big part of movies, but it was falling into disuse by 1992, and here was a writer with exceptional ear and rhythm, even if his rhapsodic badmouth talk might come from earlier movies rather than from life. Tarantino was a remarkable newcomer in film.

That promise bloomed with *Pulp Fiction,* not just an audacious film and the enactment of a beautifully structured screenplay, but a way of looking at the underworld of Los Angeles that was lit up by parody, a moderation of violence, the introduction of women, and an apparent coming to terms with the artifice of movies. The enlightenment was as if Jim Thompson material had been handed over to Nabokov in a storyline that delighted in coincidence, flashes back and forth, and the fascination of a snakelike story eating its own tail.

All of a sudden one could believe Tarantino liked people,

not just the verve of their mannered talk or the way they kidded noir archetypes. John Travolta's Vincent Vega was a stumblebum hoodlum, hounded by good luck and bad, given his quoted moment on the dance floor at Jack Rabbit Slim's and a gentle reminder of the childlike persona of Travolta. The teaming up with Samuel Jackson, and the baroque flourish of their talk, was so much more than the male allegiances in *Reservoir Dogs*. And while the film dealt in violence and sheer nastiness in the bondage scene, one could feel that Tarantino was no longer getting off on it.

He was riding along on his own movie, with a pleasure that was not far from Hawksian. In that sweeping passage where Harvey Keitel's Winston Wolfe cleans up the mess (a comic, inadvertent slaughter, let's admit), one could see that Wolfe was himself a director as good at organizing actor-characters as Dunson's men had been at getting the cattle across the Red. So it was nicer still in that scene that Tarantino was there himself, doing a good job as an actor and an assistant to Wolfe.

Pulp Fiction was a terrific title that showed Tarantino knew he was making an elegy to genre. It was akin to the Hawks of *The Big Sleep* saying, Look, see what we can do with this material. And if the women were cameos, not quite trusted with the narrative, still, Uma Thurman, Amanda Plummer, and Maria de Medeiros were memorable because they had been treated with affection. I felt that Tarantino had a surging talent and I was not alone. *Pulp Fiction* carried off the Palme d'Or at Cannes. It won the Oscar for original screenplay (shared with Roger Avary) and it earned $213 million on a budget of $8.5 million. In doing that, it became the mainstay of Miramax and a beacon for American independent pictures.

My initial disapproval was burning off in the rapture of this second film which I still regard as a masterpiece, and what might have been a fresh, subversive attitude to male supremacy. So it's sad to conclude now that it is the best thing Tarantino has ever done. But there it was, in 1994, the object of a cult, with him just thirty-one.

Jackie Brown (1997) was less ambitious, and without the uplifting formal grace of *Pulp Fiction,* but it was unexpected, ingenious, and a fond survey of oddball characters—it owed something to the wry warmth in Elmore Leonard's novel *Rum Punch,* on which it was based. (It is Tarantino's only non-original script.) In casting Pam Grier, an icon of black exploitation films, it delivered the fullest female character Tarantino had yet attempted. Robert Forster was also rescued from relative obscurity in what is the only credible love story (heterosexual, that is) in the director's work. It was also the most racially intriguing or open of his films, and Jackie had been a white woman in Leonard's novel. This likeable picture did about a fifth the business of *Pulp Fiction,* but it suggested that this level of ordinariness might be where Tarantino was headed.

That was not to be. Apparently a friendship had developed between Quentin and Uma Thurman on *Pulp Fiction,* where she presents an alluring but stunned mobster mistress, on the brink of oblivion, but oddly plausible as a prized slave of male supremacy. The two of them hatched the idea for *Kill Bill* as a vengeance vehicle for Uma, and somehow persuaded themselves that its derivation from martial arts cinema and the posturing of spaghetti Westerns might lead to "female empowerment." The two *Kill Bill*s have their enthusiasts who may be hurt at any rebuke, but I wonder if in cool hindsight many of them can justify the grisly violence or the ponderous length of the venture. Meant for one film, it became two in the first sign of Tarantino's reluctance to edit himself. The films did well, but was this because of liberated women or the mounting, gloating feeling for misogyny and violence? Years later, Thurman let it be known that she had been injured and exploited in some of the filming, as well as having to suffer the attentions of Harvey Weinstein, Quentin's fond enabler. Tarantino admitted he had been sadly inattentive to such things.

Inflation was on hand, accompanied by thematic diminution: *Kill Bill Volume 1* (2003) was an hour and fifty-two minutes; *Kill Bill Volume 2* (2004) was two hours and sixteen minutes. The sinuous narrative twists of *Pulp Fiction* gave way to block-like set pieces that were badly overextended—all instead of what might have been one deft, swift, nasty, sexy eighty-five-minute picture done in four weeks (as would befit exploitation moviemaking). Instead, the *Bill* project had occupied the better part of three years. The two films made a lot of money, but some suspicious viewers felt Tarantino was falling back on his memory bank of old movies from the video store. Movies made about movies can be a way toward a dead end.

There followed what fans of the director regard as a trilogy. That doesn't mean they were conceived as a trinity, or with any overarching narrative intent. But for me they are held together by the ignominy of the approach, the inescapable feeling that the director knows little about the world and how we live, and cares less, and by the bloated cinematic self-consciousness in pastiches of earlier and very suspect genres of entertainment. I feel they have got slower and self-conscious, and by the time of *The Hateful Eight* (2015), many prior enthusiasts had begun to be troubled by the inane length of the film, the misogyny, and the complacency over moral vacuum. As *The Hateful Eight* found fresh ways of battering and abusing the Jennifer Jason Leigh character, it was hard not to feel that the brilliant kid was going out of control.

Moreover, the three films lacked the momentum that Tarantino had commanded. They were tanker ships when once his movies had felt like sailboats. The prolonged opening sequence of *Inglourious Basterds* (2009)—where a Nazi officer (Christoph Waltz) effectively tortures a French family—may have seemed to the director like a model of suspense, but it had a luxuriating, decadent slowness that reminded me of the ear in *Reservoir Dogs*.

It began to dawn that Tarantino knew too little about the Second World War compared with the arrogant poses absorbed from casual war movies. His ability with talk, and his indulgence of actors, was congealing as we watched. A similar unawareness of racism and the history of the South buried any chance that *Django Unchained* (2012) could be a worthwhile picture. Instead, it felt like a lurid but sexually tentative reworking of *Mandingo* (1975), an unrespectable movie that had explored the sexual subcontracts in slavery. But Tarantino did not notice sexuality in his study of rampant male vengeance. It had more to do with the violent intrigue of Italian Westerns than the circumstances of the South. Only eight years after it earned $425 million, I doubt it would be acceptable now.

The trilogy did very well, with spectacle and distended suspense, even if the excitement was seeming archaic. The violence was unrestrained; the women were derided or beaten; and the code of heroism was close to schemes of white supremacy that were about to be challenged in America. The terrible blind exuberance of Trump was there in that trilogy. I meant it when I said ignominious. The chance of cinematic excellence—of real directing—was being smothered by undigested adolescent dreams. Inasmuch as Tarantino knew his American movie history, his own work was becoming a lesson on the damage that Hollywood had inflicted on us.

Such commentary seldom gets into film reviewing. But that has helped the pressure of fantasy and its fraudulent fulfillment to work on us without challenge. To go back to Andrew Sarris's policy, the stress on *how* can help us forget the *what*. Quentin Tarantino is not just a talented film-mad kid. He is a citizen going from the twentieth to the twenty-first century and an advocate for an ideology that has had woeful consequences. Film is not a closed room, a chamber for dreaming. It has to be part of the whole house of the nation.

So *Once Upon a Time . . . in Hollywood* was a title and a project that seemed necessary, yet ominous. Our fairy tales are not always wholesome.

There are good things to be said for *Once Upon a Time*. There are passages in which the lazy light of Los Angeles seems to reawaken Tarantino's eye and his interest in people. The friendship between Cliff Booth and Rick Dalton is well written, even better acted, and it becomes the heart of the film, the more intriguing for involving two "has-beens" far from any notion of supremacy. Tarantino had veered away from deadbeats before, but here we have a failing actor and a stunt double who hardly works anymore. They cling together as a way of hiding how little life they have. At moments, their bond is lugubrious, melancholy, and disconcerting. You could wonder whether Quentin felt age creeping up on him. And soon we may see their friendship as a measure of what happens to studs after male supremacy has been outlawed and they look like two stooges.

Leonardo DiCaprio and Brad Pitt enjoy these roles, and some of the sharpest things in the film involve their anxious togetherness—distinctly middle-aged—amid rapid cultural change. In their disdain for hippies one can hear disgruntled conservatism. They keep up with *Mannix* and *The FBI,* but hardly notice Vietnam, or people of color.

Yet their partnership is so tenderly done one asks for more. Cliff, the stunt double, is said to have killed his wife—long before the time of the picture—and we want to know more about that. And while Cliff is as taut and tanned as Brad Pitt, able to take his shirt off and be a statue in the sun, what really motivates him? Is he content to drive Rick here and there, to repair his TV antenna, to bolster his cracking confidence and just be "Cliff"?

He does have an eye for daughter-age girls as he drives around—and driving is what he does best. Several times, he notices Pussycat (Margaret Qualley), and he appreciates her. One day he gives her a lift, though she wants to go to Chatsworth, twenty miles away. So he has nothing else to do except drive this aimless girl out of town? She then indicates that she's willing to put out for him—in the car, in a layby or in the dusty hills on the way to Spahn Ranch. But he asks how old she is. In 1969? Do you recall how once Brad Pitt moved effortlessly on Geena Davis (to her immediate delight) in *Thelma & Louise*? That scene introduced him, and it's a tribute to vagrant sex. People, movie people, had such quick couplings in 1969. They still do. And it was hard to know why Cliff was so restrained, unless he'd had a MeToo warning, or been read a sermon by a director chastened by his own lengthy association with Harvey Weinstein.

Or was Cliff leaning just a little gay? There had always been an undertone in Tarantino—and in so much male American film—in which the guys were more comfortable with other guys than having to talk to women. Just to pose that question is to draw attention to the self-admiring and empty-headed companionship of Cliff and Rick. They are so uninteresting a couple, we settle for the inventiveness and ease of the two actors. They are charming, quite funny, and I believe in them. Hollywood has always had its share of guys who think L.A. is the world. But their hollowness alerts one to the vacancy that hovers over Tarantino. The fairy tale in the title hints that Cliff and Rick are arrested children. But the world is grown up, and surely movies have a responsibility for keeping us aware of that and better able to consider it.

I offer the point whimsically, but as they get drunk and feed the dog and their pipe dreams, Cliff and Rick could ask themselves, Why are all the women in our picture hateful, or bimbos? Margot Robbie makes a sweet, funny cartoon Sharon Tate. The scene at the Bruin Theater in Westwood where she watches herself in *The Wrecking Crew* and thrills to the audience response is delicious. That occasion is like another L.A. pool where she can sun herself and stay cool. But the scene is founded on the assumption that Tate was an idiot or an infant. Instead of an expectant mother who was cut to pieces, and a young woman so moved by reading *Tess of the D'Urbervilles* that she bought a copy for her husband, Roman Polanski. Maybe she was more interesting than this film allows. And surely she is more deserving.

The other women we meet are Manson's girls—pale, sickly, and depraved—the wife that Cliff may have murdered, and the production manager who can't stand him. Don't forget the available flesh at the Playboy Mansion, from Michelle Phillips (Rebecca Rittenhouse) to the chorus line of bikini bods. Have I left anyone out? Yes, Trudi, the wise child actress who has a couple of piercing scenes with Rick that help root the film's ethos in childishness.

But Trudi never returns; she is just one of those set pieces that Tarantino has become prey to, impressive scenes that are not integrated into a film's structure—often because the films feel more assembled than shaped. *Once Upon a Time* is crowded out with unfulfilled expectations. Did Cliff murder his wife, and what difference would that make? Why does a narrator's voice (it's Kurt Russell's unnecessary character) break into the film, unless from fears of incoherence? Why do we have the Al Pacino character? He does nothing for the storyline except provide a pretext for having Al in the picture. The same could be said for Damian Lewis's droll impersonation of Steve McQueen, and the aside to *The Great Escape*—things that stand in the way of following the picture for anyone not old enough to know who McQueen was, and he died thirty-nine years ago. He's like John Gilbert for 1969. My twenty-four-year-old son found that scene an obstacle. When I took the time to explain it, his perplexity only deepened. He likes movies to reach out to him. Without that gesture one feels indifference in the project.

My son knew enough about what happened at Cielo Drive in August 1969 to feel the portents in the film. He didn't know all the names of the dead or the killers; he hadn't read Joan Didion in *The White Album* on the lack of surprise that greeted the murders. But random slaughter has set in more during his lifetime. So he knew—just like anyone else—that the fairy story was going to end badly. Wasn't that why we were at the movie, waiting for Quentin to do his big bad thing?

That menace hangs over the Spahn Ranch scene, one of the subtlest stretches of film Tarantino has ever done. When Cliff arrives with Pussycat at the Ranch, a pack of strung-out girls are watching television in the house where George Spahn gets fucked (somehow) and sleeps away the last of his life. This is creepy; it seems to smell bad. And the way Cliff picks up on the threat puts Pitt on the frontier of unease. We hope that he is going to be all right, or what you could call safe, but we want him to get away.

This is another set piece that dodges the still pressing questions: what was Charlie really like—I mean Manson—and how did he impress himself upon those girls? It's all very well for them to be baleful apprentice witches—but how did that happen in their America of the 1960s? Tarantino isn't obliged to answer that question, but it's clear that he avoids it and lets the girls become a *Living Dead* lineup. (George Romero's great film had opened in 1968.)

But Quentin is advancing on bigger, far scarier things, isn't he? What was his plan? I think it's plain in the promise of the film (its advertising) and then in the setup that introduces Sharon Tate, that *Once Upon a Time* is going to end in violence. You expect—in a spirit of dread and anticipation—that you are going to have to witness that night at Cielo Drive. You know it's the kind of scene Quentin would want to do.

Then pause a moment. If this film is going to do significant box office and make happy suckers of us, can it really do the knives and the blood (some call it the red)? Can we see—should we require this of ourselves—blades breaking into Sharon's womb? After all, you could see the embryo—we can do anything now with CGI.

Would there be issues of taste? Sure, that's a welcome thought. And that could make the film an "X," which would hurt the box office. I'm sorry to give you grief about this, Quentin, but is it possible that the American public will not quite stand for the real horror? So will you have to trick it? Yet that same audience demands blood and outrage. And Tarantino wants to deliver it. Isn't it apparent that nothing drives him on more than that?

So how is the mayhem to be accommodated? It's like Jean-Luc Godard having Brigitte Bardot in *Le Mépris* and being told she has to be naked at some point. So he gets it over with at the start. But in *Once Upon a Time,* the violence has to be held back for the big finish, a slap-up job. Anything else will be a cheat.

The reviews didn't get into this because that would be a spoiler. But don't settle for that excuse. The film is so spoiled, it is beyond protection.

So Tarantino has the killers, in the moonlight, knives gleaming in their hands, walking up the drive on Cielo. But don't forget, Rick Dalton's house is next door. And these would-be killers are such fuckups they blunder in on Cliff, feeding the dog and reeling from the effects of an acid cigarette, while Rick is floating in his pool, locked into earphone music. Those idiot murderers! You can't trust hippies.

They say they are going to do Satan's work, but they've never held a job. So Cliff throws a loaded can of dog food in one girl's face. His dog—this deep-brown bull terrier, Brandy—launches herself at the killers, tearing at their faces and their genitals. The meanest female in the picture. Before you know it, Cliff is slamming one girl's face into a brick wall—it's loud and splashy—four times, for connoisseurs. Meanwhile the aroused Rick finds the flamethrower he has kept from one of his action movies, and thus he fries an intruder in his crazed house. Ketchup and fries—the American menu.

I've seen the film several times and the audience always rocks with laughter. While the violence is hideous, it is being visited on very bad guys by our stupefied but very dull good guys. And they deserve it as much as we do. The shaming trick of *Once Upon a Time . . . in Hollywood* is to send us out of the theatre in high spirits, well fed on brutality but with an air of righteousness, and of our $15 well spent. What a lark! What a wow! What a disgrace—and one we have been accomplices to.

Finally, Rick Dalton gets to go up to the Tate house for a drink, to tell her what has happened and to see her lovely wide eyes grow wider. And perhaps her tummy swells one touch. This is Quentin Tarantino's ninth film. He has promised that he is close to retirement, to which he looks forward heartily so that he can devote himself to writing books.

Pushing sixty, Tarantino still trades on the reputation of a hot, wild kid. But he was always a throwback, and a devotee of films made before he was born. *Once Upon a Time* is often a marvel of entertainment—Quentin is so talented—but in its violence, its regard for females, and in its curious unawareness of race, it demonstrates how far the fairy tales of Hollywood were from the realities of America by 2020.

15

THE LAST IRISHMAN

By the time Martin Scorsese's big picture, *The Irishman,* opened, in November 2019, its forbidding length had picked up other baggage. It had become more than just his baby. It might be a turning point in the picture business, and even a farewell. Do you recall?

For decades, "Marty" had been the most energetic patron of movie movies. Time and again, twenty seconds of dynamic imagery and its music had been like his fingerprint. He had his own collection of historic prints; he had seen them all; he fought for film preservation, for the recovery of lost wonders re-released to theatres or on video. He was on our side, and he was devoted to the excitement of film itself, of celluloid projected on big screens to rapt crowds of filmgoers. In being on our side, he had done so much to define the nature of that side. But was it quite there still?

At seventy-five, he faced a dilemma all directors or would-be auteurs knew. He had a vision but not enough of other people's money to realize it. He yearned to make *The Irishman*, a chronicle of badfellas, and he spoke of that feeling as if we all understood the right or the need of artists to do a film as they wished—in the way Orson Welles had made *Citizen Kane*, or Virginia Woolf had written *Mrs. Dalloway*. But she had required only pen and paper, and Welles had birthed his baby with a mere $840,000 and a band of unquestioning supporters. Those levels were far short of the $160 million talked about for *The Irishman*. Orson's 1941 budget was about $15 million in modern money. Woolf had no contract, no advance; by then she was her own publisher. She wrote for its own sake or to stop the nub of her story and its frustration making her head ache as if from a tumor.

On *The Irishman*, it was said that a lot of the money went on the CGI processing that allowed the lead actors to look like younger men, by as much as fifty years. Artistically, I think that investment was dubious, for it often jolts the viewer out of the reality of the story; sometimes the actors seem to have had a minor stroke. In *Kane*, the central character aged fifty years and a makeup artist, Maurice Seiderman, did the transitions better than they are handled in *The Irishman*.

It's possible that for the sake of his yearning over this baby, Marty received several million dollars. I don't know if he "deserved" that, even in a creative context where some people do their work for nothing, and Marty is said to have a net worth of $70 million. But these numbers matter; they always do in pictures: Malick's *A Hidden Life* cost about $10 million. Orson Welles died broke.

In the event, Paramount had backed away from Scorsese's big ask. The studio admired Marty, but they felt the budget he was calling for was too much. Perhaps they wondered quietly if the film he was intending might be too long. I think they were correct; I believe producers, studios, or the ugliest bosses can be correct sometimes on such matters: I wish Steven Bach, an executive at United Artists, had found the will, the lawyers, or even the enforcer (a Joe Pesci?) to tell Michael Cimino to abandon the Harvard scene that opens *Heaven's Gate* and stifles it as a show. I believe the wretched Harvey Weinstein was unerring in telling Simon Curtis to add a sequence of Marilyn Monroe dancing and singing at the start of *My Week with Marilyn*. And around the ninety-minute mark of *The Irishman*, it seemed fanciful to me that there were still two hours to come.

At that point, the picture is a muddle, sunk in the glorifying of gangsterese, and so addicted to badmouth, stylish violence, and the mix of grandeur and self-pity in hollow men that Scorsese seems lost in his old obsession (it's not as if he had been denied the chance to do gangsters in the past). Then something remarkable occurs. *The Irishman* rallies and begins to recognize its new message—one that Marty had not dared before—that these strutting bullies are being humbled by the universal progress of real aging. In its last hour the film is touched by greatness as hoodlums totter toward insignificance and regret. There's a feeling of sorrow, not just for these guys but even for the climate in which gangsters were unchallenged, saturnine models.

As it advances so the picture settles on De Niro's Frank Sheeran, whose betrayal of Jimmy Hoffa (a fussy and fabricated plotline) pales beside something smaller, yet larger. The greater damage is to the attention and respect of Frank's daughter Peggy, who cannot hide from her father's being a listless killer, a liar, and a source of shame. Peggy is shown first as a child (Lucy Gallina) whose admiration for her dad begins to be troubled. But then she becomes the adult Anna Paquin, essentially silent but remorselessly watchful and not to be fobbed off with any homily about women not understanding male things or knowing how to keep their place. The way Peggy looks at Dad is a force that will sweep a lot of male self-confidence off the screen. That has to mean something for Marty; there is remorse in this film. It has to mean something for every filmgoer who ever breathed the air of Philip Marlowe, Walter Burns, and Dean Martin's tender drunk in *Rio Bravo*. That was me. And was it you?

Peggy is not built up to be a redemptive moral lesson. Marty knows there is no redemption. This is not like the film I posited earlier, a *Godfather* where the woeful Kay turns state's evidence on her own Michael. But Scorsese has never done anything better than the pained way in which Paquin gazes at De Niro so he knows a world and its terrible romance are over. At two hours, done in restraint and simplicity, this might have been a great film. But there is enough left to fill one with awe. If the masterpiece needed a structure it could have adopted the way the Joe Pesci character observes but can do nothing to mend the situation. It is in Pesci's peaceful or resigned gaze that one feels Scorsese is facing mortality instead of one more string of knockout executions.

So *The Irishman* opened for three weeks as a film in theaters. It had excellent reviews and good audiences, earning about $3 million on a few hundred American screens. And then, like a Faust limo'd to hell, it began to stream on Netflix. We would never know or trust the claims of how many new subscriptions it had brought to that platform. Come to that, few people understood that the mighty Netflix empire was often close to debt. As if stung by his betrayal of an old paradise, Scorsese spoke out against the culture of "Marvel movies"; he said they were anonymous, impersonal, and regrettable. He wrote in *The New York Times:* "For anyone who dreams of making movies or who is just starting out, the situation at this moment is brutal and inhospitable to art. And the act of simply writing those words fills me with terrible sadness."

The Irishman won no Oscars. It might even prove to be Marty's last film. If he credits and inhabits the onset of age as this movie suggests, then a time will come for him to sit still, watching the classics in his collection, or letting the river of light flow over him. A Covid connoisseur.

He has been a model director and one who has come to appreciate Renoir's insight—that we do not direct life, no matter our vanity and ambition. We have to suffer the way its streaming is the tide we cannot slow or deny.

The heady cult of the director was pledged to artistry and control, to personal visions of beauty. But since 1895 there had always been the possibility that unique ambitions were all very well, but just feel the driving force of the technology and the neurotic but religious marriage of watchers and their screens. Was the great enterprise something beyond the control of talent? Was the monolith fit to be worshipped, or was it a warning?

A part of me had wanted *The Irishman* to be a noir epic, a portrait of power and the search for feeling in the large America. Instead, much of it was a lugubrious, imprisoned fantasy, so short on brave aspiration. At nearly the same time, I was watch-

ing *Ozark* on Netflix, three seasons of it. And it was everything
I had hoped for from *The Irishman*, a burning, fatalistic story
of the confounding of American energy, told not just in the
cartels of criminal industry but in the revelations of family
honor and dishonesty. Several episodes were directed by Jason
Bateman, who also played one of the lead characters and was
a producer on the show. As I watched him compose and cut
his own image—of a handsome, stricken, compromised face—
I realized that Bateman had become as demanding a director as
early Scorsese, but less egotistical.

Bateman was not alone. Long-form television is made by
teams. Alik Sakharov was born in Tashkent in 1959 and came
to America in 1985. As a cinematographer he shot thirty-eight
episodes of *The Sopranos*. From that, he graduated to directing and handling the last four episodes of season 3 of *Ozark*.
That is a momentous four-hour film, crammed with characters, action, and an unrelenting portrait of an American family
cracking under the pressure of money. It's not just that those
four episodes are "well directed." They were an essential movie
of 2020.

You may not have heard of Sakharov. Directors are shadowy
figures again.

In summer 2020, we anticipated Christopher Nolan's *Tenet*.
Wasn't he as big as Fritz Lang? The business was desperate for
his film to rescue theatres. Nolan had brooded over it for years,
the promos said; it would have sumptuous effects and a bill
for over $200 million. But could it open in the stricken Amer-
ica with breathing crowds? Was the audience still there? It was
said that *Tenet* was about saving the world, but was that storyline credible next to *Ozark*'s lucidity?

———

This chapter is for its star, Patrick McGilligan.

PRE-HISTORY

In 1984, on its publication, I felt that Richard Schickel's book
D. W. Griffith: An American Life was "the best ever written on
the man." That holds true, I think, but in 1984 neither Schickel
nor I were properly aware of the sinkholes in this very important director. Since then, for ample reason, Griffith has gone
out of fashion and it is doubtful whether a new biography will
describe the fuller picture we now confront. It would have to
be a book about a pioneer who went right and wrong at the
same time, in being both progressive and retrograde. Such a
book would talk about how the lightning of a sensational new
medium blinded as much as it illuminated, and how it laid
down stereotypes of gross sentimentality—to say nothing of
its racist confidence. It would also be a study in the aura and

dysfunction of being Southern, and that could expose how little the Civil War settled. Imagine a single book that contained Griffith, Faulkner, Louis Armstrong, and Flannery O'Connor. And Scarlett O'Hara. And Governor DeSantis.

Richard Koszarski wrote the most informative book on von Stroheim, *The Man You Loved to Hate: Erich von Stroheim and Hollywood* (1983), but it admits to big gaps in what we think we know about a man who was a pioneering trickster, or fake. The most inspiring book may be Herman G. Weinberg's *The Complete "Greed"* (1972) which reconstructs the "lost" film from script, stills, and production shots in which the Von is a modern, tanned Ozymandias.

FRITZ LANG

The best biographical study is Patrick McGilligan's *Fritz Lang: The Nature of the Beast* (1997). As its subtitle indicates, this is a book about a great director and a troubling or chilly man— that pattern is often more fruitful in directorial biographies than the lofty adulation exemplified in Lotte H. Eisner's *Fritz Lang* (published in German originally, in 1976). Eisner's book included Lang's autobiographical sketch but McGilligan's book is a searcher's map for a complex and compromised career.

That said, there is not yet a book that explores the life while giving us insight into the extraordinary body of work that concluded when Lang left Germany in 1933. That challenge is the greater in requiring the writer to come to terms with the creative links between film and authoritarianism, also known as fascism. Lang can be exiled to history, if you like, but that is a grave mistake when our fascists are becoming so agile and cute, cunning and hard to pin down. Lang is one of the more alarming and dynamic artists of the twentieth century.

We need to study his films, most of them silent, but naturally so, as if that made it easier for his terrible but naive grandeur to pass into our nervous system without being hindered by mere narrative or fortune-cookie moral lessons. Most of the films are available now for home viewing, even if their ideal forum is an awe-inspiring arena, a place for prisoners who still believe they are free.

JEAN RENOIR

The chapter spells out the place of the biography by Pascal Mérigeau, as well as the value of books by Renoir himself—*Renoir, My Father* (1962) and the novel, *The Notebooks of Captain Georges* (1966). There are two other important books: *My Life and My Films* (1974), a series of vivid sketches, and *Jean Renoir: Letters* (1994), edited by David Thompson and Lorraine LoBianco. The latter is an unmediated imprint of the warmth, the fun, and the intelligence of the man.

LUIS BUÑUEL

Buñuel was too secretive or clever to succumb to full biographical treatment. At the same time, his films are some of the hardest to write about. (No one in any film department should be given tenure unless they can make a class of freshmen desperate to see *Un Chien Andalou*—and to accomplish that in seventeen minutes, the length of the film. This requirement could unseat many chairpersons in Media Studies.) *My Last Sigh,*

Buñuel's alleged memoir, written with Jean-Claude Carrière, opens and closes doors at the same time. There is a useful biography by John Baxter (1998) and a stimulating interpretation by Raymond Durgnat (1977). But the essential implausibility of being Buñuel remains intact.

Still, we deserve a short, breathtaking provocation on the man and his work—as good as Nabokov on Gogol or Nick Tosches on Dean Martin. Carrière is the obvious author, but he would fob you off by saying he had tried it already with *My Last Sigh* (one of the few great books by, or "by," a film director).

HOWARD HAWKS

There is a full-scale biography, Todd McCarthy's *Howard Hawks: The Gray Fox of Hollywood* (1997), that is diligent and admiring but somehow distant. It doesn't get at the tricky heart of the fantasist or match a few pages from *Slim: Memories of a Rich and Imperfect Life* (1990), by Slim Keith (once Slim Hawks) and Annette Tapert. Joseph McBride did a useful interview book, *Hawks on Hawks* (1982), but it never dares question anything Hawks says, whereas most of his taciturn utterances were suspect. So an essential American artist, and perhaps the most characteristic of Golden Age directors, does not have an adequate book.

ALFRED HITCHCOCK

There are careers in film academia built on books about Hitchcock, just as there have been more seminars on him than on any other director. The first biography to begin to uncover the whole man was Donald Spoto's *The Dark Side of Genius* (1983). That book was rather resisted by Hitchcock admirers. They had their bible already: *Le Cinéma selon Hitchcock* (1966)—or *Hitchcock/Truffaut*. That was an extensive interview in which Hitch bathed in the adulation of François Truffaut and was allowed to spell out what he had done, and how, in lavish detail with beautiful sequences of illustration. The why and the what (to use Andrew Sarris's distinction) was not much attended to. By 2003, there was no escaping the darkness of the man, and that informs Patrick McGilligan's *Alfred Hitchcock: A Life in Darkness and Light* which now stands as the model biography.

There are countless books about individual films and particular aspects of Hitchcock's work, and it is increasingly apparent that the obsessive richness of the art was accompanied by an Asperger's-like isolation in the man. The cult of the director, or the auteur, has added to that tension in many directors. But the overall culture of cinephilia is reluctant to admit how often a successful movie director may be isolated from and unfeeling about life. So the job, or its opportunity, have become advertisements for enclosed obsession—as if that was our ultimate reckoning of what being an artist requires. Meanwhile, in the configuration of fear and anxiety, and the shrinking away from ease or naturalness, Hitchcock exists in the company of Kafka, Lucian Freud, and Harold Pinter.

ORSON WELLES

There is an immense biographical undertaking at work by Simon Callow, himself an actor and director, and unusually sympathetic to the variety and vitality of Welles. Three volumes are published—*The Road to Xanadu* (1995), *Hello Americans* (2006), *One-Man Band* (2015)—and there is a fourth promised. Does Welles sustain so much detail? Of course he does. But does he also require quicker treatment that grasps his bipolar personality? Yes to that too, and several of us have tried to do that book.

That said, maybe the most illuminating books are two where he expounded on himself in conversation. They show up the very narrow human range of Truffaut's Hitchcock book. For *This Is Orson Welles* (1992), the interviewer and fellow-conversationalist is Peter Bogdanovich; and on *My Lunches with Orson* (2013), Henry Jaglom is the other voice at the table.

There is also the autobiographical trilogy by John Houseman, who was producer, Horatio, and shadow to Welles—*Run-Through* (1972); *Front & Center* (1979); *Final Dress* (1983). The titles tell us that the theatre was Houseman's deepest love, but no one has ever written better on Welles—or on Nicholas Ray (Houseman had produced Ray's debut picture, *They Live by Night*). Houseman was subsequently abused in words by Welles, which may be a sign of how instrumental the producer had been in the career of a neurotically and passionately untidy loner.

JEAN-LUC GODARD

The best life in English is Richard Brody's *Everything Is Cinema: The Working Life of Jean-Luc Godard* (2008), scrupulously researched and half-aware of the shortcoming or the fallacy in its own title—because everything is *not* cinema, and the Godardian faith that it might or should be is a fatal restriction. But therein lies the dilemma in watching his great films. In so many ways he has been his surest, forbidding voice. So the reader is directed to *Godard on Godard: Critical Writings by Jean-Luc Godard* (1972), an anthology translated and edited by Tom Milne, and to the book version of his *Histoire(s) du Cinéma* (1988), a set of despairing commandments by the auteur who was always most suspicious of his glorious medium.

NICHOLAS RAY

There are two biographies that do not capture the full chaos of the man, and which want to trust in "the facts" while Nick Ray was in his own mind a fiction and a myth. The books are Bernard Eisenschitz, *Nicholas Ray: An American Journey* (1990 in French, and then 1993 in English); and Patrick McGilligan, *Nicholas Ray: The Glorious Failure of an American Director* (2011). "Glorious Failure" is a telling subtitle that fits so many directors who prefer to concentrate on their glory. One day perhaps there will be a fine novel on Ray, but as time passes there are few people left who witnessed and felt his storm. The facts will subside and legend will take over. That is a formula expressed by John Ford (in *Fort Apache* and *The Man Who Shot Liberty Valance*). It is often repeated by movie buffs as a triumphant cry—but it is a mark of cultural disaster. If you doubt that, consider Donald Trump as an actor-director who passes from reality to self-dream in an instant.

STEPHEN FREARS

It is an exact measurement of the man that there is no book about Frears, and not too much in the way of interviews. I suspect he's content with that obscurity and I can hear him saying, Well, really, there is nothing much to say. I don't trust the modesty, but I love and honor its gesture.

In a similar way, by now, too little is known about Victor Sjöström, Boris Barnet, or even Kenji Mizoguchi. The last seems to me one of the greatest directors who has ever worked. There should be a chapter on him in this book, but I feel too ignorant or distant from Japan to offer it. (So I recommend Mark LeFanu's book, *Mizoguchi and Japan*, 2005.) Movie is "international," we say, but that doesn't mean it erases cultural differences. I don't think Lang, Renoir, or Hitchcock ever understood America as well as John Boorman did in *Point Blank* or von Stroheim with *Greed*.

Still, as apology, I would urge you to seek out at least these films by Mizoguchi: *The Story of the Last Chrysanthemums, The Life of Oharu, Ugetsu Monogatari, Sansho the Bailiff,* and *Princess Yang Kwei Fei.* You have other missions—to see if you can discover a film by Yasujirō Ozu that is not worth seeing over and over again; to understand how *The Apu Trilogy* by Satyajit Ray will change your whole sense of how cinema can humbly serve the mixed moments of life.

Then there is the work of Robert Bresson, from a life that hardly seemed to exist, but is essential if only in the insight that the people in films do not need to act. It is enough to let themselves be photographed—but that possibility was clear in the opening of this book. There is a book by Bresson, *Notes on the Cinematograph* (1975 in French, and 1977 in English). It is only 140 pages, and a collection of proposals, questions, assertions, epigrams, and warnings on the nature and puzzle of film, with special emphasis on the transformation of personality and soul from life to screen. It is as essential and testing as Bresson's films.

There are a few books by film directors (and plainly written by them, not by ghosts) that need to be read and valued as books, instead of personal promotion.

Josef von Sternberg, *Fun in a Chinese Laundry* (1966). Von Sternberg's films are set everywhere or nowhere (in black-and-white), and he passed through life in a similarly unattached way. But this book is a key to the fatalism, the humor, and the passionate insouciance of his great films in which the only fixed landmark was Marlene Dietrich.

Elia Kazan, *A Life* (1988). A brilliant, insightful, egotistical, melodramatic book, as befits the outstanding American director on stage and screen in the postwar years. I think this is his finest work, better than *East of Eden* or *Wild River.* It should be read alongside a book that cannot be categorized but which draws on fact and fiction in equal measure. It centers on Kazan's second wife, Barbara Loden, who directed one film, *Wanda.* This is Natalie Léger, *Suite for Barbara Loden* (2016 in English, after French publication in 2012).

Michael Powell, *A Life in Movies: An Autobiography* (1986). Characteristically exuberant and penetrating, and ecstatically casual with facts. There was a sequel, *Million Dollar Movie* (1992), which did not feel as necessary or compelling.

John Boorman has had a constant interest in writing on film.

That led to the thirteen volumes of the *Projections* series in which filmmakers were able to write about their work and their jeopardized careers. In addition, Boorman has published three endearing books: *Money Into Light: The Emerald Forest Diary* (1985), *Adventures of a Suburban Boy* (2003), and *Conclusions* (2020).

Ingmar Bergman, *The Magic Lantern* (1987). This is not comfortable reading if you want to make a hero out of Bergman. The memoir does not spare its author as a selfish neurotic who put all his moral faith in being a genius and a practitioner who cast actors and civilians as figures in his life. He treated people badly, until he filmed them. That incisive but pitiless kindness is the engine of his films. He was a great artist but a shocking man. We cannot get deeply into the culture of filmmaking without learning to live with that conundrum.

THE AMERICAN AUTEUR

From the late 1960s, young American moviemakers became celebrities—as such, one would have anticipated many biographies or autobiographies. But celebrity may be a barrier to searching personal studies, and even to an inwardness, a self-study, that can be vital to the loneliness in a creative personality.

There is a standard, surface biography of Francis Coppola by Peter Cowie (1989), but it pales beside the anguish in *Notes* (1979), the book Eleanor Coppola wrote about her husband during the making of *Apocalypse Now*. Kay Corleone (Diane Keaton) does not register as a person in *The Godfather*, but in *Notes* we feel the resolute pained sympathy in a wife who is watching the great man in existential peril. There should be more books about directors by wives, ex-lovers, secretaries, yes-men, and maybe their lawyers. Alas, nondisclosure agreements—actual documents, or emotional pressure—have shut down that genre.

Joseph McBride wrote a well-researched, comprehensive life of Steven Spielberg (1997), and there is a good, shorter book by Molly Haskell (2017). But it's hard to believe there is a fallible human being within the empire known as Spielberg. Can an outstanding film director be that uninteresting?

Much the same could be asked about George Lucas, the subject of Brian Jay Jones's *George Lucas: A Life* (2016), where "A Life" seems more hopeful than delivered on the page.

Peter Bogdanovich has written several anecdotal and entertaining books, but not the full, candid autobiography that his up-and-down life deserves and which was touched on in *The Killing of the Unicorn: Dorothy Stratten, 1960–1980* (1984), a love letter to his murdered friend.

The fearless McGilligan attempted a life of Robert Altman—*Jumping Off the Cliff* (1989)—but I don't think it penetrates a very elusive and defensively cynical man.

Martin Scorsese has been the pretext for two books—*Martin Scorsese: The First Decade* (1980), by Mary Pat Kelly, and *Conversations with Scorsese* (2011), by Richard Schickel. The latter is serviceable public relations with a suggestion that to compose and read books in which directors talk about themselves can be like being trapped in their elevator. The Welles books are the exception to this rule.

So we do not have searching or adequate biographies of Coppola, Spielberg, Lucas, Altman, or Scorsese. Or of Woody Allen—and that is surely the book that has to be written (unless one decides that Philip Roth assembled it gradually over many years).

There is one shining writer among these auteurs: Paul Schrader is incapable of talking or writing for long without being a teacher—he does bluster, too, but life is hard. That estimate extends from *Schrader on Schrader* (2004), edited by Kevin Jackson; to many articles in magazines; a fine book on Dreyer, Ozu, and Bresson, *Transcendental Style in Film* (1972); and postings on Facebook. Schrader can be a very good director (*American Gigolo, Cat People, Light Sleeper, Affliction*), but he is a genuine writer.

Sometimes a book can suggest a larger life in exploring just one film. This rich genre includes Steven Bach's *Final Cut* (1985), on the making and unmaking of Michael Cimino's *Heaven's Gate; The Authentic Death & Contentious Afterlife of Pat Garrett and Billy the Kid* (2015) by Paul Seydor; books by Aljean Harmetz on the making of *The Wizard of Oz* (1977) and *Casablanca* (1992); Jean Cocteau's classic journal on the making of *La Belle et la Bête* (1946); all the way to Sam Wasson's *The Big Goodbye* (2020) on how *Chinatown* was both a group struggle and the victory of director Roman Polanski. Polanski did write his own book, *Roman* (1984), but it is a tame version of a very complicated life.

Books on women directors? There are a few on Jane Campion, unsatisfactory. The best work in this injudiciously phrased category is probably Steven Bach's *Leni: The Life and Work of Leni Riefenstahl* (2007), fair, thorough, and understanding of German history, but not as crazed as her own memoir (1987 in German, 1995 in English).

Can you believe there is not yet a whole book on Spike Lee,

when he is one of the best-known film directors and among the more recognizable Americans? Then ask yourself why you are not too surprised about that.

Quentin Tarantino has filled many books and interviews with his talk, but no one has dared to assess all of him. Will the books he is now promising meet that need? Or will he be talking to himself? I have a hunch and a hope that a brilliant writer may be released in this retirement project.

A final entry, and a new kind of book. *Life Isn't Everything* (compiled and edited by Ash Carter and Sam Kashner) is *Mike Nichols as Remembered by 150 of His Closest Friends* (2019). So it's a record of a very astute, top-line career (*The Graduate, Who's Afraid of Virginia Woolf?, Silkwood, Wit, Angels in America*) that also produced several inexplicable duds. Nichols was brilliant yet impersonal, as loaded with charm and skill as emptiness. As if a director really was a detached operator with extreme class, a surgeon operating on strangers.

But the story is more complicated. It may be that Nichols never did anything to match his creative affair with Elaine May, in live performance and improv, as resolutely neurotic sensibilities. They were exceptional examples of actors or voices who were directing themselves, or of creators who existed in performance. Nichols went on to be an A-list director while May wandered or drifted—*A New Leaf, The Heartbreak Kid, Mikey & Nicky, Ishtar,* and a few quirky acting jobs.

To read this enjoyable book is to face the question: which of them was the most natural or penetrating director? I don't know the answer, but the question reminds us of how often actors are uncredited directors shaping our experience through their pretending. It may be that Nichols and May in their lyrical, interrogatory conversations surpass their films, and most films of their time. Did a man and a woman ever get on better? Or feel such passionate rivalry?

CONCLUSION

In the early 1960s, there were few books about film directors. In the time of their great work, they had not been taken seriously. But Charles Chaplin's *My Autobiography* (1964) was a warning that film people might say anything and be believed because of the romantic light in which we were coming to see them; here was a plan for egotism and self-service trashing history, and thus an early step in our cultural erasure of "the news."

It followed that the great careers of professionals had gone unnoticed. So those directors were retired or dead before valuable "lives" came along. That category includes Scott Eyman's books on Cecil B. DeMille, *Empire of Dreams* (2010), and on John Ford, *Print the Legend* (1999); Joseph McBride's brave reassessment of Frank Capra, *The Catastrophe of Success* (1992); Alan K. Rode's *Michael Curtiz: A Life in Film* (2017); David Weddle's *"If They Move . . . Kill 'Em!": The Life and Times of Sam Peckinpah* (1994).

Those books are part of what is no longer just a long shelf in film studies but a whole section of the library. I have gone from owning half a dozen books on film in 1960 to five or six hundred now. But a time has come when that library is not being automatically replenished. I'm not sure that there will be books about Terrence Malick, the Coen brothers, David Fincher, Paul Thomas Anderson, or Kathryn Bigelow. But I wonder if I want those books as much as help in understanding Max Ophüls, Michael Haneke, Christian Petzold, Claire Denis, or Chris Marker. In other words, there are great gaps in our knowledge but less urge from publishers, authors, and even readers for those books. So much interview and self-justification is now available on what we call DVD extras. That matches our academic respect for directors, but does it go with diminished awe for the power of movies? This idea can be disputed but I believe the energy or the allure of the medium has shifted from great artists and moving stories to the technology of the process, the money, and the abiding faces that still draw audiences—the actors, and their embodiment of desire.

ACKNOWLEDGMENTS

———

This book began several years ago in a conversation between my agent, Laura Morris, and one of my best friends in publishing, Alan Samson. They felt that an anatomy of the film director was something I should attempt. I agreed, but then I rewarded their faith by neglecting the task. I don't know why; or why all of a sudden I felt the need to do it in 2019. Perhaps that was because I thought the luster of the director might be fading—but more likely it was the endearing, persuasive power of Laura, someone I have known and revered since 1975.

Once the book was written, and rewritten under Alan's deft, midfield play (he is a Beckenbauer in what he does), the progress of the book was taken over by Rosie Pearce. She faced first a difficult author, and then the climate of the virus. She handled both with a calm and care that brought the book to print.

Then, in America, as the book was taken on by Knopf, another old friend, Jon Segal, delivered his own wisdom and experience, under what had become very difficult circumstances.

The world might be coming apart, or trying that act, but old friends were there still. I felt very lucky in having Alan and Jon as co-editors. Further, in New York I had Jon's assistant, Erin Sellers, as an assistant director. She was representative of a core of people at Knopf who have supported me for a long time. That includes a very fine copyeditor, Kevin Bourke, plus Kathy Hourigan and Kathy Zuckerman. Most important in that crew was Sonny Mehta, who died as the early draft was being delivered. So he was spared any labor on it—but no borzoi now feels easy walking without him.

His memorial in New York was a stirring occasion for everyone there. And on that February 19, 2020, we hardly understood that it was the end of more than an era in publishing.

INDEX

David Thomson was born in London in 1941 and educated at Dulwich College and the London School of Film Technique. He worked in publishing, at Penguin; he directed the film studies program at Dartmouth College; he did the series *Life at 24 Frames per Second* for BBC Radio; he scripted the film *The Making of a Legend: Gone With the Wind;* and he was on the selection committee for the New York Film Festival. He has written many books, including the pioneering novels *Suspects* and *Silver Light,* the biography *Showman: The Life of David O. Selznick,* and the *Biographical Dictionary of Film,* now in its sixth edition. He has been called the best or the most imaginative or reckless writer on film in English, but he presses on. His residence is in San Francisco, but he lives in his head.

A NOTE ON THE TYPE

This book was set in Adobe Garamond. Designed for the Adobe Corporation by Robert Slimbach, the fonts are based on types first cut by Claude Garamond (ca. 1480–1561). Garamond was a pupil of Geoffroy Tory and is believed to have followed the Venetian models, although he introduced a number of important differences, and it is to him that we owe the letter we now know as "old style." He gave to his letters a certain elegance and feeling of movement that won their creator an immediate reputation and the patronage of Francis I of France.

Typeset by Scribe
Philadelphia, Pennsylvania

Printed and bound by Friesens,
Altona, Manitoba